"This is an absolutely wonderful book! It easily offers the best overview of the political views of Hayek, Rawls, and Cohen available today. Moreover, when Jeppe von Platz offers criticisms of the views that he outlines they are always fair, and the outlines themselves are both accurate and charitable."

James Stacey Taylor, The College of New Jersey

"With *Theories of Distributive Justice*, Jeppe von Platz does a real service for scholars and students alike. In admirably lively prose, employing clear and pertinent examples, Platz cogently lays out the most prominent positions on distributive justice, including Right Liberalism (represented by Hayek), Left Liberalism (Rawls), Libertarianism (Nozick), and Socialism (Cohen). More than a summary of arguments, this book assists readers in making up their own minds by providing a comparative critical analysis of each position's strengths and weaknesses, explaining each's basic ideas and values, its conception of justice, and the institutions needed to implement the theory. Platz's concluding chapter presents contemporary challenges and alternatives to these theories, which will serve as a valuable provocation to both discussion in the classroom and further research in the field."

Gregory Fried, Boston College

THEORIES OF DISTRIBUTIVE JUSTICE

How should we design our economic systems? Should we tax the rich at a higher rate than the poor? Should we have a minimum wage? Should the state provide healthcare for all? These and many related questions are the subject of distributive justice, and different theories of distributive justice provide different ways to think about and answer such questions. This book provides a thorough introduction to the main theories of distributive justice and reveals the underlying sources of our disagreements about economic policy. It argues that the universe of theories of distributive justice is surprisingly simple, yet complicated. It is simple in that the main theories of distributive justice are just four in number, and in that these theories each offer a distinct, well-defined theoretical approach to distributive justice; yet it is complicated in that the main theories disagree at several distinct, fundamental levels, and in that it is possible to spin innumerable new theories from the elements of the four main theories.

Key Features:

- Covers the four major theories of distributive justice and their leading philosophers, elucidating the attractions and drawbacks of each:
  - Friedrich A. von Hayek and right-liberalism;
  - John Rawls and left-liberalism;
  - Robert Nozick and libertarianism;
  - Gerald A. Cohen and socialism.
- Explains why these four theories have come to dominate most philosophical discussions on distributive justice, highlighting the essential answer provided in each that is lacking in other theories.
- Written for any reader interested in the topic, with an annotated reading list at the end of each chapter and helpful glossary at the back of the book.

Jeppe von Platz is Assistant Professor of Philosophy and in the PPEL Program at the University of Richmond.

THEORIES OF DISTRIBUTIVE JUSTICE

Who Gets What and Why

Jeppe von Platz

Routledge
Taylor & Francis Group
NEW YORK AND LONDON

First published 2020
by Routledge
52 Vanderbilt Avenue, New York, NY 10017

and by Routledge
2 Park Square, Milton Park, Abingdon, Oxon, OX14 4RN

Routledge is an imprint of the Taylor & Francis Group, an informa business

Library of Congress Cataloging-in-Publication Data
A catalog record for this title has been requested

ISBN: 978-0-367-33236-5 (hbk)
ISBN: 978-0-367-33235-8 (pbk)
ISBN: 978-0-429-31878-8 (ebk)

Typeset in Bembo
by Swales & Willis, Exeter, Devon, UK

For Marie

CONTENTS

FIGURES

TABLES

INFORMATION BOXES

PREFACE

I have been interested in distributive justice for as long as I can remember, and I have tried to make sense of my thoughts about it for almost as long. On the way I started studying theories of distributive justice. This book presents some of the results of these studies. My hope is that reading it will provide you with a much better understanding of what you should think about when considering questions of distributive justice.

A theory of distributive justice is an attempt to make sense of what we should care about, and how we should care about it, when we design the economic systems whereby the benefits and burdens of society are distributed among its members. My studies have taught me that the universe of theories of distributive justice is both simple and complicated. It is surprisingly simple in that the main theories of distributive justice are just four in number, and in that these theories each occupy a well-defined space in the universe of theories of distributive justice. It is complicated in that the main theories disagree at several distinct levels of theory, and in that it is possible to create innumerable mongrel theories out of the elements of the four main theories.

My main debts are to my parents, to my teachers – David A. Reidy, Samuel Freeman, Kok-Chor Tan, and Paul Guyer – who taught me how to think about distributive justice; and to my students, who taught me that I didn't think well enough. Lauren McGillicuddy and Sarah Millward helped edit every part of the manuscript and I am deeply grateful to both for innumerable corrections and suggestions for improvements.

1

DISTRIBUTIVE JUSTICE

1 What this Book Is About

If you've ever had dealings with children, you know that they want things – especially things that other people have. Almost as soon as they've learned to say "mom" or "dad," they start saying (well, shouting) "mine!" when another kid (or adult) holds something that looks vaguely like a toy. Try giving a piece of pie to one child without giving any to the three year old next to her, and you'll immediately hear cries of "Not fair!" Though they sometimes express themselves better, adults often share the same sentiments. While distributive justice is not in our genes, it is pervasively, permanently, and unavoidably part of the human experience. We are social and political animals living in a world of finite resources, and we face questions about the distribution of goods and burdens from the moment we start manipulating the world until we die. Whether you like it or not, you care about distributive justice, and distributive justice cares about you.

What is a fair distribution of a resource? The answer depends on the resource and the context of the question. For many goods and contexts, the answer seems obvious enough. Normally we should divide the pie equally among the children who'd like to have a piece of it. Or take medicine in a time of need: if some infection is ravaging the population, we should give antibiotics to those who are sick. Or think about seats in a restaurant: those who get there first, get to pick first, and those who show up late have to take whatever seats are left, if any. Or grades in school: those who merit higher grades should get them. Of course, sometimes the answer to how we should distribute some good is that we shouldn't try to distribute it at all. Think of dance partners at the club: the right distribution is whatever results from the free choices of the persons at the club.

These options already reveal several principles of distributive justice: distribute equally (the children each get an equal piece of pie), distribute according to need (the medicine goes to the sick), distribute on a first-come, first-served basis (seats in a restaurant, but land and natural resources have also been distributed in this way), distribute according to merit (grades in a class), and, finally, the principle of liberty tells us that the right distribution is the one that results from the free choices of individuals (dance partners at the club).

Each of these principles apply in different contexts, and we should beware of concluding that if a principle applies in one context, it applies in other contexts as well. The system of education would not work if grades were distributed according to the principles of equality, need, or liberty. Even if we could distribute dance partners according to need, trying to do it would probably destroy the fun and make people stop dancing. It would be nuts to distribute medicine in a time of crisis according to the principle of equality, and if we used the principle of liberty to distribute medicine in a time of crisis it might go to the friends and families of the doctors, or to the rich. The fact that markets are great at distributing goods efficiently might offer an argument for using the principle of liberty in this context, but if our main concern is to cure the disease rather than enrich drugmakers and purveyors, then the argument has to show that using the free market to distribute the medicine best serves the principle of distribution according to need, in which case the ruling principle is the principle of distribution according to need, not the principle of liberty.

Some important points:

- Different principles apply in different contexts.
- We should beware of the belief that just because a principle is obviously best in one context it is also best in other contexts.
- Sometimes more than one principle might be relevant for how we should distribute some good.

What about the context that is society as a whole and the fruits and burdens of society and co-operation: income, wealth, opportunities, duties (such as working, paying taxes, or caring for one's children and parents), and rights? Can we say something about how the benefits and burdens of social cooperation should be distributed among the members of society? What is a fair wage? Who should be rich, or poor? Is it unjust that there are rich and poor? Should there be poverty at all? What about access to education, jobs, or public offices? Should there be equal opportunity, and what does "equal opportunity" even mean? What about economic rights and liberties? Does the estate tax violate your right to decide what to do with your property? Can the state mandate that you buy health insurance or force you to participate in a universal system of healthcare? Can the state set a minimum wage or limit the number of hours you can work in a week? Is America more unjust than Denmark because the gap between rich and poor is wider in America than in Denmark? Or is Germany more just than England if opportunities for climbing the social ladder are more equally distributed in Germany?

These questions are not optional: we cannot ignore them or give them only a moment's thought on the way to something more interesting. As I said, whether you like it or not, distributive justice cares about you. You are a member of society, which means at least five things:

- First, you have a place in the distribution of resources, opportunities, duties, and rights. You're either rich or poor (or middle class), advantaged or disadvantaged, privileged or not, and so on.
- Second, your access to economic advantages and opportunities is determined by the rules of the economy; what you can and cannot do in life depends on how the economy is designed, as much as (if not more than) it depends on your choices or luck.
- Third, as a member of society you probably care not only how about you are doing relative to other members of society (do you get a large share of the pie?), but also about how other people are doing, and thus about what a just distribution of resources, opportunities, duties, and rights look like (what is a fair division of the pie?).
- Fourth, as a member of (a democratic) society you have a right to influence how we design the institutions that determine the distribution of resources, opportunities, duties, and rights. In a democratic society the laws that define and regulate the economy determine access to education and healthcare, and define your rights in the marketplace and beyond – these laws are all of our own making. As democratic citizens we have a right to be heard equally with other citizens in the process that makes the laws.
- Fifth, as democratic citizens we not only have a right to make laws; we have an obligation (a duty) to do so. This obligation requires us to think about lawmaking not merely in terms of our own interests (more pie for me!), but to make laws that ensure justice for all (a fair share of the pie to each!).

So, as democratic citizens we have both the right and the obligation to participate in the making of a system of laws that determines a distribution of resources, opportunities, duties, and rights that is fair and just. In the context of society as a whole, then, we *must* ask: what is a just distribution of resources, opportunities, duties, and rights? And *that is the question* that this book is about.

To recap, we face many questions of distributive justice; whether inequality is unjust, what we should do (if anything) about poverty, what sort of equality of opportunity we should seek, what rights we should enjoy, the justice of taxation and government regulation of the economy, and so on. These questions are rooted in the basic question: what is the fair and just distribution of resources, opportunities, duties, and rights for a democratic society?

In this book I present the main theories of distributive justice and show how they answer these questions. My main aim is to map out the landscape of theories of distributive justice, so that you can better understand what questions of distributive justice are about, what is at stake in these questions, and the principled answers that we may give to them.

I will not try to persuade you that any one of these theories is superior to the others. Indeed, my hope is that after reading this book you'll be just a little bit in love with every theory I present here, and a lot less confident that you know the right answers. At this moment, before reading this book, you probably think that you know the answers to the questions about distributive justice I presented above – you know what you believe about the justice of poverty, inequality, equality of opportunity, and economic rights. After reading the book, I hope that you'll better understand the arguments in defense of different views on the distribution of wealth and income, opportunities, duties, and economic rights. And because you will understand the different arguments, I hope you will see the attractions of the answers you thought were wrong, as well as the problems with the answers you thought were correct. Fair warning: after reading this book you might change your mind! And even if you don't, you'll at least know the shortcomings of your views, the attractions of alternative views, and thus be better equipped to defend your views and to poke holes in opposing views.

But, as I said, my hope is that you'll feel much less certain about what the correct view is and that you'll understand and respect those who hold opposing views. Each of the theories of distributive justice that we meet in this book is attractive and has persuasive arguments in its favor, so choosing among these theories (and the answers they defend) is hard. Yet we must choose, for if one theory is true, then the others are false.

2 The Elements of Theories of Distributive Justice (The Basic Version)

To draw a clear map of the landscape of theories, and to avoid some common confusions, we need to distinguish among the main elements of theories of distributive justice. For our present purposes we can distinguish among three elements that are part of all the main theories of distributive justice. Later, I add several more elements so the map becomes increasingly detailed as the book progresses, just as zooming in on Google Maps lets you see the smaller – but still important – streets. The three elements (or levels) are principles of distributive justice, the institutional implications of these principles, and the story that each theory tells about why these are the right principles (i.e. the grounds or justification of the principles of distributive justice that the theory defends). To be clear, here are the main elements of theories of distributive justice:

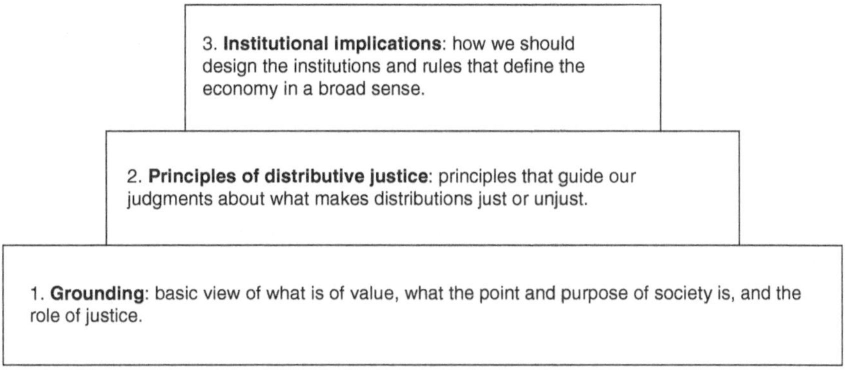

FIGURE 1.1 The main elements of theories of distributive justice

I have listed these elements in inverse order of justification to indicate how the institutional implications of a theory of distributive justice rely on the principles of distributive justice that it defends, and these principles, in turn, express its underlying commitments at the grounding level. The pyramid shape is meant to illustrate this relation: institutional design rests on principles, which, in turn, rests on the grounding views of society and justice (this justification relationship will become much clearer in later chapters). The important point is that to justify answers about institutional design, we have to appeal to principles of distributive justice; and to justify the principles, we have to appeal to more basic considerations about the nature and values of society and the relations that ought to obtain among the members of society. If you favor a progressive income tax and you'd like to defend your position, you might appeal to a principle of equality, but then you still face the task of showing *why we should care about equality*. The three main elements of a theory of justice (grounding, principles, and institutional design) are also three levels of theories of distributive justice, where grounding is more basic than principles, which are more basic than institutional implications. Discussions of distributive justice are often confused by failure to clearly distinguish these levels – I discuss this sort of confusion later. First, though, I offer a more thorough description of each of the three levels.

2.1 Grounding/Justification

At the foundation of theories of distributive justice, we find understandings of what the subject and role of justice is and accompanying visions of what society is about and what values a good and just society achieves. Here we meet a basic division of different views on the relation between *the right and the good*. Some theories of justice work from the assumption that the good is prior to the right in the sense that rightness is the set of rules that best allows us to achieve what is truly good (and avoid what is truly bad). Such theories of justice are called *teleological*, since they maintain that justice is about the optimal achievement of human ends (and the Greek word for "end" is *telos*). Other theories of justice reject that justice can be defined by reference to antecedently given ends. Such theories are called *deontological* for reasons that need not bother us here (but see the Glossary). Deontological theories say that justice/the right is *independent from and prior to the good* in that justice tells us *how* we may permissibly pursue our various ends, *and also* constrains which ends we may pursue. We might agree that the satisfaction of human desires is good, but also agree that justice constrains what may be done in the pursuit of desire satisfaction and that immoral desires should not be pursued at all. Below I describe these two families of theories of justice in more detail and introduce the most prominent members of these families.

Teleological theories focus on what makes it good (or rational) to live in societies in the first place. By living in societies, human beings get access to a number of desired and desirable goods, including (but not limited to):

- Security (of person and property);
- Community;
- Stability and predictability (of rules and relations and the supply of desirable goods and services);
- Learning and education;
- Culture and science;
- Healthcare and housing; and
- Technology and the means of commodious living (agriculture, heating and cooling, plumbers and plumbing, and so on).

Following this line of thought, we might believe that justice is the rules that best allow us to get what we want, or what we really should want.

There are two kinds of teleological theories of justice, corresponding to whether they see these ends in terms of objective or subjective good. The first kind, called *perfectionism*, focuses on what is *objectively good* for human beings, so that theories of this kind say that the just society is that which best allows us to live objectively good human lives. Different theories of objective goodness produce different varieties of perfectionism – some of them religious, some of them not.

Historically, perfectionism was the dominant way to think about justice. More recently, it has been relegated to the fringe of contemporary political philosophy, since most contemporary political philosophers accept some sort of minimal liberalism that says that it is wrong to force other people to live according to a conception of the objectively good life with which they disagree.

The second family of teleological theories of justice avoids this problem by saying that what matters is not that people live objectively good lives, but that they live *subjectively good lives*, meaning that people are happy in the sense that they get what they want. Pursuing this line of thought, society is the cooperative venture by which we together produce the goods that people desire; what really matters is that people get what they desire, so we should create the society that best provides these goods. People will disagree about what the good life is (about objective human goodness) and they will desire different things, but it is rational to be in society and to cooperate, since doing so provides more for each of what they individually desire. Some goods are desired by most (even all) and will, of course, have more weight – peace, liberty, stability, and prosperity in the broad sense. If we follow this line of thought, we arrive at the idea that justice is the rules that allow us to live together with liberty in peace and prosperity, and the true principles of distributive justice are those that best allow us to achieve these ends of society. This position is called *utilitarianism*.

Other philosophers think that teleological approaches to justice are mistaken. Theories that reject the teleological framework are called *deontological*. Here, again, there are two main types of deontological theories of justice. Both kinds reject that justice is about the ends of society and direct our attention instead to *how we may go about pursuing these ends*.

According to the first deontological variety what really matters is that the cooperative pursuit of social prosperity is conducted in a manner that is *fair* to all the cooperators. These theories say that living in society is a precondition for the production and distribution of desirable outcomes. While we should aim for an efficient system of production and distribution of the things we want, it is also true that we produce all the good things by working together, by *cooperating*. If we think of society as a system of social cooperation, we also think of the members of society as coming together to cooperate. This cooperation should benefit (and burden) each member of society fairly, rather than simply lead to the greatest possible aggregate sum of goods produced. In other words, when we think of society as a system of cooperation, we also think of the members as freely cooperating and as having an equal claim to the benefits, and equal responsibility for the burdens, of cooperation. Since all members cooperate, the division of goods should be fair to all members of society. Where the utilitarian approach allows a society to sacrifice the interests of some when doing so leads to the production of more goods, the cooperative approach leads to the *contractualist* idea that the distribution of benefits and burdens should be justifiable to each, so that each member of society can agree to the terms of their cooperation – in a slogan, the utilitarian approach requires us to pursue the best aggregate outcome (we should produce the biggest possible pie), whereas the contractualist approach cares also about the distributive outcome (we should make sure that the pie and the labor that goes into creating the pie are fairly distributed among the members of society).

Another sort of deontological framework says that the subject of justice is actions and how the actions of one person relate to the rights of other persons. Apart from the existence of societies, every person has certain rights – to their person, to their property, to the fruits of their labor, to trade with others, and so on – and the role of justice is to secure a situation where the actions of each do not violate the rights of others. On this view, societies exist and political authority is legitimate because they help us secure that rights are respected, and the

TABLE 1.1 Frameworks/grounding

Teleological theories: the just society is that which best achieves the good (the good is prior to the right)		*Deontological theories*: justice is not about the good, but restricts how we may pursue it (the right is prior to the good)	
Focus on *objective* goodness: good human living	Focus on *subjective goodness*: getting what we want, happiness	Basic requirement is *fair social cooperation among free and equal persons*	Basic requirement is that all rights are respected and protected
Perfectionisms	Utilitarianisms	Contractualisms	Rights theories

extent of political authority is defined by the need to protect rights. A just society is simply one where rights (whether natural or acquired) are respected. If justice is all about protecting and respecting natural and acquired rights, then it is mistaken to focus on the aggregate goods that are produced or how these goods are distributed, for justice is not about creating nice outcomes, nor about ensuring fairness in the division of benefits and burdens of social cooperation; justice is about protecting people's rights and liberties.

To summarize, Table 1.1 above shows four frameworks for thinking about distributive justice.

There are other views of the nature and role of justice, and accompanying visions of a good and just society, but these four have been tremendously important in the history of ideas and remain influential in both academic and political debates today.

2.2 Principle(s) of Distributive Justice

The main principles of distributive justice are equality, sufficiency, priority, utility, merit, and liberty. In this section I sketch these principles, but I do not discuss the arguments that we might give for or against them – the arguments are presented and discussed in conjunction with the theories of distributive justice in later chapters.

According to *the principle of equality*, inequalities are unjust, so we always have a reason to prefer an equal distribution to an unequal distribution. Thus, the principle of equality judges the justice of a distribution in terms of the relative holdings of its members – if some have more than others then there is an injustice, and we have a reason to try to move in the direction of a more equal distribution – no matter how much those who have less actually hold. Of course, other considerations might matter as well, so sometimes we should allow inequality; but, in that case, we also should recognize that we are allowing injustice. Because the principle of equality cares only about relative holdings and insists that it is unjust when some have more than others, it is vulnerable to the leveling down objection (see Information Box 1.1 The leveling down objection).

INFORMATION BOX 1.1 THE LEVELING DOWN OBJECTION

The principle of equality claims that we always have a reason to prefer an equal to an unequal distribution. This claim invites the objection that sometimes the way to a more equal distribution is to make the richer less well-off *without improving the lot of the poorer*. To take a simple example: if we have a population where half are blind and the other half can see, and we cannot make the blind see, then the principle of equality says that we have a reason to blind the seeing, since that is the only way to ensure equality. But no one would gain by blinding half the population, so that seems absurd. It also seems absurd to say that a situation where all are blind is better or more just than a situation where half can see.

Even worse, the egalitarian principle seems to require that we sometimes *make everyone worse off*. Imagine a situation where there are rich and poor, but the poor benefit from the inequality (it might be that allowing inequalities motivates people to productive behavior that benefits everyone). According to the egalitarian principle, we would have reason to create a more equal distribution, *even if the poor thereby become worse off*, and that seems absurd: why would justice require that we do something that makes *everyone* worse off? Is a society where all live in extreme poverty better than a society where some are poor and others are rich, but no one lives in extreme poverty?

The egalitarian can respond that, no, the society where all live in extreme poverty is not *all things considered* a better society, but it is better in one respect, namely, that it is a society of equals. Such a response allows that the principle of equality cannot be the only principle of distributive justice, for other things matter as well. The reply also leaves us with the question: why should we care about equality, if no one benefits from it?

The principle of sufficiency says that what matters is that everyone has enough, *not* whether some have more than others. Enough of what, and for what? That depends on the details of the theory that hosts the principle, but for the present purposes we can say that the principle maintains that all should have enough resources to enjoy a worthwhile human life.

The principle of sufficiency says nothing about the relative holdings of members of society, but focuses instead on the absolute holdings of the poorest members of society (see Information Box 1.2 Absolute and relative poverty). If the poor have less than enough to enjoy a sufficiently worthwhile existence and society is rich enough that the poor could be helped, then there is an injustice and we have reason to redistribute from the rich to the poor to the point where the poor no longer suffer extreme poverty. Once every member of society meets the standard of sufficiency (i.e. has enough), then distributive justice is satisfied and there's no further cause for redistribution, no matter how great the degree of inequality is. Since the principle of sufficiency focuses on the absolute holdings of the least well-off and whether these holdings meet the standard of sufficiency, the principle of sufficiency is immune to the leveling down objection; the principle gives us no reason to take from the rich and give to the poor unless we thereby improve the lot of the least well-off.

INFORMATION BOX 1.2 ABSOLUTE AND RELATIVE POVERTY

There are two ways to talk about the poor and the rich (or poverty and wealth). First, we might measure poverty in relative terms, so the poor are those who have less than others, who we can then count as rich. The poor are poor relative to the rich, who are rich relative to the poor. Even if a person is quite wealthy, she still counts as (relatively) poor when compared to those who are super-wealthy.

Second, we might measure poverty in terms of some absolute standard, be it $5/day or access to some bundle of goods (housing, food, water, clothing, etc.). In that case, a person is poor insofar as she does not have enough to meet the standard, no matter if other people have more or less than her.

The difference between these two measures of poverty is relevant to the disagreement between the principle of equality and the principle of sufficiency. *The principle of equality says that all relative poverty is unjust,* for justice requires that all have (at least roughly) an equal share of the wealth (or whatever other good we want to distribute). *The principle of sufficiency says that only absolute poverty is unjust,* for justice requires simply that no person should live in the extreme sort of poverty where she cannot enjoy a worthwhile life.

The principle of priority agrees with the principle of sufficiency that what matters is the lot of the least well-off, not how much they have relative to what others have. Unlike the principle of sufficiency, however, the principle of priority does not focus on a threshold standard of adequacy (that all have enough), but instead says that we should create a situation where the least well-off are as well-off as they could possibly be, meaning that there is no accessible alternative distribution where the least well-off group has more.

To illustrate these three principles, imagine a society divided neatly into three groups: the least well-off (LWO), the middle class (Middle), and most well-off (MWO), and imagine also that we have a choice among three distributions of a resource (see Figure 1.2).

The black line illustrates the level of resources that is the threshold for having enough by the principle of sufficiency. The principle of equality favors the first distribution, since it is the only one that achieves equality. The principle of sufficiency is equally satisfied by the first and the third distributions, since in both of these every

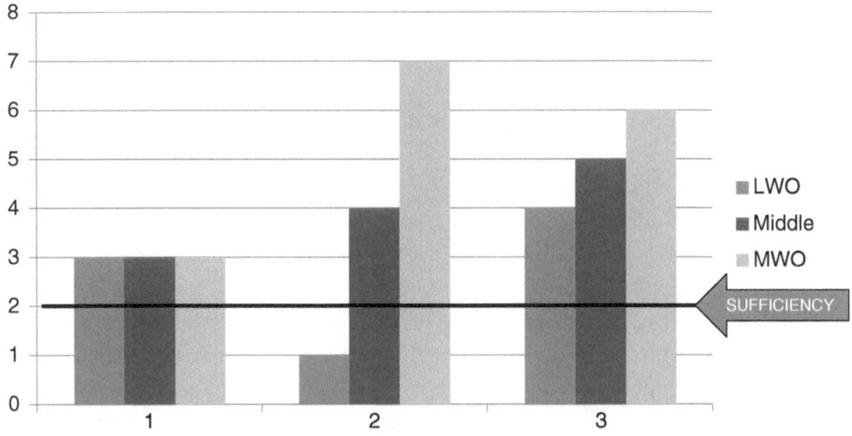

FIGURE 1.2 Simple distributions

member of society has enough, but it rules out as unjust the second distribution, since in that distribution the least well-off have less than enough. The principle of priority favors the third distribution, since of the three distributions this is the one where the least well-off have the most.

Notice that from the point of view of the principle of priority, it does not matter for the justice of the distribution how much the other groups in society have – the distribution is just if it maximizes the lot of the least well-off compared to other accessible distributions, unjust if it doesn't. For the same reason, the principle of priority will judge all distributions where the least well-off have the same level of resources as equally just, no matter how much the other groups in society have. Thus, the principle of priority says that all three distributions in Figure 1.3 are equally just.

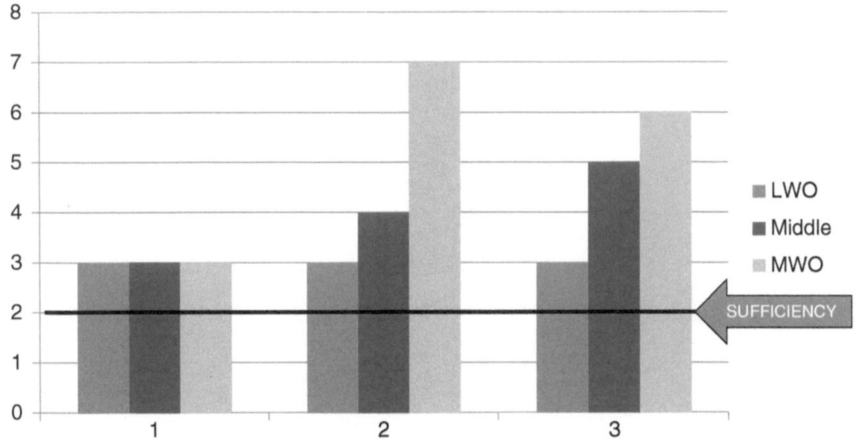

FIGURE 1.3 Simple distributions without poverty

Since the principle of priority focuses on maximizing the absolute holdings of the least well-off, it gives us no reason to criticize inequalities (i.e. relative holdings), but by the same token the principle of priority is immune to the leveling down objection. The principle of priority only tells us to change a distribution if we can make the least well-off better-off and does not justify a redistribution that either does not improve the lot of the least well-off or makes them worse off.

The principle of utility tells us that the just distribution is that which maximizes the sum of utility, where utility measures the sum of benefits and costs, or desirable minus undesirable consequences. Different theories of value offer different ways to make sense of this principle. In the simplest versions, the principle of utility tells us to maximize either the sum of the good that is distributed, or the number of preferences that can be satisfied by the distribution. Thus, if we can increase the sum of utility by allowing inequalities or poverty, then we should do so. To illustrate, think again of the simple case of a society with only three groups and three possible distributions (Figure 1.4).

The principle of utility says that in Figure 1.4 the third distribution is just (and the other distributions are unjust), since that is the distribution that maximizes the sum of utility. Note that the principle of utility would say the same even if the least well-off fall below the line of sufficiency, *as long as the sum of utility is higher* than in any other available distribution.

The principle of merit says the justice of a distribution of a resource or burden depends on how well it tracts the merit or desert of the relevant persons. There are two versions of the principle of merit. In the stronger version, the principle says that people should get what they merit. In the weaker version, the principle says that equally meritorious people should receive the same or be equally well-off. The stronger version implies the weaker version, but not *vice versa*, for if all receive what they merit, then the equally meritorious receive the same, but

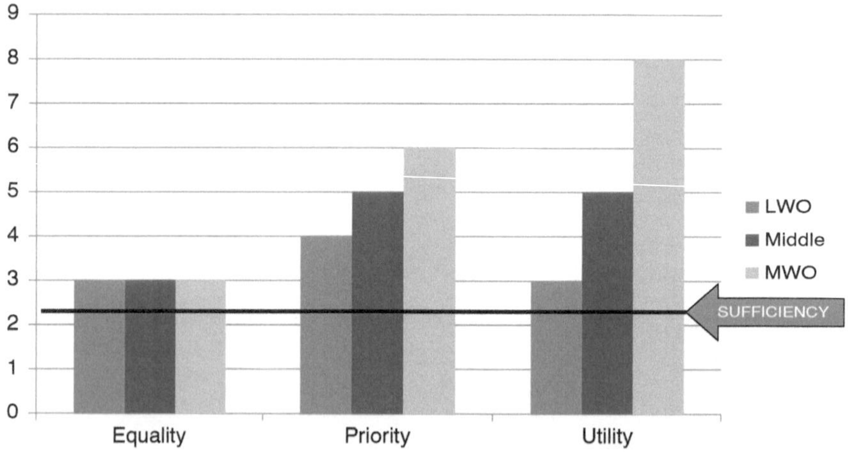

FIGURE 1.4 Simple distributions favored by principles of distributive justice

equally meritorious persons could receive the same without any of them getting what they merit – indeed the weaker version could be satisfied in a world where everyone receives the opposite of what they merit!

Different theories of merit produce different principles of merit. The most common definition is merit as desert, so that the strong principle states the desertist position that people get what they deserve, but there are other options. One popular alternative to the desertist version of the principle of merit defines merit in terms of contribution to a shared product (or marginal contribution to surplus of production). While desert is tied to personal virtue and how hard persons work, the notion of merit as contribution swings free of notions of virtue and effort: the most productive person could be a dishonorable slacker who just happens to be extremely good at what she does.

Different principles of merit can be combined with different subjects of distribution (resources, welfare, etc.). But all such principles permit and even require absolute poverty, inequality, worse-than-necessary conditions for the least well-off, and sacrifices of total utility, when these sorts of conditions correspond to people getting what they merit. So, no matter the definition of merit and the distribuendum that the principle covers, the principle of merit is *not* an egalitarian principle, for the principle of merit requires inequalities in situations of unequal merit. The principle of merit is a *principle of equity* (those who are equal in some respect should get the same, and those who are unequal in that respect should not get the same). The principle of equity contradicts the principle of equality, for the principle of equality requires that some who are unequal in the relevant respect get the same.

Finally, *the principle of liberty* says that we cannot judge the justice of distributions by looking at what people have, and that there is no pattern, such as equality or equity, that distributions ought to satisfy. According to the principle of liberty, a distribution is just if it arose by voluntary transactions. Any of the distributions sketched in Figures 1.2, 1.3, and 1.4 above *could* arise by voluntary transactions and, if one did, then, according to the principle of liberty, it is just, no matter what else is true about it; if it did not, it is unjust, no matter what else is true about it. Whether a distribution contains extreme poverty, or extreme inequality, or fails to maximize utility is irrelevant. Only the history of the distribution matters; if the history is a history of voluntary transactions, then the distribution is just. The principle of liberty, then, judges the justice of a distribution by looking at its history, and since we do not know the histories of the distributions of Figures 1.2, 1.3, and 1.4, the principle of liberty cannot determine the justice of these distributions – by the principle of liberty, each of the distributions in these figures could be just or unjust. By reducing the justice of a distribution to its history, the principle of liberty exemplifies the idea of *pure procedural distributive justice* (see Information Box 1.3 Procedural justice).

These, then, are the main principles of distributive justice: equality, sufficiency, priority, utility, merit, and liberty. Later in this book we shall see how these principles find their homes in the different theories of distributive justice. In the next part of this first chapter, we'll take a brief look at the third element and level of theories of distributive justice, namely, their institutional implications.

INFORMATION BOX 1.3 PROCEDURAL JUSTICE

Procedural justice is the idea that the justice of an outcome is a function of the process (or procedures) that led to the outcome.

Think of the outcome of a game: who the prize for winning a game should go to depends on how the game went (e.g. who scored the most goals), not on any features of the players or how they are related, and there is no way to answer the questions of "Who won?" or "Who should get the prize for winning?" other than to actually play the game.

The principle of liberty is a principle of pure procedural distributive justice; if a distribution came about from another just distribution by voluntary transactions, then it is just. We cannot say what a just distribution looks like in advance of transactions – as in a game, there is no way to tell in advance who should get what. Entitlements are the result of persons playing the game (i.e. voluntary transactions).

Pure procedural justice can be contrasted with *perfect procedural justice*, where there is an independent criterion for what the outcome should be and we can design the procedure that will produce the right outcome: if we know that the right outcome is that each child gets an equally sized piece of the pie, we might have an adult cut it, rather than letting the kids go at it on their own.

Sometimes we know the right outcome, but cannot design a procedure that brings it about. These are cases of *imperfect procedural justice*. An example is the criminal trial system: the right outcome is that all, and only, the guilty are convicted of crimes, but no matter how hard we try we cannot design a system where the guilty are never acquitted and the innocent never convicted. The rules of the court aim at getting us as close as we can to this outcome, while also erring on the side of preferring the acquittal of a guilty person to the conviction of an innocent.

The idea of procedural justice is important for distributive justice, since any theory that allows free transactions among individuals must allow that, to some extent at least, the justice of a distribution depends on the fairness of the procedure by which it came about (i.e. the fairness of the marketplace wherein the transactions take place), rather than on the intrinsic features of the situation, such as whether it conforms to a pattern of equality or maximizes utility.

2.3 Institutional Implications (Institutional Design)

The whole point of a theory of distributive justice is to guide our judgments about how we should design society. That is, theories of distributive justice guide our judgments about the design of the system of institutions that (as a whole and in complex ways) define the rules of the game by which the advantages (wealth and income, opportunities, and rights) and burdens (work, risks, care, and much else) are distributed among the members of society – in a word: the economy.

The institutions that together define the economy of a society form a very complex system of rules, roles, and permissible actions. The following is an incomplete list of these (presented in no particular order):

i. Legal rules that define the economic sphere of society – the institution of property, laws that regulate contracts for services or goods, and laws that regulate the rights and obligations of capital and labor.
ii. Rules that define the system of education (elementary and higher) and how it can be accessed.
iii. Rules that define the system of healthcare and how it is accessed.
iv. Rules that define how the state's activities are funded (the tax code) and whether the state should be involved in public investments.
v. Rules governing the maintenance and transfer of resources.
vi. Rules that define the social safety net.
vii. Rules that regulate the system of pensions.
viii. Rules that define the family and familiar obligations.

This system of institutions comprises the rules of the complex game that we, as members of society, play when we try to get what we want, be that apartments in Manhattan, iPhones, academic degrees, surgery, jobs, or the means of a decent retirement (or basically anything else that we pursue by interacting with other people apart from love, friendships, honor, and similar intangible goods). A theory of distributive justice guides our design of these systems of rules. The institutional implications of a theory of justice are what the theory tells us about how we should design these rules.

One big issue is how we should define rights to hold and use *productive property*; property that is used in the production of goods and services. Think of stuff like natural resources, technology, buildings used as factories, farmland and farms, and so on. Historically, one of the heated disagreements about distributive justice has been between those who believe that productive property should be owned by private persons (whether individual persons or corporations) and those who believe that productive property should be owned by the state (i.e. by all of us as a collective). This division leads to the split between capitalist and socialist systems for the control of productive property. In *a capitalist system* the means of production (natural resources, technology, buildings used in production) are owned by private individuals (capitalists), the system of production is geared towards maximizing profits, and the productive processes (the flow of inputs and outputs of production) are determined by market forces. In *a socialist system* the means of production are owned by the state (the members of society collectively) which aims to use them for the advantage of all. The choice between these two systems (and variations of mixes of these two systems) is an important social choice, and one that theories of distributive justice should help us make.

Another (and related) social choice is the design of the system of economic rights; the rights that define and protect spheres of economic agency. If, for example, we believe that all members of society have a basic right to do what they want with their labor (time and body), then society cannot regulate working hours or working conditions, or set a minimum wage. Conversely, if we don't have this basic right, then society can regulate all these aspects of work as needed to further other social concerns, such as a fair distribution of wealth and income, or an efficient system for the production and consumption of goods and services, or the safety of workers. If we have a basic right to hold and use productive property, then the economic system must be a variety of capitalism; if we don't have this as a basic right, socialism is permissible. And so on.

Another important topic of institutional design is how society should regulate and support access to jobs, whether in the private or public sector, the education that qualifies members for jobs, and the healthcare needed to stay fit and healthy. Most of the theories discussed in this book agree that society should prohibit discrimination based on race, gender, religious affiliation, or sexual orientation (the exception is libertarianism, which can permit such discrimination in the private sphere), but should society also actively seek to promote equality of opportunity? Is it fair if wealth can buy better opportunities for one's children (is it fair if the rich kids get better education, jobs, and healthcare)? Should we try to negate the effects of luck – whether social or natural – on access to education and jobs? Should society provide education (primary or higher) free to all members? Why or why not? These also are important institutional questions that a theory of distributive justice should help us answer.

Finally, there are, of course, questions about taxation, welfare, family support, and so on. These questions tend to dominate the political debate about distributive justice: Are we paying too much/too little in taxes? Should we tax inheritances and bequests? Should society provide relief for those who find themselves in poverty? Should society guarantee healthcare for all? Can it mandate that we all buy health insurance? Should society guarantee adequate pensions for all? Again, these are questions of institutional design that a theory of justice should help us answer.

We should, however, be careful not to expect too much of a theory of distributive justice. Theories of distributive justice primarily give us visions of society, justice, and principles we can rely on when we approach the (hard and divisive) questions of institutional design – rarely does a theory of justice actually provide a clear and decisive answer to these questions. Instead, we must take the principles the theories offer and apply them to the questions we face. This shortcoming, however, is simply one of the limits of *any* theory: theories cannot tell us what to do, but they can provide general principles that we should use when we think about what to do.

3 A Source of Confusion

Distinguishing among the different levels of theories of distributive justice as outlined in the preceding sections allows us to avoid one source of confusion about distributive justice. This source of confusion is, I believe, the root of much bewilderment, frustration, and animosity. And it certainly makes it hard to understand what's actually going on in the current political debates about distributive justice.

The source of confusion is that the names of the main theories of distributive justice are used to refer to any one of the levels of theories of distributive justice *and also* to the theories as a whole. To illustrate, one definition of *socialism* is the idea that we should have collective ownership of the means of production (as sketched in the description of a socialist system for the control of productive property above). By this definition, socialism is about how we should design economic institutions. Another frequently offered definition of socialism is that anyone who affirms the principle of equality is a socialist, a claim that defines socialism in terms of a principle of distributive justice. Still others define socialism in terms of a vision of society as a community of equals relating to each other with solidarity and friendship. By this definition, socialism is about the grounding communitarian vision of society by which we might defend the egalitarian principle of distributive justice and its institutional implications. In this book, however, socialism is defined as a theory of distributive justice *that includes all three levels*: it is a communitarian vision of society that supports an egalitarian principle of distributive justice, which, in turn, can be used to defend an institutional design that involves collective ownership of the means of production.

The same confusion applies to other theories. Libertarianism is often depicted as a view about institutions (that the state should be as small as possible), or a principle of distributive justice (the principle of liberty), or as a claim about the nature of justice and the justification of society (justice consists in respect for individual rights). In this book, libertarianism is the theory that grounds the principle of liberty in a claim about the nature of justice and the legitimacy of political authority and, therefore, supports institutional implications in the direction of a minimal state, sometimes called a night-watchman state (that is, a state whose only function is to protect its members from having their rights violated).

We could run similar analyses for right- and left-liberalism, but the main points should be clear. First, people often lose their way or talk past each other when they're debating questions of distributive justice, because they fail to distinguish among the different levels of theories of distributive justice (there are many nonsocialists who care about equality, many nonlibertarians who affirm the principle of liberty, and so on). Second, people often get confused about what is really being discussed when they disagree about distributive justice, because the main terms used to discuss theories of distributive justice (socialism, libertarianism, liberalism, etc.) sometimes refer to different levels of theories, and sometimes refer to the theories as a whole. Third, in this book the terms that

I use for the theories of distributive justice (right-liberalism, left-liberalism, libertarianism, and socialism) refer to the theories as wholes, meaning the systemic ordering of all three levels (and views on equality of opportunity, economic rights, and much else; but we get to that later).

4 The Distribution of What?

Again, the subject of this book is what defines a fair and just distribution of resources, burdens, opportunities, and rights. The focus, then, is on the sorts of stuff that are produced, distributed, and consumed in accordance with the rules of society: wealth and income, opportunities for access to education and employments, economic rights, access to housing and healthcare, the means of a decent retirement, and so on.

Some philosophers think this focus is a mistake, since what matters is our well-being, not how many resources or opportunities we have at our disposal. For example, if we care about equality, then what we should care about is equal well-being, not equal wealth or income. And equal resources do not translate into equal well-being, for some people need more resources than others to obtain the same amount of well-being – some people have expensive special needs, others have expensive tastes, and still others live good lives without owning much.

This shift from resources to well-being is not without problems. For one thing, it is not clear that distributive justice is about well-being, even if well-being is the value that explains why we care about resources in the first place. The rules of the game (the laws of society) are more directly about our access to resources than our access to well-being; the tax code regulates flows of income and wealth, not our subjective experience. What's more, if we sought equality of well-being (or priority of well-being, or to maximize well-being), then we would make those whose needs are easily satisfied pay for the satisfaction of expensive wants and tastes. If I am happy only when I drink champagne and eat caviar with Snoop Dogg, then making me as happy as a normal person would require an inordinate amount of resources and these must be taken from those with less expensive tastes – and that doesn't seem fair.

Other philosophers argue that what matters is neither resources nor well-being, but the actualization of our capabilities; that is, the real opportunities that people have for doing the things that they have reasons to enjoy doing. The capabilities approach has many attractions, but also suffers many (though not all) of the same problems as the focus on well-being.

In either case, since the laws that define and regulate the economy and other spheres subject to principles of distributive justice define the rules of the game by which we distribute resources, opportunities, and rights – *not* well-being and capabilities – I take the distribution of these more direct goods as the main subject of distributive justice. Questions about the distribution of these goods are the main questions of distributive justice that occupy our public discourse and about which we find ourselves in deep disagreement. There is, of course, another set of questions about why we do, and should, care about resources, opportunities, and rights, but to properly answer that question we would need to decide what makes human existence better or worse, and that question (about the meaning of life) is beyond the scope of this book.

5 Synopsis

In the following four chapters I present four different theories of distributive justice: right-liberalism (sometimes called classical liberalism), left-liberalism (sometimes called high-liberalism), libertarianism, and socialism. These are, I believe, the main theories of distributive justice and these four chapters together provide an overview of the landscape of theories of distributive justice. In Chapters 6 and 7 I offer some reflections on what we can learn by studying these theories of distributive justice.

6 A Note on Method and Limits

I use a single political philosopher to present each of the theories of distributive justice that I treat in this book: I use Hayek for right-liberalism, Rawls for left-liberalism, Nozick for libertarianism, and Cohen for socialism. The attractions of this way of presenting the theories are several. In addition to introducing the main theories of distributive justice, this book also serves as an introduction to some of the most influential (and in my opinion most important) political philosophers of the 20th century, and using these political philosophers also allows me to present each theory of distributive justice clearly and coherently.

There are, however, two dangers to this method that the reader should be aware of. *First, each of the theories of distributive justice introduced here is really a family of diverse theories*, and by focusing on the presentation it has been given by a particular philosopher, there is a risk that I fail to give due attention to this diversity. Accordingly, there might be philosophers working within each of the theories that would disagree with the presentation I give it, because they don't believe that the philosopher I have chosen provides a good presentation of the theory.

Second, I risk doing violence to the thought of the individual philosophers that I use to represent the different theories. As I show in this book, each theory presents a coherent and systematically ordered set of answers to the questions of distributive justice, but there is a risk that the thinkers I use do not actually affirm this coherent and ordered set of answers – except when I read them tendentiously as fitting my preconceived view of the theory that I'd like them to represent.

I flag these two worries, not because I believe that I commit either of the mistakes that I'm worried about, but to invite you to approach this book with a critical mind. I truly believe that the philosophers I focus on are the best representatives of the theories that I introduce and that I give an honest and true presentation of these philosophers. But I also hope that after finishing this book you will have an appetite to read these and other political philosophers and think more about what the best theory of distributive justice looks like.

I should also acknowledge that there are a number of questions related to distributive justice that I do not treat in this book. I'm especially troubled that I leave out questions about justice in the family, justice and disabilities, and particular injustices that many suffer today. The current treatment and relative positions of women, immigrants, and various racial and ethnic groups are clearly unjust, but this book is mostly silent on these injustices. The reason is that this book examines what distributive justice is, not what we should do about particular injustices. It is not that I think that particular injustices don't matter (clearly, they do!) or that they don't deserve philosophical treatment (clearly, they do!), they're simply not questions that fall within the scope of this book, which, again, is what we can say *in general* about how we should distribute the benefits and burdens of society, not what we should do to correct particular injustices.

Finally, the theories I discuss in this book were developed as answers to how we should organize the economic systems of societies, a question that presumes a context where there is a body politic that faces this question. It remains an open question whether and how the theories discussed in this book apply to questions of international or cosmopolitan distributive justice. Again, this limitation does not express the viewpoint that such questions are uninteresting (clearly, they are interesting) or that we don't have to answer them (we do), but the fact that these questions are interesting does not undermine the interest or necessity of the questions of how we should design the economic systems in the domestic context that is the primary subject of the theories discussed in this book.

Further Reading

There are few book-length introductions to theories of distributive justice. One exception is:

Nathanson, Stephen, 1997. *Economic Justice*, London, UK: Pearson.

The *Stanford Encyclopedia of Philosophy* entry on distributive justice offers a comprehensive overview of recent debates with special attention to the luck-egalitarian position:

Lamont, Julian & Christi Favor, 2017. "Distributive Justice," *The Stanford Encyclopedia of Philosophy, Winter 2017 Edition*, Edward N. Zalta (ed.), https://plato.stanford.edu/archives/win2017/entries/justice-distributive/.

Distributive justice is frequently treated in a chapter or two in general introductions to political philosophy, including the following:

Bird, Colin, 2007. *An Introduction to Political Philosophy (Cambridge Introductions to Philosophy), 2nd Edition*, Cambridge, UK: Cambridge University Press.

Christman, John, 2017. *Social and Political Philosophy (Routledge Contemporary Introductions to Philosophy), 2nd Edition*, London, UK: Routledge.
Kymlicka, Will, 2001. *Contemporary Political Philosophy: An Introduction, 2nd Edition*, Oxford, UK: Oxford University Press.
Wolff, Jonathan, 2016. *An Introduction to Political Philosophy, 3rd Edition*, Oxford, UK: Oxford University Press.

A limited but useful overview of some of the history of theories of distributive justice is:

Fleischacker, Samuel, 2005. *A Short History of Distributive Justice*, Cambridge, MA: Harvard University Press.

Important contributions to the debate about the distribuendum of distributive justice include:

Cohen, Gerald A., 2011. *On the Currency of Egalitarian Justice, and Other Essays in Political Philosophy*, Princeton, NJ: Princeton University Press.
Daniels, Norman, 1990. "Equality of What: Welfare, Resources, or Capabilities?" *Philosophy and Phenomenological Research*, 50: 273–296.
Dworkin, Ronald, 2000. *Sovereign Virtue: The Theory and Practice of Equality*, Cambridge, MA: Harvard University Press. Chapters 1 and 2.
Sen, Amartya, 1979. *The Equality of What? The Tanner Lectures on Human Values*, Delivered at Stanford University, May 1979. Available from https://tannerlectures.utah.edu/_documents/a-to-z/s/sen80.pdf.

Important feminist contributions to the field of distributive justice include:

Held, Virginia, 1994. *Rights and Goods: Justifying Social Action*, New York, NY: Free Press.
Okin, Susan Moller, 1991. *Justice, Gender and the Family*, New York, NY: Basic Books.
Pateman, Carol, 1988. *The Sexual Contract*, Stanford, CA: Stanford University Press.

Important contributions to the debate about how we should think about international and cosmopolitan distributive justice include:

Beitz, Charles, 1973. *Political Theory and International Relations*, Princeton, NJ: Princeton University Press.
Brock, Gillian, 2009. *Global Justice: A Cosmopolitan Account*, Oxford, UK: Oxford University Press.
Moellendorf, Darrel, 2002. *Cosmopolitan Justice*, New York, NY: Westview Press.
Pogge, Thomas, 2008. *World Poverty and Human Rights: Cosmopolitan Responsibilities and Reforms, 2nd Edition*, London, UK: Polity Press.
Rawls, John, 1999. *The Law of Peoples*, Cambridge, MA: Harvard University Press.
Tan, Kok-Chor, 2004. *Justice without Borders: Cosmopolitanism, Nationalism, and Patriotism*, Cambridge, UK: Cambridge University Press.

2

RIGHT-LIBERALISM/HAYEK

1 Introduction

What justifies political authority? Why do we have a state that issues laws – and should we have such a state? A long-standing tradition responds that we do, and should, have states and laws because without them we cannot have the things that make human lives go well: peace, security, stability, freedom, science, culture, education, comfort, inventions and innovations, wealth, and the things we use every day (roads, bikes, books, sewers, computers, and so on). In short, we have states and laws because without them we cannot have peace, liberty, or prosperity.

To support this idea, we can point to the fact that rules and the societies they define evolved as *tools* that help us live together in peace and prosperity. These rules include unwritten rules, traditions, and customs, but also many types of laws. The laws may directly regulate our behavior, such as the laws of traffic, which tell us what side of the road to drive on, how fast we can go, in what sort of physical state we and our vehicles must be in, what sort of insurance we must carry when we do it, and so on. There are also many types of law that do not regulate behavior directly – here is a list of other types of law:

i. Laws that define the system of roles and rules of law enforcement (i.e. police, courts, penal system, and related functions).
ii. Laws that define the service functions of government, such as how government should be involved in supplying national and personal security, environmental protection, fire departments and healthcare, support for science and education, support for the unemployed, and the other functions of governments.
iii. Laws that govern how the state can collect the revenue needed to pay for all these government activities.

iv. Second-order laws that define the various branches of government, their authorities, and how laws of the three previously mentioned kinds can be made and executed: these include the constitutional laws that define and govern elections for public offices, the functions of parliament and the executive offices, and so on.

There are more kinds of laws than these, but this list provides an idea of the complex system of rules that defines the legal dimension of society. We live in law's empire; our rights and opportunities, our privileges and obligations, the rules of the economy and the games we play for advantages in various marketplaces, and much else, is defined by the legal system. What we do and how we do it are both defined by, take place within, and are largely determined by the system of written and unwritten laws that define society.

Right-liberalism (sometimes called classical liberalism) consists in the marriage of liberty and utility and the assumptions that hold this marriage together. For right-liberals, liberty is both desirable for its own sake *and* the primary tool of social prosperity. As we shall see at the end of this chapter, the marriage of liberty and utility is not without tensions. First, however, we need to understand how right-liberals bring them together. In the following I use Friedrich Hayek's political philosophy to explain right-liberalism.

2 Grounding Elements: Hayek's Consequentialism

Hayek's theory of justice is built on a variation of indirect, pluralist consequentialism. *Consequentialism* is the view that we ought to do what best promotes desirable outcomes; that we should look for good consequences from our actions. According to consequentialism, the main virtue of a just system of laws and institutions is *efficiency*: that the system is the most efficient system for bringing about desirable goods.

Different theories of value – of what is desirable and undesirable – produce different sorts of consequentialism. Historically, the dominant versions are:

- *Hedonistic consequentialism*, which says that the only truly good thing is pleasure and the absence of pain;
- *Preference consequentialism*, which says that the truly good thing is the satisfaction of preferences (and dissatisfaction is bad); and
- Varieties of *perfectionist consequentialism*, which say that the truly good thing is the achievement of admirable human living. (Of course, different views of admirable human living produce different sorts of perfectionism, but we need not examine these for the purposes of this book.)

Hayek believes that preference satisfaction is an important political end – one of the main attractions of society is that it allows us to get what we want – but he is not working with any of these sorts of consequentialism.

Consequentialisms comes in two main forms – *monist* and *pluralist* – depending on whether they reduce the universe of value to a single value or permit more than one value. Hedonism and preference satisfaction consequentialisms are *monist* sorts of consequentialism, since they reduce the universe of value to a single value (pleasure or preference satisfaction). Hayek is not a monist. Hayek's consequentialism is *pluralist*. He recognizes at least two distinct sorts of value: *preference satisfaction* (happiness, utility) and *individual liberty*. Liberty is both good in itself and good because the exercise of liberty leads to societal prosperity and thus increases the prospects for happiness for members of the society. This connection between liberty and utility is a defining feature of right-liberalism, and we'll return to it below.

Hayek's consequentialism is a variety of indirect consequentialism (cf. *CoL*, 156–61; *LLL* 1, Chapter 3; *LLL* 2, Chapter 7). *Indirect consequentialism* (often called rule-consequentialism) is best described by contrasting it with direct consequentialism (often called act-consequentialism). *Direct consequentialism* says that an act is morally right to the extent that it brings about the most desirable outcome. Indirect consequentialism says that an act is right if it conforms to a rule (or a law or an institution), where the general observance of that rule (or law or institution) brings about the most desirable outcome. For example, direct consequentialism will tell you that whether you should keep a promise depends on the consequences – if the consequences of breaking it are better than keeping it, you should break it. Indirect consequentialism, by contrast, tells you that you should keep your promise, if and because the general observance of the rule that promises should be kept leads to a better overall outcome for society as a whole and in the long-term.

The idea behind indirect consequentialism is that in many areas of human conduct, the most efficient way to bring about desirable outcomes is to make sure that everybody acts in a certain way. Take the example of killing: it is generally good for society if people do not kill one another, so we have a general rule that killing is impermissible except in self-defense. In contrast with direct consequentialism, which sanctions killings when they bring about a net benefit, indirect consequentialism says that killings are morally wrong, even when they bring about a net benefit. Similar rules typically defended by indirect consequentialism are prohibitions against lying, the rules of the road, and respect for individual rights. Hayek advocates for a variety of indirect consequentialism, since his theory tells us that we should construct the system of laws that best promotes happiness and liberty, whereas individual acts within the system are permissible only when they conform to this system of laws.

Hayek's consequentialism is further complicated by the fact that he takes an unusual view of how we should seek to measure utility. Hayek tells us that we should aim to improve the chances for a good life for *all* (*LLL* 2, 70, 114–5, 122, 129–30); the system of laws should aim "at increasing for any person picked out at random [...] his chances of attaining his ends [...] not at every moment, but only 'on the whole' and in the long run." (*LLL* 2, 114–5) For Hayek, the best and most just system is that where the average person has the best chances of realizing her ends (i.e. satisfying her preferences). To illustrate this principle, Hayek says that the best society is "that in which we would place our children if we knew that their position would be determined by lot" (*LLL* 2, 132).

To see what results from this principle, we must first look at another distinction. In addition to monist/pluralist and direct/indirect forms, consequentialisms can be distinguished by how they measure the good results. To illustrate, imagine a society of three persons with four possible distributions of a resource as shown in Table 2.1.

Aggregate consequentialism says that the third distribution is best, since it has the highest sum (33.6). *Average consequentialism* says that we should pick the outcome with the best average, which means that it selects the same distribution as aggregate consequentialism, except in cases where the population size varies. In this case, average consequentialism also picks the third distribution (average of 11.2).

It is not immediately clear how we should interpret Hayek's principle of aiming to improve the chances of a good life for all, or whether it leads to other conclusions about institutional design than those of aggregate or average consequentialisms. However, I believe that we should read Hayek as rejecting both aggregate and average consequentialism in favor of *product consequentialism*, since reading him in this way makes sense of his care for the well-being of the least well-off members of society and justifies provisions for a sufficientarian minimum that prevents extreme poverty. *Product consequentialism* says that the third distribution in the graph above is *worst*, since it has the lowest arithmetic product (16.5), whereas the second distribution is best, because it has the highest product (168).

Of course, this illustration is not an argument *for* anything – the result is a function of the numbers made up for the purpose of the illustration. The point is simply to show that there is a consequentialist way to worry about poverty and not simply to require the highest aggregate (or average). Who would place their children in a society where it is highly probable that they will live in absolute poverty, if there are alternatives where everybody has enough to live a decent life? Hayek is clearly sensitive to this concern, which means, I believe, that we should read him as defending a variety of product consequentialism.

TABLE 2.1 Four distributions

	Poor person	*Middle person*	*Rich person*
Sufficiency guaranteed	1	4	18
Strong middle class	2	6	14
Extreme inequality	0.6	3	30
Sufficiency and extreme inequality	1	3	29

To summarize, the grounding principle (the first level of the pyramid for Hayek's right-liberalism) is a form consequentialism, as follows:

- It is *consequentialist* because we should create the society that most efficiently produces desirable outcomes.
- It is *pluralist* because it identifies more than one basic value as a metric of desirability; in fact, it values two things – happiness (preference satisfaction) and individual liberty.
- It is *indirect* because it applies to systems of laws rather than actions.
- Outcomes are ranked by the *multiplication product* of the distribution of benefits among members of society, rather than the average or aggregate of such distributions.

The principles of distributive justice that, Hayek argues, best satisfy this consequentialist grounding are the principles of utility (laws should aim to maximize happiness), liberty (a just distribution of goods results from free transactions), and sufficiency (no one should live in abject poverty).

The next sections explain why these (and only these) are the principles of distributive justice in Hayek's right-liberalism.

3 Spontaneous Orders and the Game of Catallaxy: Hayek's Defense of Free Markets

What system best secures the ends of society? Hayek's answer is that we best secure the ends of society by unleashing the creative powers of a free civilization; we should allow free markets to work their magic, restricting the functions of the state to security, support for the market, and provisions for the goods and services that the market does not supply efficiently.

Perhaps surprisingly, Hayek's defense of the free market starts with ignorance (*CoL*, Chapter 2; *LLL* 1). As Hayek sees it, *either* we try to use some sort of central planning for running the economy, *or* we use free markets. If we use central planning, politicians or experts define the ends of society as best they can and then try to design the system of rules and institutions that most efficiently brings about these ends. The planners can then specify what sorts of factories there should be, what they should produce, how much of it, and using what resources; how much goods should cost, how much workers should be paid, and so on – all with an eye to most efficiently satisfying the ends of society as they understand them.

However, the planners that do both the defining and the designing are individual persons (experts or politicians or technocrats), who work from their personal understanding of the ends of, and their particular knowledge of, society. They might know various general facts, such as the laws of sociology, psychology, and economy, and the availability of natural resources, the climate of the society, and so on, and they know their own local circumstances; but they cannot know the local circumstances of other members of society, nor what they value or how much they value it.

The only alternative, as Hayek sees it, to central planning is to let the economy define itself – to let the free market define who produces what, let producers decide how to go about the production of goods, let the laws of supply and demand set prices and wages, and let those with excess capital invest it where they think they'll get the best return on their investment. (Please note that this is Hayek's view of our choices. There are problems with this view, discussed below.)

One of the central claims of Hayek's philosophy, and of right-liberalism in general, is that the free market is much more efficient than central planning even if we assume complete non-corruption of public officials. Why? Because central planners are human beings and as such have limited knowledge; they are, in a word, *ignorant* of most of the relevant facts. Since central planners do not know the local circumstances of other people, nor what they want or how badly they want it, central planners have to make educated guesses at things like demand for and availability of resources, desires for work versus leisure, and much else.

A free market is an ongoing spontaneous order. *Spontaneous orders* are systems where individual members coordinate spontaneously to create an orderly arrangement – the contrast is designed orders (organizations) where individual members are guided by some design (and designer) to produce the ordered system. A brick wall is a designed order – the wall is an orderly construction, created by some person to produce a well-defined end, whether that end is to support the roof, keep heat inside, or keep strangers outside (or all of these). Spontaneous orders are not organized by anyone; they are not designed, there is no designer behind them, and their orderliness is not for the sake of some end or ends, but simply emerges as the result of the coordination of the individuals in the order. Of course, that does not mean that they do not bring about desirable ends.

Chemistry provides examples of spontaneous orders. Think of the crystals that form on a string when you make rock candy. The individual molecules follow no design made by a designer, and yet the molecules create the crystal in the most orderly fashion. The result is tasty, pretty, and well ordered – it is *as if* it was designed to be that way, though of course it is not. Biology offers many other examples of spontaneous orders. Think of how the fish in a school act in the presence of a predator. By each individual fish coordinating its movements with the fish around it, the school forms an ordered whole that increases the chances of survival for each individual fish. Similar things happen when a murmuration of starlings is approached by a bird of prey; each individual bird coordinates its movements to the birds next to it, and the result is a compact mass of birds that is capable of chasing away the predator.

Human activities also present numerous examples of spontaneous orders. One of the most remarkable of these is the distribution of goods and services in a free market. In such a market, goods and services flow according to the laws of supply and demand. Wherever goods are in demand and the demand is backed by purchasing power, goods will be supplied – and not only supplied, but supplied at a competitive price. The producers of goods need not care for their customers, or even know who their customers are, apart from the fact that they are able and willing to pay a profitable price for the goods in question – facts that are clearly communicated by the price mechanism. The producers, pursuing only their own profit, supply the demanded goods at a competitive price to the benefit of the consumer. The price mechanism lets producers know what to produce and where to supply it. Think of how you can buy heaters and air-conditioning when you need heating or cooling, or milk, or bread, or coats, or an electrician, or pencils, or … The list of things that you have at your easy disposal (if you have money) is almost infinite – with few exceptions, if you have money, the market supplies whatever you need.

Do you need a pencil? There are thousands available for next day delivery. Does that mean that somewhere someone tried to guess whether you – you personally – needed a pencil? Or that someone cares for your personal well-being and therefore produced a pencil? No. All that the producers of pencils have to know is conveyed to them by the price mechanism, and all they have to care for is their own profit; they know that they can make a profit by producing pencils at a certain cost and supplying them at a certain price, and that's all they need to know for you to have a pencil when you want it.

What's more, there is no single producer of a pencil. Producing a pencil involves a huge network of producers that coordinate their activities – the result is a pencil, and there is one factory that produces the end result, but that factory relies on easy access to the huge number of things that go into the production of a pencil, and probably subcontracts large parts of the production, and yet that factory too can rely on the supply of whatever it needs. Not because somewhere someone is guessing that they'll need these things, but because, guided by the price mechanism, the market provides what is needed, where it is needed, at a competitive price.

Add to the price mechanism and the laws of supply and demand the way the market harnesses each person's self-love to entice productivity from them, the division of labor, the advantages of specialization, and technological innovations (many of which are driven by market incentives), and we have the desirable result: *a spontaneous and orderly process* where individuals, guided by their own preferences, using their own knowledge, and coordinating with individuals in their local spheres of action, create an efficient and orderly system for the production and distribution of goods and services.

Using a Greek term, Hayek calls this spontaneous order produced by a free market a "*catallaxy*" (*LLL* 2, 109), and the ongoing orderly processes that are the economy at work and by which economic advantages are distributed the "game of *catallaxy*" (*LLL* 2, 71, 115).

The idea that self-interested pursuits best serve the public good goes back at least to Mandeville's idea in *The Fable of the Bees* that private vices are public virtues (in today's parlance: "greed is good"). Coupling this idea to the economy and the way that self-interested pursuits in a free market produce a spontaneous order beneficial to all goes back at least to Adam Smith's *The Wealth of Nations* (first edition published in 1776). There, Smith shows how self-interested pursuits in a free market lead persons to act in ways that best promote the interests of others and the good of society as a whole:

> by directing that industry in such a manner as its produce may be of the greatest value, he intends only his own gain, and he is in this, as in many other cases, led by an invisible hand to promote an end which was no part of his intention.
>
> (The Wealth of Nations, *366)*

The wonder of the free market economy is that it harnesses the knowledge and talents of the individuals involved in it without appealing to anything *but* their self-interest. Simply by pursuing their self-interest in the way they know best, and using whatever knowledge they have available, each individual ends up working in a coordinated fashion with other individuals involved in the economy to create the most efficient system for the production and distribution of goods and services. No amount of central planning could achieve the same desirable result, for any individual politician or expert must be ignorant of most of the values and desires of most other individuals, nor will they have good knowledge of the particular circumstances of most other individuals. Thus, the free market economy is a more efficient system for the production and distribution of goods and services than is any system of planning.

The free market economy has two advantages when compared to a system that involves central planning. First, because the free market economy is the most *efficient* system for the production and distribution of goods, it is the system that achieves the highest total level of economic prosperity. Though economic prosperity will not be equally shared, the free market system offers the best aggregate system of opportunities for the satisfaction of preferences for goods and services – including houses, cars, food, water, and so on.

Second, because the free market economy allows individuals to decide what to buy, what to consume, how to work, where to invest, and how much to charge when they supply their goods and services to others, it secures a very high degree of *individual liberty* in the economic sphere of life. In a centralized economy, where planners try to decide how to run the economy, who produces how much, at what costs, and so on, the will of the central planners unavoidably determines what other individuals do. This restricts liberty in two ways: first, the values of the central planners determine the structure of the economy, and thus also the choices individuals can make in the economy, which means that the individuals involved in the economy are made to pursue other persons' ends. Second, since the design of the planners determines what individuals choose to produce, how to produce it, and how to distribute it, individuals are not at liberty to choose these things for themselves. If a central planner decides how much you can charge for your labor, or for the goods you produce, then that limits your liberty.

In sum, Hayek argues that a centralized, planned economy is inefficient and lacking in liberty. A free market economy, by contrast, is efficient and allows a wider range of liberty. Thus, if we care about individual happiness and liberty, a free market economy is better (and thus more just) than a centralized economy. Accordingly, the task of politics and legislation is "not to set up a particular order but merely to create conditions in which an orderly arrangement can establish and ever renew itself" (*CoL*, 161).

4 The Dual Attractions of Liberty

The discussion above brings out how Hayek (and right-liberals more generally) values liberty in two distinct ways. First, *liberty is good in itself*, and the justice of laws depends at least in part on whether they respect and promote liberty. Second, *liberty is a tool of prosperity*, meaning that only a system that allows liberty in the economic sphere unleashes the creative powers of a free civilization, offers an efficient system for the production and distribution of goods and services and, therefore, secures a society where the average person has the best opportunities for happiness. Hayek even goes so far as to say that the main value of liberty is the benefits it gives to others, for it is from the liberty of others (and the whole system of liberty working its magic) that a person receives most of its benefits: "The benefits I derive from freedom are thus largely the result of the uses of freedom by others" (*CoL*, 32).

5 The Rule of Law, Not Men

But what is liberty? While Hayek's answer to this question is murky, the question itself is notoriously hard to answer, so in this he is no different from other philosophers who value liberty (and *all* the thinkers we meet in this book do, in fact, value liberty). Hayek says that whether a person is free or not depends on "whether he can expect to shape his course of action [...] or whether somebody else has power so to manipulate the conditions as to make him act according to that person's will rather than his own" (*CoL*, 13). Liberty, accordingly, "describes the absence of a particular obstacle – coercion by other men" (*CoL*, 19). But defining liberty as the absence of coercion just raises another hard question: What is coercion?

Coercion, Hayek says, "occurs when one man's actions are made to serve another man's will, not for his own but for the other's purpose" (*CoL*, 133). But this too leaves us with questions. When, exactly, are one man's actions "made to" serve another man's will? Of course, the robber that holds a gun to your head is coercing you to act in a manner that serves his rather than your will; when you hand him your money, you're not really doing what you want, but what he wants. But even such cases are tricky. Surely, you *also* serve your own will (to not be shot) when you hand the robber your money. And don't you also serve the car salesman's will, when you hand him your money? And what about the sales tax that is part of the price of the car – the money you hand to the state?

In any case, suppose that we say that a person is coerced to do or not to do X, when her choice is influenced by threats of harm from other persons, and that the person is at liberty with respect to doing X when she is not coerced. It would seem to follow from this definition that most laws are coercive, for when there is a law, your choice about whether to break it or not is influenced by the threat of punishment for lawbreaking, whether that punishment takes the form of fines, imprisonment, or something else. Does that mean that a friend of liberty should prefer anarchy? Hayek does not think so. To see why, we need to take a look at his distinction between *laws* and *commands*.

There are three important differences between commands and laws: their source, their audience, and the manner in which they direct their audience. In the pure version, *a command* is an imperative whereby one person determines the act of another person, "and leaves those to whom it is addressed no chance to use their own knowledge or follow their own predilections" (*CoL*, 150). To illustrate, think of the officer commanding a private to run from point A to point B. The private does not decide where to go, her knowledge and preferences did not inform the decision that she should do it, and she does not go there to serve her personal ends. Commands are issued from specific persons to specific persons and concretely determine the acts of their receivers, leaving little or no room for them to use their own knowledge to pursue their own ends. *A law*, by contrast, is issued by a proper legislative body; it binds all members of society equally, and does not command anyone to any particular actions, but instead "provides merely additional information to be taken into account in the decision of the actor" (*CoL*, 150). To illustrate, think of the law that prohibits drunk driving. The law binds all citizens; only under the most unusual circumstances (to save another person's life, for example) is it permissible to drink and drive; even then, you are breaking the law. The law does not tell people what to do, but merely provides a rule they must take into account when they decide what to do – the law does not tell them that they must stay sober at the party, but that if they drink then they cannot drive. Laws are issued by a legislative authority that purportedly represents all members of society, it is addressed to all members of society, and it issues abstract, general directions that the members of society can take into account when they use their own knowledge to pursue their own ends.

Commands and laws are both coercive, but laws that satisfy the requirements of *the rule of law* are nevertheless consistent with liberty: "When we obey laws, in the sense of general abstract rules laid down irrespective of their application to us, we are not subject to another man's will and are therefore free" (*CoL*, 153). The rule of law avoids the sort of objectionable interpersonal coercion that obtains under the rule of men. In *the rule of men*, some persons rule and the rest are subjects; some use coercion to make others serve their ends. Under the rule of law, the system of the state is designed to prevent the political authority from serving or expressing the will of any particular members of society. When the coercive powers of the state serve or express the will of particular members, the rest are subjected to the arbitrary will of the rulers, as was the case in most societies of human history. Under the rule of law, by contrast, the coercive power of the state serves no particular will, but instead serves the general or common good of society as a whole.

Commands work well in the army, but if you want a free society that unleashes the creative powers of a free civilization to the benefit of all, then political authority must speak the language of laws, not commands. Where political authority speaks the language of commands, some are subjected to the wills of others (which destroys their liberty to use their own knowledge to pursue their own ends) and the economy is organized according to the designs of politicians or experts; it becomes the rule of men, and cannot provide the benefits of the spontaneous order process of the game of catallaxy.

To realize the rule of law (rather than men), laws must have certain properties (*CoL*, Chapter 10):

i. Laws must be abstract and general so that they do not bind specific groups of people, and they must determine no particular actions, but bind all members to follow abstractly stated rules in the indefinite future.
ii. Laws must be publicly proclaimed and promulgated so that all members know what the laws are, which means that they know the general rules of what they must, may, and may not do when they apply their particular knowledge in the pursuit of their own ends.
iii. Laws must apply equally to all, meaning that they cannot issue any specific privileges or create discriminations between groups of citizens.

To reliably secure that laws have these properties, Hayek believes that we should adopt the following constitutional rules:

i. To ensure that all political authorities express the rule of law rather than men, there should be a division of powers, where the legislative function is clearly separated from the executive and judicial functions and the executive function is limited to applying and administering the laws.
ii. There should also be various procedural safeguards in place to ensure that the executive power cannot transgress its mandate: the rules of a fair trial, habeas corpus, no punishment without a crime, judicial review, and so on, are examples of these safeguards.
iii. In addition to procedural protections, various rights such as freedom of speech, freedom of assembly, freedom of religion, and security of property should be guaranteed for all.

The properties of the rule of law are not themselves laws, but serve as metalaws. They might be explicit constitutional provisions, but often they will simply be norms and assumptions of the legal culture of the society in question. They work as part of or alongside the constitution to define and limit the genesis and extent of political authority and the various powers and offices of government. Each metarule presents an ideal to strive for, and it will often be unclear exactly what it requires – but the closer a society gets to satisfying these metarules, the more secure is the rule of law and the lower the risk that political authority is merely the rule of men. The point of enumerating rights in a bill of rights is not to single out especially important rights and liberties, and especially not to say that other rights and liberties are not important, but simply to make vivid and secure some of the salient components of individual liberty (*CoL*, 216–7). Hayek doubts that we really need a bill of rights, and sometimes seem to prefer a general presumption of liberty to the enumeration of a list of rights (*LLL* 3, 109–11).

This, then, is Hayek's reply to the anarchist: under the rule of law, the exercise of political authority avoids the sort of coercion where some persons are made to serve the will of others. In fact, in a well-regulated society the laws protect, respect, and enlarge individual liberty. With this belief in the liberating potential of law Hayek enlists himself in a long republican tradition nicely expressed by Locke in the following passage from his *Second Treatise on Government*:

> The end of law is, not to abolish or restrain, but to preserve and enlarge freedom. […] where there is no law there is no freedom. For liberty is to be free from restraint and violence from others; which cannot be where there is no law; and it is not, as we are told, a liberty for every man to do as he lists. […] but a liberty to dispose, and order as he lists, his person, actions, possessions, and his whole property, within the allowance of those laws under which he is, and therein not to be the subject of the arbitrary will of another, but freely follow his own.
>
> (Second Treatise, II, *sect. 57)*

Again, the rule of law is desirable because, *first*, we need laws to have liberty, peace, security, and prosperity, and, *second*, only laws that satisfy the requirements of the rule of law are consistent with the liberty of those subjected to them. Liberty, in turn, is attractive both as an end in itself and because liberty is necessary for the sort of spontaneous market order (the game of catallaxy) that is the most efficient system for the production and distribution of the many goods and services that are the ingredients of societal prosperity.

The rule of law is necessary, but not sufficient for liberty. Liberty also requires that the laws have a certain content and that the state actively enforces the laws and in other ways protects citizens. In addition, the system of liberty can be supported and promoted in many ways by the state – there are many functions of government which are not coercive functions. In the following we take a look at some of these functions.

6 The Coercive and Noncoercive Functions of Government

The rule of law allows us to distinguish between the prohibited, permitted, and required functions of the state (see *CoL*, especially Chapters 14 and 15).

The state is *prohibited* from using coercive power in a way that is inconsistent with the rule of law. This means that the state cannot command any particular person or group of persons to perform particular actions, the state cannot make retroactive laws, the state cannot issue privileges or discriminate between groups of persons or make anyone exempt from the laws, and the state cannot micro-manage the economy – it cannot decide who produces what or in what quantities, at what price or to whom they should sell it, or the supply or prices of services (*CoL*, 227–8).

Conversely, there are many functions that the state is *required* to perform: it must provide for the security of persons, property, and contracts, and it must generally provide for a system of law that allows for a well-functioning society (rules of the road, rules governing pollution and other externalities, the basic rules of the economy, and so on) (*CoL*, 228–30).

In addition, the state is *permitted*, but *not required*, to do a number of things (cf. *CoL*, part III). The state may provide for public goods that the market does not supply efficiently: the construction and maintenance of infrastructure, sanitation, and power supply; provide support for research; and provide a system of emergency management and assistance (fire departments and the like). The state may also support the monetary system (though Hayek argues that the state should not have a monopoly on issuing money), set standards of weights and measures, and conduct and provide information from surveys. More dramatically, Hayek also suggests that the state may be involved in securing that basic education and healthcare are available to all, though it should do so by supporting a private market in these goods rather than by supplying them directly. In addition, Hayek argues that the state should offer a system for poor relief so that no person falls into extreme poverty. Finally, the state may also regulate the market as needed to ensure that it functions efficiently: it may regulate working hours and working conditions, limit freedom of contract, require licensing for certain professions (say, doctors and gun vendors), and implement other regulations that secure an efficient and safe economy.

Of course, to fund its various activities the state has to collect revenue. So, the state is permitted to tax income or wealth, as needed, to finance its various activities – including poor relief – and that provides a second justification for coercive state power (i.e. in addition to issuing the rules of society that protect and enable liberty). Hayek summarizes his view on the functions of the state as follows:

> The task of government is to create a framework within which individuals and groups can successfully pursue their respective aims, and sometimes to use its coercive powers of raising revenue to provide services which for one reason or other the market cannot supply. But coercion is justified only in order to provide such a framework within which all can use their abilities and knowledge for their own ends so long as they do not interfere with the equally protected individual domains of others.
>
> *(*LLL *3, 139; see also* CoL, *143–7, 220–2)*

Though the state may tax to fund its activities, the state should not be involved in *redistributive* taxation in the pursuit of satisfying some principle of distributive justice. Hayek is adamant that the idea of distributive justice has no place in a just society – for, according to Hayek, the idea of distributive justice is conceptually confused, and its pursuit inevitably violates the rule of law and destroys economic prosperity (we return to this topic below).

7 Principles of Distributive Justice: Utility, Liberty, and Sufficiency

Hayek tells us that just civil societies deliver the goods: peace, liberty, knowledge, culture, economic prosperity, and opportunities for happiness. Hayek also argues that a system of liberty is the system that best achieves these goods, and so the coercive power of the state is justified only insofar as it is needed to uphold and enforce the laws of society and to fund its various coercive and supporting functions. The state is permitted to supply and support a number of service functions, and to use its coercive power to fund these, when the state's supply and support of these is more efficient than simply leaving it to the market to supply these goods on its own. Even so, the main idea of Hayek's political philosophy, which is also the core idea of right-liberalism generally, is that liberty is both an end and the only sure means for achieving the various other ends of society. Here is how Hayek expresses this idea:

> It was in effect the discovery that playing a game according to rules improves the *chances* of all, even at the risk that the outcome for some might be worse than it would be otherwise, which made classical liberalism aim at the complete elimination of power in determining relative incomes earned in the market. [...] if the aim is to provide maximum opportunity to men as they are, without any arbitrary coercion, we can achieve our ends only by treating them according to the same rules irrespective of their factual differences, leaving the outcome to be decided by those constant restructurings of the economic order which are determined by circumstances nobody can foresee. [...] This game serves not only the winner, because his gain from having served the others best is only part of what he has added to the social product and it is only by

> playing according to the rules of this game that we can assure that high degree of utilization of resources which no other known method can achieve.
>
> (LLL *3, 141, 142, 143)*

If we look closely at this passage, we see that Hayek combines two principles of distributive justice. First, he tells us that we should design the system of laws and institutions so that it best achieves the desirable ends – or, more precisely, so that it offers the average person the best chances for realizing their *own* ends, whatever these ends are. He thus affirms *a principle of utility* that tells us we should aim to design the system that maximizes opportunities for happiness (preference satisfaction). Of course, in addition to maximizing opportunities for happiness, the best society also secures liberty – happiness and liberty are equally important goods of society. Though Hayek is not clear about this, we can imagine that he would say that the value of peace, stability, economic prosperity, and perhaps also knowledge and culture, is that these goods make it easier to gain access to happiness and liberty.

Second, Hayek tells us that the system that best delivers opportunities for happiness and liberty is the system of *liberty*, where no person is coerced except in accordance with the rule of law and where the laws that regulate the economy aim simply to define and secure the background rules of a free market system. So, since liberty is an end in itself, and since the economic system should be designed to define and support a free market, it is clear that Hayek's principle of utility both supports and stands next to *a principle of liberty*, which says that the distribution that results from the voluntary exchanges of persons is just no matter if it conforms to some pattern. (Maybe it would be more correct to say that it is "not unjust" since Hayek prefers to use the term "justice" only for intentional actions; the distribution that results from the game of catallaxy is not intended, but simply emerges as the result of individual choices as these are coordinated with the choices of others.) Hayek thus endorses a proceduralist view of distributive justice; if the rules of the economy are well designed, then the outcome of the game of catallaxy is just: "justice is not concerned with the results of the various transactions but only with whether the transactions themselves are fair" (*LLL*, 1, 141).

So, the core of Hayek's theory of distributive justice, and of right-liberal theories of distributive justice in general, is a combination of two principles:

The principle of utility which tells us that the just society (and just laws and institutions) is that (or those) that best promotes the ends of society – which we can condense to just two, namely, happiness and liberty.

The principle of liberty, which says that the just distribution of resources is the distribution that results from voluntary transactions in a free market.

Right-liberalism is defined by the marriage of these two principles and the empirical assumptions needed to hold their marriage together.

Hayek also affirms a principle of sufficiency:

The sufficientarian principle that says that society must not permit extreme poverty, but should secure that every member of society has enough to live a minimally decent life – a principle that can be satisfied by guaranteeing a minimum basic income (*CoL*, 259–60; *LLL* 2, 87; *LLL* 3, 54–6, 141–3, 150).

The sufficientarian principle is derivative; justified by the principle of utility. Poverty is bad both for the poor and for everyone else, so society is generally better served if it satisfies the sufficientarian principle. Utilitarian arguments also justify Hayek's support for public provisions for education, healthcare, investments in research and science, and other service functions.

In this fashion, the principle of utility and the principle of liberty can support secondary principles that should guide the activities of the state, but the heart of Hayek's theory of justice – and of right-liberal theories in general – is the marriage of the principle of liberty and the principle of utility, a marriage that is based on the two values that society is all about: happiness and liberty.

This marriage is not without tension, for the principle of utility and the principle of liberty are naturally opposed to each other. *The principle of utility* says that the justice of something, in this case of laws and institutions, is a function of its consequences. The justice of laws and institutions is decided by a cost-benefit analysis that counts both the benefits and the costs and then tells us that we should institute the system of laws and institutions that has the highest net benefit. When we decide whether a law or other state action is just, the principle of utility tells us that we should *look to the future* and see whether it promotes good consequences. The principle of liberty, by contrast, tells us that we should design the system of laws and institutions to best allow the members of society to use their own knowledge in the pursuit of their own ends – that is, the state should regulate as little as possible – and that the justice of distributions is a function of *the past*, since a distribution is just no matter if it conforms to some pattern and *no matter how conducive it is to happiness*. The liberty principle does not require cost-benefit analysis.

The tension between the two principles should be clear: the most efficient system of laws and institutions might *not* be the one that also best respects, protects, and preserves liberty. It might be that we sometimes have to choose between liberty and maximizing opportunities for happiness. The optimal distribution might not be the one that arises from the voluntary exchanges of the members of society, for it might be that we could increase happiness by limiting voluntary exchanges or by redistributive efforts.

The way that Hayek and right-liberals marry the two incongruent principles is by denying that such possibilities are realized. To do so they rely on a crucial empirical premise: that the system of liberty is the most efficient system, and the distribution that arises from voluntary exchanges is the optimal accessible distribution. Without this premise, Hayek would either have to choose between utility and liberty or accept that politics is a matter of striking a balance between satisfying the demands of utility and the demands of liberty, which would undermine his defense of the free market as well as his rejection of redistributive policies. Indeed, for all right-liberals, the premise that the system of liberty is also the system that best secures opportunities for happiness must be true, for if it is not, then the right-liberal defense of the system of liberty falls apart. In fact, it may be that some alternative to the free market system does better at striking a balance between the imperatives of utility and liberty.

The importance of this premise explains Hayek's insistence on the epistemic foundations of liberty, for Hayek's defense of the premise is that the epistemic shortcomings of human beings (our inevitable ignorance) entails that any attempt to improve on the system of liberty will be counterproductive and inefficient, since it requires knowledge that we do not have. An omniscient being might do better at achieving the various goods of society, but human beings cannot:

> [T]he case for individual freedom rests chiefly on the recognition of the inevitable ignorance of all of us concerning a great many of the factors on which the achievement of our ends and welfare depends. [...] If there were omniscient men [...] there would be little case for liberty.
>
> (CoL, *29; likewise* LLL *2, 8, 39, 127)*

It is, of course, questionable whether the argument from ignorance gets Hayek the conclusion he needs (we return to this question at the end of this chapter).

8 Hayek's Critique of Other Principles of Distributive Justice

Hayek argues that the pursuit of any other principles of distributive justice such as distribution according to merit, the principle of equality, or the principle of priority violates individual liberty, destroys the productive powers of society, and frustrates access to the desirable ends. His main argument for these conclusions is that any pursuit of these principles of distributive justice requires government micromanagement of the economy:

> Distributive justice requires an allocation of all resources by a central authority; it requires that people be told what to do and what ends to serve. Where distributive justice is the goal, the decisions as to what the different individuals must be made to do cannot be derived from general rules but must be made in the light of the particular aims and knowledge of the planning authority. [...] Within the limits set by the rule of law, a great deal can be done to make the market work more effectively and smoothly; but within these limits, what people now regard as distributive justice can never be achieved.
>
> (CoL, *232–3)*

The pursuit of distributive justice, therefore, is inconsistent with the rule of law: "The restrictions which the rule of law imposes on government preclude [...] the pursuit of distributive, as opposed to commutative, justice" (*CoL*, 232–3).

To explain, take the principle of equality. According to this principle, inequalities in, say, income and wealth, are unjust and the state should seek to decrease inequality, presumably by redistributive policies. Such policies could be a redistributive taxation scheme, or measures that aim to determine how much people are paid for goods and services. Both of these courses of action would violate the rule of law. If the state pursues the first option, it creates a system of perverse incentives, stifles the economy, and singles out particular people (the relatively poor) for special treatment, i.e. by taking from another particular group of people (the wealthy and those with high incomes) to give to them (*LLL* 2, 80–4). If the state pursues the second option, it gets involved in the sort of planning of the economy that both limits economic liberty and stifles the productive powers of the economy. Thus, Hayek believes that any pursuit of distributive justice both violates liberty and destroys the creative powers of the economy, to the detriment of all.

Hayek also argues that in a free society the mere idea of distributive justice (or social justice) is nonsense, since in a free society, the distribution of resources like wealth and income is not the result of intentional actions:

> Since only situations which have been created by human will can be called just or unjust, the particulars of a spontaneous order cannot be just or unjust [...] what is called 'social' or 'distributive' justice is indeed meaningless within a spontaneous order.
>
> *(*LLL *2, 33; likewise,* LLL *2, 64–5, 70, 83, 96)*

In a free society the distribution of wealth and income is the result of everybody playing the same economic game in accordance with the general rules that secure the best opportunity for access to resources of each, and "there is no need morally to justify specific distributions (of income or wealth) which have not been brought about deliberately but are the outcome of a game that is played because it improves the changes of all" (*LLL* 2, 117).

There will, of course, be losers of the free market economic game, and there is no reason to suppose that the distribution between winners and losers will follow some metric of merit so that the distribution that results from playing the game tracks socially productive behavior (or, as an economist might put it, marginal contribution to the social product). Some who are deserving will be poor; some who are undeserving will be rich. This result does not, however, give the poor a complaint against the distribution, for it is the unavoidable price we pay for having a system that both respects the liberty of each and maximizes the chances of access to resources for each:

> [T]he effects of the processes of a free society on the fates of different individuals are not distributed according to some recognizable principle of justice. Where we go wrong is in concluding from this that they are unjust.
>
> (*LLL 2, 69–70)*

Note what Hayek's reply to the hypothetical complaint of the poor does *not* say. A standard right-liberal reply to inequalities is that the poor are better-off in a free market system than they would be in any other system, which means that even though they are poor in *that* system, they too have reason to prefer that system, because in absolute terms (i.e. in access to desirable goods) they're better-off in that system than they would be in any of the accessible alternative systems. Interestingly, this reply claims that the free market system will satisfy the *principle of priority*, since of the available alternatives it is the system that makes the least well-off as well-off as they can be, even if it does not satisfy this principle by design. Rather, as a fortunate side effect, the free market system produces the most of the desirable goods and also ensures that wealth "trickles down" or that the "rising tide lifts all boats," so that this productive power also benefits those who lose out in the economic game. This is *not* Hayek's reply, and that's good, for this reply is clearly false; often redistribution would make the poor better-off.

Hayek's reply to the complaint of the poor is that, even though some persons who are poor would be better-off in an alternative system, this does not justify a complaint against the free market system (from them or from anyone else), for it is true of everybody, and thus also of the poor, that they had the best *chances* for having access to the most goods by living in a free market economy. With the principle of sufficiency guaranteed, the free market system *maximizes the average probability* for access to the means of happiness, though for those who lose the game of catallaxy it might also be true that they would be better-off in an alternative system such as a welfare state. The free market system provides the best average opportunities for happiness and liberty of any of the available systems, which means that it is preferable to every person if they think about the choice of system without knowing their actual position in it. Hayek's reply allows him to say that even the poor would choose the free market economy from any of the available alternatives, if they were to choose where to send their children without knowing what position their children would end up occupying:

> we consent to retain, and agree to enforce, uniform rules for a procedure which has greatly improved the chances of all to have their wants satisfied, but at the price of all individuals and groups incurring the risk of unmerited failure.
>
> (*LLL 2, 70)*

The existence of (relative) poverty is the price we pay for maximizing opportunities for happiness.

9 Hayek on Equality of Opportunity

We have seen that Hayek rejects the principle of equality, since any pursuit of equality of wealth and income violates the rule of law and undermines the efficiency of the economy. But there are other ways to care about equality. One principle of equality focuses on *equality of holdings*, so that what matters is that people have more or less the same wealth and income (so-called material equality), but there are other types of equality we might care about. First, we might care about *equality before the law* so that all citizens are equal in the eyes of political authority and the laws cannot issue privileges or discriminate between classes of citizens (so-called formal equality). Second, we might care about *equality of opportunity*, which requires that all members of society have equal opportunities for success, so that inequalities in the outcome (material inequality of holdings) reflect what people do, rather than their initial endowments. The idea of equal opportunity has close affinities to the principle of merit, which requires that distribution tracks merit. The principle of merit provides a justification for equality of opportunity, since merit is a function of our choices and efforts, rather than the resources we were handed by nature or nurture or the contingent circumstances we find ourselves in. (The principle of merit implies the principle of equality of opportunity, but not *vice versa*.) Hayek affirms formal equality (equality before the law), but rejects equality of holdings, equality of opportunity, and the principle of merit.

There are different ways to think about equal opportunity. In the most minimalist form, equality of opportunity requires *nondiscrimination*; access to careers is a function of talent, so that the state (and perhaps also private employers) cannot discriminate against applicants for positions based on irrelevant characteristics such as gender, religious affiliation, race, or sexual orientation. Under nondiscrimination the job market is equally open to all, so that how one is remunerated for what one brings to the market (talents, goods, services) depends on market value rather than on biases.

Of course, discrimination is not the only source of unequal opportunities, and to get to a stronger principle of equal opportunity we can look at the factors that normally determine what opportunities persons have in life. There are two main sorts of contingencies at work here: social and natural.

One strong version of equal opportunity focuses on *social circumstances* and requires that one's luck in the so-called social lottery should have minimal effect on one's opportunities. Unless we do something to counter such effects, those born into a family with resources (wealth, education, musical or artistic skill, etc.) tend to have better chances for a good life than those who are born into a family with fewer resources. If we should have equal opportunity to succeed in life, then our chances for a good life should not depend on our parents' resources or other such social contingencies. Thus, this principle of equal opportunity recommends that we limit the effects of inheritance on wealth and the influence of family resources (whether in terms of capacities or wealth) on relative access to education and other ingredients of success.

Another strong version of equality of opportunity notes that how we fare in life also tends to depend on our *natural endowments* and on whether these are valued in the societies we live in. The beautiful, the smart, and the sociable tend to do better in life. The math genius does great in a society that values math skills, the strong in societies that value strength, and so on. This version of equality of opportunity requires that we minimize the extent to which differences in natural talents translate into unequal opportunities.

The preceding gives us a way to understand the main positions on equality of opportunity:

1. Ultra-minimalist (libertarian nondiscrimination): no public discrimination in hiring, but private discrimination is permitted.
2. Minimalist (right-liberal nondiscrimination): careers should be open to talents, so there should be no discrimination in public or private hiring.
3. Stronger (left-liberal equality of opportunity): we should minimize the effects of the social lottery, but allow for the effects of the natural lottery.
4. Very strong (socialist equality of opportunity): we should minimize the effects of both the natural and the social lotteries.

Hayek embraces the minimalist position that there should be no discrimination in hiring (of careers open to talents) (*CoL*, 92–3; *LLL* 2, 84–5), but he rejects that we should try to minimize the effects of social and natural contingencies, which means that he rejects the stronger positions on equality of opportunity (*CoL*, Chapter 6; *LLL*, 2, 85). Hayek's argument against limiting the effects of the natural lottery tracks the dual principles of his theory: liberty and utility. *In terms of liberty*, the effects of the natural lottery cannot be countered without violating liberty, either by restricting what people are allowed to do with their talents, or by deciding how people should be remunerated for the use of their talents. *In terms of utility*, Hayek argues that differences in natural talents, and the material inequalities that result from the exercise of our different talents, are some of the main factors that drive economic progress. It is because we are different and have different talents that we develop competitive human enterprise, the division of labor, inventions and innovations, and much else that drive a productive economy.

Hayek's argument against limiting the effects of the social lottery splits into arguments against interfering with child-rearing in the family, equal access to education, and limits on inheritance (*CoL*, 88–93). In each case, the argument is that attempts to minimize the effects of the social lottery violate liberty and lead to a less productive economy (and thereby lower average expectation for opportunities for happiness). Hayek's argument boils down to the claims that the pursuit of equal opportunity will require government interference with liberty and lead to *less opportunities for the average person*. Of course, if the principle of merit is true, then Hayek's arguments lose much of their power – but Hayek argues that the principle of merit is false.

According to *the principle of merit*, resources should be distributed according to merit. How exactly we measure merit is, of course, a hard question, but let us say that merit is a function of virtuousness, choices, and effort. When a good person chooses carefully and puts in a real effort, then they are meritorious and ought to do well. Hayek agrees with the sentiment, but he thinks it is wrong-headed to turn the sentiment into a principle of distributive justice.

Hayek's argument against this principle starts by noting that there is a distinction between merit and value. Merit is about the person (their mind-set and effort), whereas value is a function of how useful their actions, products, or services are to others. While the notion of merit naturally invites the thought of reward (and demerit that of penalty), we often reward value rather than merit. The Nobel Prizes go to those who have produced the most interesting and useful discoveries, not to the nicest and most hardworking scientists. At the Olympic Games, the gold medal goes to the fastest runner, not to the nicest and most hardworking runner.

Markets are extremely good at tracking value, since the prices of goods and services are a function of the demand for those goods and services. If you bring valuable skills to the market, then you'll be paid well for them – no matter if you are a nice person or how hard you worked to acquire those skills. The math wizard who is just naturally good with numbers will likely be paid much more in the current market than an average and hardworking person trying to get a job using his or her math skills.

Could we design an economy where market value tracks merit, so that people are remunerated for their virtue and efforts rather than their usefulness? No, says Hayek, we could not. We are epistemically unable to gather and process all the required information. But, even if we could, the result would be a disaster. The wonder of the free market, where value tracks usefulness, is that whatever people do in pursuit of their self-interest turns out to be more or less the most socially useful thing that they could do, because they receive the highest remuneration by doing what is most valued. The free market invites the math wizard to work with math (if market value tracked merit, she should work hard at what she is *not* good at to receive the highest rewards!), the baker to supply bread at a competitive price, and the person who is a naturally talented athlete to pursue athletic excellence. In this manner, in a well-functioning market, everyone self-interestedly does the thing that is most useful to others, because this is how they get the highest remuneration, and the result is a society with maximal average opportunity for access to the various desirable goods for each.

What about those who lose out in the economy? Is that fair? Do they deserve their (relative) poverty? No, it is not *fair* and they do not deserve their relative poverty, but it is not *unjust*. In a free market economy, the distribution of wealth is a function of choices, brute luck, effort, talents, economic events that no one could foresee, and much else, and that means that sometimes (often, even) people end up poor and rich through no fault or merit of their own. But that the distribution of rich and poor is not fair does not mean that it is *un*fair, for, Hayek tells us, the notion of fairness has no real application to the distribution of opportunities, wealth, or income in a free market economy. The distribution that results from the workings of the free market is just (or at least not unjust), whether it tracks merit or not, for it is the only sort of distribution that satisfies the principle of liberty and ensures an efficient system for the production and distribution of goods and services (and thereby maximizes access to the means of happiness for the average person). The principle of merit is false, unworkable, and trying to implement it would destroy the economy and stifle the creative and productive powers of society. So, "attractive as the phrase of equality of opportunity sounds [...] any attempt concretely to realize it is apt to produce a nightmare" (*LLL* 2, 85).

In sum, there are many sorts of equality that one might care about: equal resources (material equality), varieties of equality of opportunity, and equality before the law. According to Hayek, justice *requires* equality before the law and nondiscrimination, but justice *prohibits* the pursuit of material equality and any of the stronger principles of equality of opportunity.

10 Hayek on Economic Rights

Following Hume and Smith, Hayek believes that certain economic rights and liberties must be respected in any free society: security and control of person and property, freedom to contract for goods and services, freedom to produce, use, and consume goods, and freedom to buy from and sell to whom we want (*CoL*, 140, 158; *LLL* 2, 40).

While Hayek argues that any free society must secure these economic rights and liberties, he is also skeptical of giving them a special status as fundamental rights protected in a constitution, for he is generally skeptical that *any* rights can be singled out as more important than others (*CoL*, 216–7; *LLL* 3, 110–1, 119). Historical experience may teach us that it is prudent to enshrine various rights and liberties in a constitution – including freedom of speech, religion, movement, and assembly – simply because these help to keep the reach of power within its legitimate limits; however, the constitution of liberty respects and protects all liberties equally, for what matters is individual liberty to use one's own knowledge to pursue one's own ends. We cannot say in advance what rights and liberties best secure these conditions – apart from what we can say about the rule of law and the legitimate form and content of the generation and exercise of political authority. In the last resort, a bill of rights is "no more than part of the safeguards of individual liberty which constitutionalism provides" (*CoL*, 217).

What's more, Hayek rejects the idea that economic rights, or any other rights for that matter, are natural, sacred, or absolute. Rights are political tools, and the system of rights should be designed to best serve the ends of society: in other words, liberty and utility. Take, for example, the right to contract for services and goods. Hayek rejects that there is anything especially sacred or natural about freedom of contract, and he has no problem with regulation of freedom of contract if such regulation helps create the system that best serves the desired ends:

> Freedom of contract, like any other freedom, means merely that what kind of contract is enforceable in the courts depends only on the general rules of law and not on the previous approval by authority of the particular contents of the contract. Many kinds of contracts, such as gambling contracts, or contracts for immoral purposes, or contracts for life-long service, have long been held invalid and unenforceable.
>
> (LLL *3, 86–7; also* CoL, *230–1)*

So, Hayek is not an economic rights fundamentalist, but he endorses a very strong general presumption of liberty that also covers economic liberties. *The presumption of liberty* generally says that laws cannot restrict individual liberty without sufficient reason. Hayek's version of this presumption is especially strong, since he says that laws that limit liberty, and so all coercive acts of government, are legitimate only if they are needed to secure a system of liberty or to finance the various functions of the state, including the service functions enumerated under the permissible government activities above. However, with this presumption satisfied, there is no need for further special protection of economic rights. Rather, we should design the system of economic rights, including what rights should enjoy constitutional protection as fundamental rights, so that it best defines the rules of an efficient economy. There is nothing sacred, holy, or natural about economic rights, though the main economic liberties (of person, property, and contract) are necessary elements of the rules of a free market economy.

11 Summary

Right-liberalism consists in the marriage of liberty and utility (social prosperity). Illustrated by the pyramid figure introduced in Chapter 1, the theory can be depicted as follows (Figure 2.1).

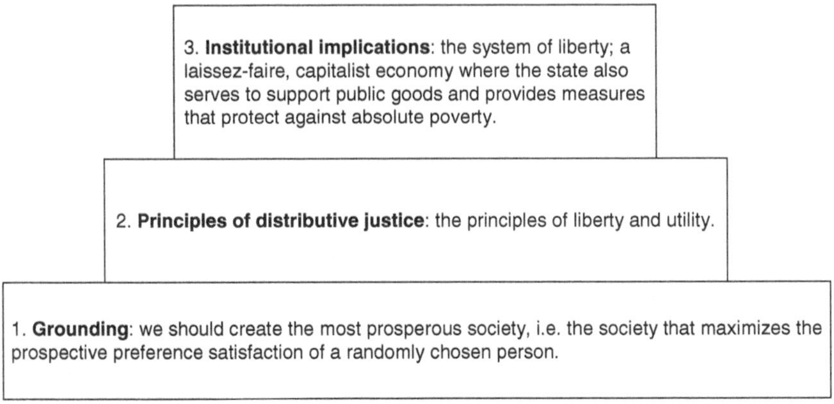

FIGURE 2.1 The main elements of right-liberalism

In more detail, right-liberalism can be characterized as the combination of the following propositions:

- First, the whole *point of society and laws* are that they help us access the things we need to live good lives. The basic principles of justice are simply the general principles that tell us how we can design the system of laws that best allow us to access these good things.
- Second, the *main values* are liberty and happiness. Each of these supports a distinct principle of distributive justice: the principle of liberty and the principle of utility.
- Third, *liberty works*: the surest way to social prosperity (i.e. to maximize the prospects for the means of happiness for the average person) is to unleash human competitiveness, creativity, and enterprise; to leave people free to pursue their own desires in their own ways in their own contexts. So, the most efficient way to organize the economy is the free market, properly defined by laws and supported in various ways by the state.
- Fourth, because extreme (absolute) poverty is destructive, for those who are poor and also for the stability and productivity of society as a whole, right-liberalism assumes that the principle of liberty should be tempered with a principle of *sufficiency*: no member of society should live in extreme poverty. Once extreme poverty is removed, the distribution that arises from voluntary changes in a free economy – the distribution that results from playing the game of catallaxy – is just, no matter what sorts of inequalities it contains.
- Fifth, *egalitarian principles* of distributive justice and equality of opportunity are confused and destructive and *should be rejected.*
- Sixth, right-liberalism is *not an enemy of the state*, nor does it defend a minimal or night watchman state. Though the free market is the best system for the design of the economy, the state may serve various supporting and servicing functions. The state should define and enforce the rules of the market, make sure that there is a functioning system of education, that there a functioning system of healthcare, that no one lives in extreme poverty, that infrastructure is built and maintained, that pollution is limited, and much more.

Right-liberalism is attractive, but as we shall see below, the right-liberal marriage of liberty and utility is not without tensions.

12 Discussion: An Uneasy Marriage of Liberty and Utility

A defining feature of Hayek's political philosophy, and of right-liberalism more generally, is how it marries two distinct values: utility (happiness) and liberty. These values support different principles of distributive justice: *the principle of utility* tells us we should seek to design the system of laws that secures the best opportunities for happiness, and *the principle of liberty* tells us that the distribution of resources resulting from the voluntary transactions of individuals in a system that secures individual liberty is just, no matter what else is true about it. The problem is that the system of liberty might not offer the best average chances for happiness. Right-liberalism tries to deny this possibility by arguing that the system of liberty is the best system for achieving the ends of society (and the happiness that they support): "The only moral principle which has ever made the growth of an advanced civilization possible was the principle of individual freedom" (*LLL* 3, 151). The premise that holds together the marriage of liberty and utility is empirical: given facts about human nature and the human condition, liberty is the only sure route to prosperity.

Right-liberalism falls apart if this empirical premise is false, for then it is no longer the case that the system that satisfies the principle of utility is also the system that satisfies the principle of liberty. What are the reasons in favor of this crucial premise? Here is the short version of Hayek's argument:

1. The only alternative to a system of liberty is a planned economy.
2. Because of human ignorance, a system of liberty does much better than a planned economy at producing and distributing goods and services efficiently.
3. The more efficient a system for the production and distribution of goods and services is, the higher is the likelihood for the average person to succeed in achieving their ends.
4. So, utility and liberty go hand in hand.

There are several problems with this argument. Taking a weaker problem first, the third premise is questionable. Why should we believe that an efficient system is also the system that offers the highest likelihood for the average person to succeed in their ends? An efficient system brings about the largest aggregate amount of goods, but the likelihood of the average person succeeding in their ends need not correlate strictly with the aggregate amount of goods, for it is also a function of how the goods are distributed. It might be that a system producing an abundance of goods in the most efficient manner fails to distribute these goods in a way that leads to a high likelihood for the average person to succeed in their pursuits. If most of the efficiently produced goods and services go to a select few members of society (say, the top 1%), then the most efficient system is *not* the system that maximizes the likelihood for success. In that case, a redistributive system would actually do better than the system of liberty at satisfying Hayek's principle of utility.

Hayek could reply that if the population size is constant, the largest aggregate amount is also the highest average amount, which means that the third premise is true. Yet, Hayek cannot rely on this argument without abandoning one of the attractive features of his consequentialism. Above I indicated that Hayek's consequentialism offers a way to care about distributions (and the plight of the poor), since it directs us to increase the chances for the random person attaining her ends. If Hayek reads the requirement to increase the prospects of the *average person* simply as increasing the *average*, then his consequentialism is a version of average consequentialism and he cannot care directly for distributions or the plight of the poor.

Hayek might reply that the factual evidence supports his claim that the system of liberty leads to higher average expectations for success. Look at the economic developments that have taken place since the early 18th century: worldwide productivity has increased dramatically and almost all classes of society have benefitted from this increase. In societies that have embraced capitalism and free markets, the poor are much better-off today in terms of access to housing, edibles and potables, healthcare and education, culture and entertainment, and so on, than the poor were 100 years ago – and the poor of 100 years ago were much better-off than the poor of 300 years ago, but then the train of improvement slows and stops. The poor of 500 years ago were not much better-off than the poor of 600, 800, or 1,000 years ago. What changed? What brought about the sudden growth in prosperity that we have seen since the 18th century? The answer, Hayek would say, is *liberty*: capitalism, free markets, and the rule of law (here he could draw on a large literature of economic history). Likewise, if you compare the wealth of different nations today you will see that the more prosperous nations have free market economies and that the poor in free market economies are better-off than in other systems. Where would you rather be poor: in Mexico or in the US? In North Korea or in South Korea?

Yet, even if we accept the facts of this argument, they do not support the conclusion that the system of liberty is *best* at securing average expected happiness. Of course, the rise of capitalism is part of the explanation of the great fact of economic growth since the 17th century, but there is no reason to think that it was the whole explanation, or even that it was the most important factor driving economic growth. What's more, economic progress was also achieved in equal measure by countries that did not embrace the system of liberty. It cannot be said that France, Germany, or the Scandinavian countries embraced the system of liberty, for while they increasingly used free markets for the production and distribution of some goods and services, they also had (and still have) state-run firms, sectors of the economy in public hands (e.g. health and education), redistributive taxation, and regulations of the market that are prohibited by the system of liberty. Did they do well in comparison with other countries because they got closer to the system of liberty? Perhaps – but perhaps not. The difference might instead lie as much in the expansion as in the retraction of the powers and reach of the state. A similar problem besets the argument that compares countries in the present. Sure, Mexico does poorly when compared with the US, and North Korea does very poorly when compared with South Korea. And part of the explanation undoubtedly lies in the different shapes of their economies; the capitalist systems of the US and South Korea are more productive than the planned economy of North Korea. But to say that this is the whole difference is a further move – and to infer that the system of liberty is *the best system* remains unjustified.

A more serious issue arises with the first premise of Hayek's argument. It is false that there are no alternatives to the system of liberty except a planned economy. These are not opposites of the sort that exhausts the options, but are like the opposite ends of a ladder of options. The system of liberty is toward the bottom of the ladder where a fully planned economy is at the top. But the ladder is high and there are many possible systems between these – many ways that we could design an economy that is neither entirely planned, nor fully free; where regulation goes far beyond what is allowed in the system of liberty, yet is not of the sort that we know from planned economies. There is, in short, not just a third way, but a fourth, fifth, sixth, and more ways to design an economic system than the options Hayek presents. Hayek's argument relies on false exclusive choices between planning and spontaneous order, between the system of commands and the rule of law, between totalitarian socialism and free market capitalism, between dictatorship and the system of liberty. Here is one of many passages where Hayek asserts such a fundamental choice:

> There exists no third principle for the organization of the economic process which can be rationally chosen to achieve any desirable ends, in addition to either a functioning market in which nobody can conclusively determine how well-off particular groups or individuals will be, or a central direction where a group organized for power determines it. The two principles are irreconcilable, since any combination prevents the achievements of the aims of either. [...] We face an inescapable choice between two irreconcilable principles, and however far we may always remain from fully realizing either, there can be no stable compromise.
>
> (LLL *3, 151)*

But there are third principles and third ways. The Scandinavian welfare states pursue a third way – and seem to succeed fairly well at securing the prospects for access to the means of happiness for the average citizens. More importantly, there are plenty of theoretical options for alternatives to the system of liberty and the planned economy.

These alternatives are well illustrated by discussing some shortcomings of Hayek's critique of principles of distributive justice and equality of opportunity. Hayek's critique of principles of distributive justice is that the pursuit of any of these requires a turn to a planned economy – here is an example of the argument:

> The predominant view today appears to be that we should avail ourselves in the main of the ordering forces of the market, indeed must in a great measure do so, but should 'correct' its results where they are flagrantly unjust. Yet, [...] we can do so only by replacing the whole spontaneous order by an organization in which the share of each is fixed by some central authority. [...] The current endeavour to rely on a spontaneous order

> corrected according to principles of justice amounts to an attempt to have the best of two worlds which are mutually incompatible.
>
> (LLL *2, 142)*

It is true that if we think of distributive justice in terms of a pattern that must be satisfied at any given moment, then distributive justice requires micro-management of the economy, which might be contrary to liberty and would very likely frustrate economic prosperity. But it is not true that principles of justice have to be directive in this way. To take a simple example, if we're impressed with the productive powers and efficiency of free markets, but we also care about equality and worry that the tendency of a free market is toward inequality, then we might try to design the rules in a fashion that counters the tendency to inequality. We might institute a system of progressive taxes on income, or we might tax wealth or inheritance, and there are many other things we could do. None of these things require that we directly take from *particular* rich people and give those funds to *particular* poor people in the manner that Hayek fears. A progressive tax system defines the rules of the economic game – it leaves individuals free to pursue their own ends using their local knowledge, and (except for extreme versions that tax nearly 100% of the top bracket) does little if any damage to the economy. Thus, a well-designed system of progressive taxation is consistent with the rule of law, liberty, and efficiency.

A similar argument defeats Hayek's criticisms of the stronger principles of equality of opportunity. Say, that equality of opportunity requires that we try to minimize the effects of the social lottery on access to education and healthcare. Hayek argues that there is nothing we could do to satisfy these requirements that would not violate liberty and frustrate the economy. But that is not true: we can have state-funded education, ensuring that the wealth, income, or social positions of parents have limited influence on access to education. We can have universal healthcare, so that access to healthcare is not a function of personal wealth and income, and thus not of parents' wealth and income either. We can supply education and healthcare and fund these via taxes, without being forced to create the sort of micromanagement of people's affairs, socialist planning of the economy, or violations of the rule of law that Hayek worries about. Providing education and healthcare would simply serve as background conditions wherein the game of catallaxy takes place.

The general point is that the game of catallaxy is consistent with regulations that aim to limit material inequality or equality of opportunity (or other principles of distributive justice). To illustrate, think again of making rock candy crystals: it is true that you cannot make rock crystals by placing the individual molecules on the string – at least, it would be really, really hard to do it, and it would also be stupid to try, for all you have to do is to create the conditions where the ordered crystal is created spontaneously by the individual molecules responding to the conditions. However, you still need to create and control the conditions – you have to provide a clean glass, the right solution, the string, and various other conditions. What is more, we can control aspects of the outcome without destroying the spontaneous order. We can decide the color of the crystal (add food coloring), its length (the length of the string), its size (duration of immersion), and probably much else – all this while still relying on the spontaneous order process to do all the work of making the crystals for us. Likewise, when we decide the rules of the game of catallaxy there is much we can determine – including how opportunities, wealth, and income are distributed – while still relying on the free market to spontaneously generate the ordered economy that efficiently produces and distributes goods and services. The inherent conflict between distributive justice and the free market that Hayek describes does not really exist, and the choice between the system of liberty and planned organization is a false choice.

Hayek's political philosophy is optimistic. He believes that if we allow liberty to work its magic, it improves the prospects of all: liberty is good in itself and the system of liberty is the recipe for peace, stability, and economic prosperity. This optimistic position may be true, but even if it is, we might continue to worry that the system of liberty results in a distribution of opportunities and resources that is unfair and unjust. Hayek also believes that nothing but liberty works – that only the most extensive system of liberty provides the desirable goods, and thus that any pursuit of distributive justice and equality of opportunity is wrongheaded and destructive. I have argued that Hayek's argument for this conclusion fails, for the demands of liberty and efficiency are also consistent with those of distributive justice and equality of opportunity. In the following chapter we shall see how John Rawls's left-liberal theory of justice, *justice as fairness*, defends this union.

Further Reading

Historical sources mentioned in this chapter:

Locke, John, 1988 [org., 1689]. *Two Treatises of Government*, Cambridge, UK: Cambridge University Press.

Mandeville, Bernard, 1988 [org. 1714]. *The Fable of the Bees, Or Private Vices, Publick Benefits*, Indianapolis, IN: Liberty Fund, Inc.

Smith, Adam, 2012. [org. 1776]. *An Inquiry Into the Nature and Causes of the Wealth of Nations*, Hertfordshire, UK: Wordsworth Editions, Ltd.

The primary sources used in describing Hayek's political philosophy are (abbreviations for in-text citations in parenthesis):

Hayek, Friedrich A. v., 1960. *The Constitution of Liberty*, Chicago, IL: University of Chicago Press. (*COL*).

Hayek, Friedrich A. v., 1973. *Law, Legislation, and Liberty, Volume 1: Rules and Order*, Chicago, IL: University of Chicago Press. (*LLL* 1).

Hayek, Friedrich A. v., 1976. *Law, Legislation, and Liberty, Volume 2: The Mirage of Social Justice*, Chicago, IL: University of Chicago Press. (*LLL* 2).

Hayek, Friedrich A. v., 1979. *Law, Legislation, and Liberty, Volume 3: The Political Order of a Free People*, Chicago, IL: University of Chicago Press. (*LLL* 3).

Other works by Hayek that are useful for understanding his theory of distributive justice include:

Hayek, Friedrich A. v., 1944. *The Road to Serfdom*, Chicago, IL: University of Chicago Press.

Hayek, Friedrich A. v., 1969 *Studies in Philosophy, Politics, and Economics*, London, UK: Routledge.

Hayek, Friedrich A. v., 1978. *New Studies in Philosophy, Politics, Economics, and the History of Ideas*, London, UK: Routledge.

Hayek, Friedrich A. v., 1991. *The Fatal Conceit: The Errors of Socialism (The Collected Work of F.A. Hayek, Vol. 1)*, W.W. Bartley, III (ed.), Chicago, IL: University of Chicago Press.

Hayek, Friedrich A. v., 1998. *Individualism and Economic Order, Reissue Edition*, Chicago, IL: University of Chicago Press.

Worthwhile discussions of Hayek's philosophy include:

Gray, John, 1998. *Hayek on Liberty, 3rd Edition*, London, UK: Routledge.

Feser, Edward, ed., 2006. *The Cambridge Companion to Hayek*, Cambridge, UK: Cambridge University Press.

Kukathas, Chandran, 1989. *Hayek and Modern Liberalism*, Oxford, UK: Clarendon Press.

For an intellectual biography of Hayek, see:

Caldwell, Bruce, 2004. *Hayek's Challenge: An Intellectual Biography of F.A. Hayek*, Chicago, IL: University of Chicago Press.

For variant defenses of right-liberalism, see:

Epstein, Richard A., 1998. *Principles for a Free Society: Reconciling Individual Liberty with the Common Good*, New York, NY: Basic Books.

Friedman, Milton, 2002 (org. 1962). *Capitalism and Freedom: Fortieth Anniversary Edition*, Chicago, IL: University of Chicago Press.

Gauthier, David, 1987. *Morals by Agreement*, Oxford, UK: Oxford University Press.

Schmidtz, David, 2006. *Elements of Justice*, Cambridge, UK: Cambridge University Press.

3

LEFT-LIBERALISM/RAWLS

1 Introduction

In the preface to *A Theory of Justice*, John Rawls says that his aim is to "generalize and carry to a higher order of abstraction the traditional theory of the social contract as represented by Locke, Rousseau, and Kant" (*TJ*, xviii). In the preface to the revised edition, Rawls adds that he hopes "to work out a conception of justice that provides a reasonably systematic alternative to utilitarianism" (*TJ*, xi). These aims go together: the social contract theory that Rawls works out is an alternative to utilitarianism.

Interestingly, Hayek could agree with Rawls's aim of finding an alternative to utilitarianism as it is normally understood, but their disagreements with utilitarianism are very different. Hayek would not endorse Rawls's contractualism or the conception of justice that it supports. Utilitarianism, recall, is the view that we ought to do what maximizes utility. In politics, this view often translates into welfare economics, which tells us to pursue the policies that maximize welfare. Hayek departs from this sort of utilitarianism in two ways. First, Hayek rejects the sort of value monism that classical direct utilitarianism involves: welfare is not the only thing of intrinsic value, for liberty is also of intrinsic value. Second, given human ignorance, the plurality of human ends, and the complexity of human societies, Hayek believes that attempts to set policies that maximize utility must fail – only the system of liberty in which politicians and bureaucrats *do not* try to maximize utility directly may actually bring about the desirable outcomes.

By contrast, Rawls offers at least four complaints against utilitarianism:

- First, utilitarianism has a mistaken view of society as simply a forum for the coordination of activities that produce the ingredients of utility. Rawls says that this view fails to recognize that society ought to be a *democratic* society, which means that it is not merely a forum of *coordination* of activities for mutual benefit, but is, rather, a system of *cooperation* between individuals coming together as free and equal moral persons to produce shared benefits.

- Second, utilitarianism regards individuals primarily as vehicles of utility, but in a democratic society individuals must be seen as distinct moral persons, each with their own moral claim on the laws and institutions of society.
- Third, utilitarianism focuses exclusively on aggregation and therefore fails to show proper concern for the question of how resources, opportunities, burdens, and rights should be distributed.
- Fourth, utilitarianism fails to recognize that certain basic rights function as constraints on what we can do in the pursuit of utility, and so fails to adequately protect these basic rights equally for all.

Underwriting these complaints is the disagreement about the relation between the right and the good that I mentioned in Chapter 1. Utilitarians define the right in terms of the good: justice is the set of rules that best allow us to realize desirable outcomes (usually understood in terms of preference satisfaction). Rawls rejects this view. According to Rawls, the right is independent of the good, both in the sense that the right constrains what we may do to pursue desirable outcomes, and in the sense that the right constraints what outcomes are desirable in the first place; the satisfaction of unjust preferences is not desirable.

Rawls could also direct at least the first of the four above critiques at Hayek, for Hayek's commitment to democracy is lukewarm at best. Hayek assigns primary value to the *outcome* of the political process rather than to the process itself; what matters is whether the laws and institutions respect and protect liberty and lead to an efficient economy. Democracy, by which Hayek understands a decision procedure where the majority decides, is not an end in itself, but the least worst of the ways we can generate laws: "I do not regard majority rule as an end but merely as a means, or perhaps even as the least evil of those forms of government from which we have to choose" (Hayek, *The Constitution of Liberty*, 403). The "true value of democracy" is that it prevents abuse of power by enabling the members of society "to get rid of a government and try to replace it by a better one" (Hayek, *Law, Legislation, and Liberty 3*, 137).

Rawls, by contrast, starts from a commitment to democratic society and moves from that commitment to a *contractualist* approach to justice. The contrast is sharp: Hayek's commitment to democracy is a result of his theory of distributive justice; Rawls's theory of distributive justice is a result of his commitment to democracy. This disagreement, moreover, points to their differing conceptions of democracy. For Hayek, democracy is a decision procedure – it is the democratic political process with free debate, political association, and voting whereby the will of the majority determines what the law is. For Rawls, by contrast, democracy is an ideal of living and cooperating together as free and equal persons, an ideal that *implies* we should make laws through democratic politics – with free debate, political parties, voting, and so on – but the ideal of democracy is much more than this implication, and it carries many other implications; among these, implications of distributive justice in light of which we should design the economic system.

What, then, is the contractualist alternative to utilitarianism? The idea of the social contract has ancient roots, but it gained prominence through 17th and 18th century theories of political legitimacy and political obligation such as those of Hobbes, Grotius, Locke, Rousseau, Pufendorf, Vattel, and Kant. Followers of this tradition say that political authority is based on the consent of those subjected to it. For some writers, the consent that matters is *actual* consent, so that political authority is legitimate only if it was created by an actual social contract (such as a constitution); for others, the consent that matters is hypothetical, so that political authority is legitimate if it is exercised in accordance with principles that all citizens *could* agree to in a social contract. Rawls adopts a version of the second option and tries to identify the principles that all citizens could agree to as authoritative prescriptions for the design and execution of the system of political institutions and laws.

However, we must recognize that Rawls's contractualism expresses more basic commitments. Rawls does *not* start with the idea of consent and then design his theory of justice from there; rather, Rawls begins with the idea of democratic society as a system of cooperation between free and equal citizens. This is the organizing idea of Rawls's theory of justice; it explains why we should care about consent in the first place, what the subject of consent is, and how we should conceive of the consenting persons.

The basic ideas of Rawls's theory of justice, then, are ideas of democratic society and democratic citizenship. These ideas lead him to the contractualist framework for theorizing justice, and it is in light of these ideas that he rejects varieties of consequentialism – whether utilitarianism or the indirect consequentialism defended by Hayek. The principles of justice that Rawls defends express the normative requirements of these ideas of democratic society and citizenship. In a sense, the ideas of democratic society and citizenship are ideals – they describe the society that we ought to create. The principles of justice tell us how we should go about creating it by spelling out the requirements of justice that a truly democratic society realizes.

2 Justice for a Democratic Society

Rawls asks the following question: What is the best conception of justice for a democratic society? (see *JaF*, 5–8, 39–42). The question itself brings resources that help us answer it; the idea of *justice* and the idea of *democratic society*.

3 The Idea of Justice

The idea of justice directs us to the concept of justice, which, in turn, leads us to the subject and role of justice, the circumstances of justice, formal constraints of justice, a history of conversations about justice that presents us with a list of candidate conceptions of justice, and the idea of a well-ordered society.

3.1 The Concept of Justice

The concept of justice is part of the area of normative thought concerned with what is right and wrong. The concept of right is one of the three main concepts of practical reasoning; the other two are the concepts of value (the good) and moral worth (*TJ*, 94). Rawls follows the contractualist tradition and argues that the concept of right should be understood in terms of what appropriately situated and motivated parties would agree to. On this contractualist understanding of the concept of right, we can identify the best conception of right for a given subject by asking what principles would be agreed to by all parties in an appropriately defined initial situation (*CP*, 59, 63, 222–3; *TJ*, 95).

The concept of justice can be further defined in terms of the role, subject, and basic form of justice. A theory of justice provides a way to specify the concept of justice in light of the grounding ideals of society and personhood that lead to definite principles of justice, which can guide our design of society. A theory of justice answers a specific set of questions about how we ought to live together. There are, of course, many other questions that we would have to answer to have a complete vision of an ideal society, but the questions of justice are inescapably part of living together and of thinking about how we should live together. One part of a theory of justice is the principles of justice it defends as the primary requirements of justice. Rawls calls these sets of principles *conceptions of justice* (*TJ*, 5, 9; see also Information Box 3.1 The concepts and conceptions of justice).

INFORMATION BOX 3.1 THE CONCEPT AND CONCEPTIONS OF JUSTICE

A concept is the general definition of a contested idea shared by different conceptions of that idea. For example, the concept of the good is "that which is desirable and that we have reason to pursue." Different conceptions of the good share this meaning, but define the good in different ways, say, as pleasure and the absence of pain, preference satisfaction, or the achievement of human perfection.

Rawls says that the *concept of justice* is defined by the *role* that different conceptions of justice agree that justice should play. The concept of justice, then, is "a proper balance of competing claims," and a conception of justice is "a set of related principles for identifying the relevant considerations which determine this balance" (*TJ*, 9).

The *role of justice* is to specify fair terms of social cooperation and thereby help us choose between the various ways in which we might design the laws and institutions of society. Different ways of designing the laws and institutions of society will lead to different systems for the distribution of society's benefits and burdens. Principles of justice "provide a way of assigning rights and duties in the basic institutions of society as well as defining the appropriate distribution of the benefits and burdens of social cooperation" (*PL*, 4; also *TJ*, 109; *JaF*, 7).

The *subject of justice* is this system of institutions and laws that defines basic rights and duties; access to offices and positions and power; the institution of property, contracts, and other economic rights; the laws of taxation, inheritance, and bequests; and the rules that define access to healthcare, education, and the many other goods of society. Rawls calls this system of institutions the basic structure of society, because it is the structure that defines the basic rules whereby the benefits and burdens of social cooperation are distributed (*TJ*, sect. 2; *PL*, lecture VII).

There are, of course, subjects of justice other than the basic structure: the justice of actions, international justice, justice of associations, and so on. But the basic structure of society is an important subject of justice. Rawls says it is the "primary subject of justice" (*TJ*, 7; *PL*, 257), and it is the subject where the principles of distributive justice that are the subject of this book have their primary application.

The basic *form of justice* is a form of impartiality: "institutions are just when no arbitrary distinctions are made between persons in the assigning of basic rights and duties and when the rules determine a proper balance between competing claims to the advantages of social life" (*TJ*, 5). Of course, this concept is too abstract, vague, and lacking in content to settle any contentious issues of justice.

Each of the theories of distributive justice discussed in this book – right-liberalism, left-liberalism, libertarianism, and socialism – offer a way to specify the concept of justice by articulating and defending different principles of justice. In Rawls's terminology, the different theories of justice articulate and defend competing conceptions of justice. Each of these different *conceptions of justice* provides a way to give concreteness, meaning, and content to the concept of justice by defining what arbitrary and nonarbitrary distinctions are, what a proper claim is, what a proper balance of competing claims is, and so forth.

3.2 The Circumstances of Justice

Based on the above, justice is only relevant in certain circumstances – these are called the circumstances of justice. The idea of the circumstances of justice dates back at least to David Hume. According to Hume, justice is artificial in the same manner as the rules of grammar or cultural mores; something that evolved to help us live and flourish together. That justice is artificial does not mean that justice is accidental or foreign to human nature. Like grammar, justice is necessary but conventional. There are, Hume believed, two sets of circumstances which necessitate the rise of justice: objective and subjective. The objective circumstances are those of moderate scarcity and interaction among men, the subjective circumstances are selfishness and limited generosity:

> [I]f every man had a tender regard for another, or if nature supplied abundantly all our wants and desires, that jealousy of interest, which justice supposes, could no longer have a place; nor would there be any occasion for those distinctions and limits of property and possession, which at present are in use among mankind. Encrease to a sufficient degree the benevolence of men, or the bounty of nature, and you render justice useless, by supplying its place with much nobler virtues, and more valuable blessings.
>
> *(Hume,* Treatise, *Book III, sect. II, 494–5)*

Both subjective and objective circumstances of justice lie between two extremes. Were human nature incapable of even limited generosity or lacking all sympathy, or were resources too scarce or cooperation impossible, justice could not come into being. Conversely, were human nature perfectly sympathetic or benevolent, or were resources abundant so that no person needed assistance from other persons to satisfy his or her material needs, justice would have no use. The conventions of justice, then, evolve because self-interested but partially generous men and women find themselves in conditions of limited scarcity where cooperation mutually benefits all.

Rawls elaborates on Hume's rendition of the circumstances of justice; the circumstances of justice are the subjective and objective conditions that make fair social cooperation both necessary and possible (*TJ*, 109–12). In addition to limited altruism and moderate scarcity, Rawls adds "the fact of pluralism," which is that a pluralism of comprehensive doctrines is a permanent feature of democratic societies (*PL*, 36–7; *JaF*, 33–5). Disagreements about religion, philosophy, the meaning of life, and about what ends are worth pursuing for their own sakes are permanent features of democratic societies; societal consensus on a comprehensive doctrine can only be established through impermissible coercive state power (*PL*, 37; *JaF*, 34).

That candidate conceptions must respect the fact of pluralism primarily affects the sort of justification(s) that can be used to establish the superiority of a conception of justice. A conception of justice that is acceptable only to those who affirm a particular metaphysical system, such as a particular religion, will be less attractive than conceptions that can appeal to citizens independently of their particular beliefs about religion or views of the good life.

A conception of justice directs the use of coercive state power. If it relies too heavily on a particular set of metaphysical beliefs, then the use of coercive state power is predicated on judgments that many of those subjected to it have no reason to accept. This use of coercive state power violates the liberal principle of legitimacy – that "our exercise of political power is proper only when we sincerely believe that the reasons we offer for our political actions may reasonably be accepted by other citizens as justification for those actions" (*PL*, xlvi). Another way to state this implication of combining the fact of pluralism and the liberal principle of legitimacy is that a democratic society can never be a community (*PL* 40–3, 144–50; *JaF*, 20–1, 198–202). A *community* is an association of persons united and working together for a common end supported by shared beliefs (e.g. a church). A democratic society cannot and should not aspire to this sort of sharing of a particular end, for there will be reasonable disagreement between citizens about what the right ends are and agreement would be possible only through the illegitimate use of political coercion.

3.3 Formal Constraints of Justice

Since the choice of principles of justice is an interpretation of the concept of right for the basic structure of society, the choice of principles takes place within the formal constraints of the concept of right. These constraints are not a matter of semantics, but are elicited from the role that the principles of justice are to play – they spell out the basic conditions that principles of justice must satisfy to play their role of defining the rules for a fair distribution of the benefits and burdens of social cooperation.

Rawls identifies five formal constraints of the concept of right, five conditions that candidate conceptions of justice should satisfy (*TJ*, sect. 23; *CP*, 291–5; *JaF*, 85–7): generality, universality, order, finality, and publicity:

Generality: the principles should be general – it must be possible to state them without the use of proper names, definite descriptions, or similar ways of distinguishing one person from another.

Universality: the principles should be universal in application, meaning that they must hold for all persons simply by virtue of their moral personality and that it must be possible for all moral persons to act on them.

Order: the principles must order conflicting claims, providing a principled basis for adjudicating the various claims that citizens might raise.

Finality: the principles must be the final court of appeal when negotiating competing claims; when these principles have decided a matter, no other principles or arbitrary provisos can affect the order of competing claims – "reasoning successfully from these principles is conclusive" (*TJ*, 116).

Publicity: the principles must be publicly recognizable as first principles of justice; that is, it must be possible for all members to willingly accept and act upon them as if they were the outcome of a public agreement between them.

All five conditions taken together provide a set of minimal requirements for conceptions of justice. Rawls summarizes the idea thus:

> Taken together [...] these conditions on conceptions of right come to this: a conception of right is a set of principles, general in form and universal in application, that is to be publicly recognized as a final court of appeal for ordering the conflicting claims of moral persons.
>
> (TJ, *117)*

Candidate conceptions of justice can be ranked according to how well they satisfy the requirements of generality, universality, order, finality, and publicity.

3.4 Candidate Conceptions of Justice

A candidate conception of justice consists of sets of principles of justice that interpret the concept of justice. Rawls says that we can gather the list of candidate conceptions from history and public culture. It should include the usual suspects: utilitarianism, perfectionism, right-liberalism, libertarianism, and so on. The only real constraint on candidate conceptions is that they must be able to satisfy the formal constraints of the concept of right.

Most conceptions of justice satisfy these constraints, but varieties of *egoism* do not, and so are not considered true candidate conceptions. Rawls distinguishes between three kinds of egoism (*TJ*, 107): first-person dictatorship (all should serve my interest), free-rider egoism (everyone but I should act justly), and general egoism (everyone should advance their interests as they please). First-person dictatorship and free-rider egoism both fail by the generality condition; they apply to a named individual. General egoism satisfies the generality condition, but fails by the ordering condition, since it rules out an impartial ranking of competing claims. Accordingly, no version of egoism is on the list of candidate conceptions of justice. This is Rawls's way of showing what most people accept already, namely that the "significance of egoism is not as an alternative conception of right but as a challenge to any such conception" (*TJ*, 117).

3.5 Well-Ordered Societies

The rule, subject, circumstances, and formal constraints of justice give us a start to thinking about what makes a conception of justice an attractive candidate. To model how well candidate conceptions satisfy these various requirements, we can use the idea of a well-ordered society (cf. *PL*, 35–40; *JaF*, 8–9). A *well-ordered society* is a society where:

- First, everyone accepts and knows that others accept the same conception of justice;
- Second, the basic structure of society satisfies and is publicly known to satisfy the principles of this conception of justice; and,
- Third, the citizens have an effective sense of justice, which means that they willingly comply with the terms of cooperation spelled out by these principles and adjudicate matters of disagreement by appeal to these principles.

We can imagine a well-ordered society for every candidate conception of justice. Such an imagined society fully satisfies the principles of justice of that conception, and the principles also govern the political psychology of citizens. We can then assess how well that conception of justice does in terms of the various requirements of justice, by looking at the relevant well-ordered society: Will this society respect the fact of pluralism? How does this society fare in terms of publicity? Will this society be stable by engendering the political psychology (the sense of justice) that leads citizens to support the institutions that best express this conception's principles of justice?

4 The Idea of Democratic Society

The idea of democratic society is the idea of society as a fair system of social cooperation between free and equal citizens.

4.1 Social Cooperation, Reciprocity, and Fairness

The idea of *social cooperation* brings together Humean, Marxist, and Kantian insights. The Humean insight is that societies exist (descriptively and normatively), because societies produce the goods and services that make for good human living: security (of person and property), stability (of roles, rules and regulations, and the supply of desirable goods and services), learning and education, culture and science, healthcare and housing, technology and the means of commodious living (agriculture, heating and cooling, plumbers and plumbing, and so on). Society is the cooperative venture by which we together produce all these goods. The Marxist insight is that these goods are produced by the *work* that the members of society do together. The Kantian insight is that social cooperation should be seen as taking place between free and equal moral persons, which implies that the terms of cooperation (the terms by which goods are produced, distributed, and consumed) must be agreeable (fair) to all members as free and equal moral persons.

Combining these Humean, Marxist, and Kantian insights, we get the Rawlsian idea of cooperation: free and equal citizens working together for mutual benefit and on fair terms to produce the many material (and many immaterial) goods that they need to live well. Since cooperation is an ingredient in the organizing idea of the Rawlsian system, the economy (the forum of cooperation) and economic activities are essential rather than incidental parts of the ideals of democratic society and democratic citizenship that are the heart of the Rawlsian theory of justice.

The idea of *reciprocity* guides the move from the idea(l) of cooperation to that of fairness. Recall the distinction between cooperation and coordination (*PL*, 16–7; *JaF*, 6–7); coordination takes place when individuals coordinate their activities with other individuals in their environment (like a school of fish). Coordination in a spontaneous order may be advantageous to each person, but this benefit is incidental rather than deliberate. Coordination may be regular, but is not rule-governed in the sense that persons coordinate because of their knowledge of the rules that regulate their behavior. Coordination is politically attractive when it serves the expected advantage of each and all (think again of Hayek's embrace of the system of liberty). Cooperation, by contrast, is where individuals deliberately work together for the production of shared social and material goods.

Cooperation is always to the benefit of each cooperator, and this benefit explains why it takes place. Cooperation is governed by rules that specify the division of labor among the cooperators, their rights and obligations, and also how the benefits of cooperation are divided among them. The cooperators deliberately cooperate in accordance with these rules – the rules define their behavior not merely in the sense of its regularity (as with coordination), but by virtue of the recognition and acceptance of the rules by the cooperators (the difference is, perhaps, captured as the difference between regularity and regulative: we regularly brush our teeth in the morning; but pay our taxes to comply with regulations).

Cooperation implies that the cooperators come together voluntarily and consent to work together in accordance with the rules that govern their cooperation. Thus, by contrast with coordination, the idea of cooperation implies a notion of *reciprocity*: that the benefits and burdens of cooperation are divided according to rules that recognize the equal claim of each cooperator to a fair share of the benefits, and to carrying only a fair share of the burdens (cf. *PL*, 16; *CP*, "Justice as Reciprocity"; *JaF*, 49). Reciprocity thus assumes a baseline of *equality*: when we come together to cooperate, we have at least an initial claim to an equal share of the benefits of cooperation, and to only carry an equal share of the burdens. Of course, when we cooperate, we might decide together – that is, *agree* – to divide the benefits and burdens differently. It might be smart, for example, to reward extra efforts with extra benefits and so on – but such departures from equality should be acceptable to each cooperator when he or she considers them from the assumption that without any such additional agreements,the benefits and burdens will be divided equally. Reciprocity thus implies that the rules that regulate the division of labor and benefits are *fair* to all cooperating persons. Fairness need not mean equality in the share of burdens and benefits (material equality), but it does imply a notion of equal standing among cooperators (a sort of formal equality), and that the rules of cooperation are equally acceptable to all.

Reciprocity and fairness are not always the relevant standards. When you go to the store to buy food, there is no presumption of reciprocity or fairness; all that is assumed between you and the storekeeper is that you'll trade for mutual advantage, not that you'll cooperate as equals for the production of anything. But Rawls believes that reciprocity and fairness are the relevant standards for assessing the rules wherein these interactions take place, that is, the rules that decide the overall division of the benefits and burdens of social cooperation.

Because the idea of social cooperation between free and equal citizens is the central organizing idea of Rawls's theory of justice, and because this idea directs us to the notion of *fairness* as the property that the rules of cooperation should be aimed at, Rawls gives the name *justice as fairness* to his theory of justice. The principles of this theory are meant to specify the main requirements that must be met for the rules of society that define fair terms of social cooperation.

4.2 Free and Equal Citizens

The idea of free and equal citizens defines the capacities of citizenship that make social cooperation both individually desirable and politically possible. The idea thus defines some of the main interests that social cooperation must respect and promote, and also offers further support for the contractualist approach to justice. To define the idea of free and equal citizenship, Rawls uses the ancient idea of *moral powers*; the moral capacities of persons that explain their ability to cooperate, their willingness to cooperate, and why they each have an equal claim to the fruits of cooperation.

The moral powers are political analogues of prudential and moral practical reason. Together they define the capacities of citizenship (*PL*, 18–20, lecture II, 302; *TJ*, Chapters 7 and 8). Rawls says there are two:

> The *first moral power* is the capacity to devise, revise, and rationally pursue a conception of the good (in short, the capacity for a conception of the good). This moral power is a capacity to develop a vision of the good life and to order one's ends and activities in light of this vision.
>
> The *second moral power* is the capacity to understand, apply, and abide by principles of justice (in short, the capacity for a sense of justice). This moral power is a capacity to understand the demands of justice, to willingly comply with these when others do so as well, and to participate in the political processes that lead to the expression of these demands in laws.

Citizens are thus conceived as *rational* – they can order their ends and desires into a coherent plan of life (a determinate conception of the good) – and as *reasonable* – they design and pursue their plans of life consistently with the requirements of justice, and thus on terms that respect the equal standing of other citizens (*PL*, lecture II). Here, again, we see the importance of the distinction between the right and the good: democratic citizens are not pure utility maximizers, but are willing to constrain their individual preferences and the means they employ in the pursuit of satisfying preferences (i.e. their rationality) by principles of justice; i.e. to pursue their rational self-interest only in a reasonable manner that respects the standing of other citizens as equal moral persons and fellow cooperators.

Moreover, by virtue of these moral powers, citizens are free and equal: *free* both in the sense that they have the capacity to devise and rationally pursue their own determinate conception of the good, and in the sense that they are legally free to do so as long as their actions are consistent with the rights of others. The standing and public identity of citizenship are independent of what determinate conception of the good citizens endorses – if, say, one converts from one faith to another, or loses faith altogether, such changes in one's religious, moral, or philosophical beliefs have no bearing on one's rights and duties as a citizen (the rare exception being when the law recognizes religiously or philosophically motivated exemptions, such as when a draft exempts conscientious objectors). Citizens are *equal* in that they all possess the capacity for moral personality and this capacity is sufficient for full and equal standing as a citizen (*TJ*, section 77; *PL*, 19, 74, 79–81, 109, 183, 302–3; *JaF*, 20–1).

Citizens are *moral persons* in that they have, and view each other as having, an effective sense of justice and a conception of their own good in light of which they order their ends (*CP*, 255, 309). As moral persons, citizens view themselves and each other as *self-authenticating sources of valid claims*, meaning that "they regard themselves as being entitled to make claims on their institutions so as to advance their conceptions of the good" (*PL*, 32; *JaF*, 23).

The development and exercise of the moral powers make fair social cooperation individually desirable and collectively possible (*PL*, 18–20, 48–43, 108; *CP*, 315–20). As rational beings, citizens have a higher-order interest in developing and exercising their capacity to devise and pursue a determinate conception of the good, and in securing the social conditions hospitable to their pursuit of it. As reasonable beings, citizens have a higher-order interest in offering and abiding by fair and mutually respectful terms of social cooperation.

5 The Original Position

Recall that we started with a question: What is the best conception of justice for a democratic society? Taking a closer look at the terms of this question has provided us with a number of clues to its answer. From a closer look at the idea of justice we got the role, subject, circumstances, and formal constraints of justice. From a closer look at the idea of a democratic society we got the idea of social cooperation between free and equal citizens, which led us to the ideas of reciprocity and fairness, and the moral powers and general interests of democratic citizens. The best conception of justice for a democratic society is the conception of justice that best satisfies and expresses these many ideas.

Different conceptions of justice will do better at satisfying different ideas – some will do very well at satisfying the formal constraints of generality, publicity, and stability, while others might do better at capturing the notions of fairness and equality. How, then, can we find a way to rank candidate conceptions of justice in a manner that allows us to say that one of these does better than the rest at satisfying and expressing these ideas?

Rawls's answer to this question is the *original position.* The original position is constructed to turn the scatter of ideas enumerated above into a selection device that accurately filters conceptions of justice according to how well they satisfy and express them. In this manner, and if Rawls is right about what the ideas of justice and democratic society imply, the original position models what we generally believe and hope for when we think about justice for a democratic society.

The aim of the original position is, accordingly, to answer exactly the question we asked: What is the best conception of justice for a democratic society? It allows us to do so by modelling what we already believe about justice and democratic society. The original position is not meant to introduce any new materials into the argument, but to take the materials we already have at hand and use them to construct a way to make clear what they imply. In a sense, then, the original position is simply a device that helps us think through our commitments and considered convictions, and come to clarity about what we already believe.

The original position is a *thought experiment.* We imagine that representatives of all members of society come together and choose a conception of justice that those they represent will live by. The parties are given a list of candidate conceptions that they then rank by running a pairwise comparison of the candidates until they arrive at a definite order. The highest-ranking conception of justice is the best conception of justice for a democratic society. (See below for a more detailed discussion of what the original position is and is not.)

The original position models our beliefs about justice for a democratic society by defining the knowledge and interests of the parties and by requiring that all candidate conceptions of justice satisfy the formal constraints of the concept of right.

5.1 Knowledge of the Parties: The Veil of Ignorance

To ensure that the parties satisfy the requirement of impartiality and do not favor principles partial to those they represent, the parties are placed behind a *veil of ignorance.* This veil shields them from knowledge about who they represent: about their gender, race, skills, wealth, or similar facts. The parties are also ignorant of particular facts about their society, such as the distribution of religious beliefs, what sorts of natural resources the society has access to, or the distribution of wealth and opportunities among different classes of citizens. The veil of ignorance shields the parties from knowledge that could lead them to propose unfair terms of social cooperation, but lets them know enough to rank candidate conceptions of justice. So, the parties know that those they represent have a conception of the good (but not what that good is), and they know general facts about their situation: that they are in circumstances of justice (as described in Section 3.2); facts about human nature, psychology, and needs; the general laws of social theory and economics; and that the members of their society affirm a diversity of philosophical, religious, political, and social doctrines (*TJ*, sect. 24 and pages 110, 137–8).

5.2 Interests of the Parties: Primary Goods

The veil of ignorance leaves the parties without any knowledge about the particular interests of those they represent or even about the distribution of interests in society. Their ignorance leaves us with the question of how they can rank conceptions of justice at all – for what interests do they have that could lead them to have preferences between different candidate conceptions? Rawls's answer is that they know that those they represent are in circumstances of justice, and they know various general facts about human nature, economics, and so on, so they have an interest in procuring for those they represent certain goods that are needed to develop and exercise the powers of democratic citizenship and to pursue determinate conceptions of the good (*JaF*, 88). Rawls calls these generally desirable goods *primary goods*. The primary goods serve three general interests of democratic citizens: first, their interest in developing their capacity for a conception of the good (their first moral power); second, their interest in developing their capacity for a sense of justice (their second moral power); and, third, their interest in having adequate all-purpose means for pursuing their determinate conception of the good – whatever it is. This account of the three basic interests of democratic citizenship supports the following list of primary goods (*PL*, 181; *JaF*, 58):

1. Basic rights and liberties;
2. Freedom of movement and free choice of occupation;
3. Power and prerogatives and opportunities for access to positions and offices;
4. Income and wealth; and
5. The social bases of self-respect.

The interests of the parties, then, are the following: first, to enable those they represent to engage in social cooperation as free and equal persons by securing for them whatever basic rights and liberties are necessary to adequately develop and exercise the two moral powers; second, to secure that those they represent have opportunities for access to offices and positions and receive as much income and wealth as possible. (I return to the "social bases of self-respect" below.)

Note that the parties are "mutually disinterested" (*TJ*, 111–2), in that they care only to maximize the absolute position of those they represent and do not aim to increase or decrease the positions of others. This mutual disinterestedness expresses both that the parties know that those they represent are in circumstances of justice and that they have an equal claim to the fruits of cooperation. It also expresses a rejection of envy. The fact that others have more or less than oneself is not by itself a reason to suspect injustice in the system – what matters is whether the distribution wherein they have more or less arose from cooperation according to rules that are fair and just. If the system of rules (the basic structure) is just, then the fact that others have more than oneself gives no cause for complaint. In this fashion, Rawls also builds into the argument an assumption that leads away from the sort of egalitarianism that is vulnerable to the levelling down objection (more on this below).

The parties are also interested in choosing a conception of justice that can be stable in the sense that it generates its own support. If, for example, a conception of justice is prone to create distrust or resentment among citizens, this will undermine its ability to support a stable system of institutions – in effect, it will make it harder to have a society that is well ordered by this conception of justice – and this would count as a reason against this candidate conception.

5.3 Rawls's Contractualism and the Original Position

The original position is inspired by the social contract tradition. In this tradition, the legitimacy and obligating power of political authority stems from the wills of those who are subjected to it, as these wills either were actually expressed in the past, or as they could be expressed in the present. The social contract tradition draws on two powerful strands in Western moral philosophy. First, the principle that no person has natural authority over another person and that interpersonal coercion, therefore, is permissible only when it is needed to protect against or to correct rights-violations. And, second, the obligating force of consent and promises: if I voluntarily consent to some agreement, then this consent creates new rights and obligations.

If we bring these two ideas together, we get the idea that there is no natural political authority, so no person has a natural authority to legislate for others or to coerce them to do things, except insofar as their actions threaten the rights of other persons. Thus, originally, there is no political authority – all political authority must be generated by the acts of those party to the authority relation, that is, through a social contract where people agree to create and respect political offices authorized to legislate and enforce laws on behalf of all.

Rawls draws on the social contract tradition, but the original position is *not* a social contract. The original position is a thought experiment that helps us to think clearly about what justice requires. The hypothetical agreement of the original position is not the source of political authority or political obligation.

Rawls's contractualism is found in his endorsement of the liberal principle of legitimacy which says that the exercise of political authority must take place in accordance with principles that all those subjected to it could agree to, in a situation that respects their status as free and equal moral persons. The original position helps us identify what these principles are and shows what we can agree to as free and equal moral persons.

It is worth emphasizing how far removed from any actual situation the original position is. The original position is not some legislative assembly that might happen or could have happened. The original position is a thought experiment where we construct imaginary characters that think about justice using only knowledge and interests relevant for the question – this *could not happen*. It is safer to think of the original position as an algorithm or a filtering device that sorts conceptions of justice according to how well they fit the basic ideas of democratic society and democratic citizenship, rather than as a bargaining situation where parties negotiate for principles.

That the original position is hypothetical, imaginary, and impossible is *not* an objection to it. If it truly expresses the fundamental normative commitments of democratic society and sorts candidate conceptions of justice according to how well they satisfy these commitments, then it can help us to think clearly about what the best conception of justice is for a democratic society.

One important contractualist feature of the original position is that it makes us think of principles of justice as the object of an agreement rather than as a choice made by a collective person. Agreements carry a sort of commitment that choices do not; I might choose to take a risk, but then later try to undo my choice when it turns out that the worse outcome came about. If I *agree* to take a risk, by contrast, then I cannot decide to undo my choice when the worst outcome comes about (at least not without the permission of the persons I made the agreement with). Rawls calls this feature of agreements the *strains of commitment* and they restrict the parties to agree only to principles that those they represent can willingly comply with, even if it turns out that they represent the least well-off members of society (cf. *TJ*, 153–4; *JaF*, 102–3).

6 Fair, Fair, Fair, Fair

One way to think of the original position is to think of it as a way to use pure procedural justice at the level of theory (cf. discussion of procedural justice in Chapter 1). From the ideas of social cooperation, reciprocity, and free and equal citizenship we know that we are looking for principles of justice that ensure a distribution of benefits and burdens of cooperation that is fair to all members of society. To identify these principles, Rawls designs the original position as a situation that is fair through and through, since it removes all sources of unfairness – in the original position the parties are equal to the point where they have exactly the same knowledge and interest and so cannot try to influence the principles in any way that would advantage any particular members of society. *The fairness of the situation then transfers to its outcome*, so that the principles that are chosen are fair in three relevant senses:

- First, they would be agreed to in fair conditions, so the principles themselves are fair;
- Second, the basic structure that is designed in accordance with those principles, therefore, defines the rules of society as a fair game of social cooperation;
- Third, the distribution of the benefits and burdens of cooperation that results from this game is, therefore, fair.

Since the principles of justice in this context are simply the principles that ensure a fair game of social cooperation, the original position serves to identify the best principles of justice for a democratic society conceived of as a fair system of social cooperation.

The reader might get the feeling that Rawls keeps moving the ball further and further away from the goal, and also that Rawls keeps saying that things are "fair," but then explains what fair means by saying that something else is fair. Does he ever explain it? He does, and it is instructive to see how.

First, Rawls tells us that when we conceive of democratic society as a system of social cooperation between free and equal citizens, it follows that distribution of the benefits and burdens of cooperation must be fair. This raises the first and basic question: What is a fair distribution of the benefits and burdens of social cooperation?

Fairness is not a function of outcomes, but of the rules of the game by which the outcome is created. The notion of fairness directs us to the idea of procedural distributive justice; we cannot look directly at a distribution and tell whether it is fair, we have to look instead at the rules of cooperation by which it was created. A distribution is fair, if it arose by permissible moves under rules that are fair. So, we must ask, what rules are fair?

Rawls designs the original position to answer this question. In the original position, Rawls uses procedural justice once more: the design of the original position removes all sources of unfairness in the choice of principles of justice in light of which we can design the rules of social cooperation. So, because the original position is fair, the outcome of the original position (principles of justice) is fair – meaning that when we design the rules of social cooperation to satisfy the principles of justice agreed to in the original position, then the rules of cooperation are fair. That, in turn, means that the distribution of benefits and burdens of social cooperation that arises from citizens playing by the rules that express the principles of justice agreed to in the original position is fair – and we have now answered the basic question.

Here, then, is the structure of Rawls's argument:

1. The distribution of benefits and burdens ought to be fair.
2. The distribution of benefits and burdens is fair if it takes place according to rules that are fair.
3. Rules are fair if they express principles of justice that would be agreed to in an original position that is fair.
4. *The* original position that Rawls employs is fair.
5. So, the distribution of benefits and burdens is fair if it takes place in accordance with rules that express the principles of justice that would be agreed to in the original position.

The next step is to explore the principles of justice that issue from the original position.

7 Principles of Justice

What is the result of the original position? What are the best principles for a democratic society? The answer, Rawls tells us, is the following set of principles (*TJ*, 266; *PL*, 5–6; *JaF*, 42–3):

1. *The principle of equal basic rights*: each person has an equal claim to an adequate scheme of equal basic rights and liberties compatible with the same scheme for all.
2. *The principles of democratic equality*:
    a. *The principle of fair equality of opportunity*: social and economic inequalities must be attached to offices and positions open to all under fair equality of opportunity.
    b. *The difference principle*: inequalities in wealth and income are permissible only if they are to the greatest benefit of the least advantaged.

Priority rules: the first principle has priority over both parts of the second principle, and part a. of the second principle has priority over part b.

Priority here means that a principle with higher priority cannot be compromised for the sake of even large gains to a principle with lower priority. So, we cannot permissibly sacrifice or restrict basic rights, even if doing so would somehow increase equality of opportunity, and we cannot sacrifice equality of opportunity even if doing so would lead to a higher share of income and wealth for the least well-off. The priority rules allow restrictions of rights and liberties, as well as compromises with equality of opportunity. We can restrict basic rights and liberties as needed to ensure an adequate scheme of basic rights and liberties *for all*. We can compromise with equality of opportunity for the same reason and also when adjustments to the principle allow us to better satisfy it. For example, policies of affirmative action might violate equality of opportunity in some respects, but might nevertheless be justified to secure equal rights or equality of opportunity in some other respect.

We can summarize the role of the different principles of justice by sorting for the primary good they govern and how governing that good secures a particular democratic ideal as illustrated by Table 3.1.

The below schema (Table 3.1) is too schematic in that the principles of equal basic rights and fair equality of opportunity issue requirements also for the primary good of wealth and income. That is, securing, say, the fair value of the political rights as required by the first principle might require that there are limits to inequalities of wealth.

These, then, are the principles of justice that, Rawls argues, best express and secure our commitment to democratic society as a system of social cooperation between free and equal citizens. Of course, what exactly these principles require and why these are the principles that the parties in the original position choose is not yet clear. The rest of this section aims to clarify what these principles mean and why they are best.

TABLE 3.1 Primary goods

Primary goods	*Principle*	*Role of principle(s)*
1. Basic rights, including freedom of movement and occupation	First principle: equal basic rights	To enable each citizen to participate in social cooperation as a free and equal person
2. Opportunities for access to powers, prerogatives, positions, and offices	Democratic equality, part 1: fair equality of opportunity	To secure a fair distribution of the burdens of cooperation
3. Income and wealth	Democratic equality, part 2: the difference principle	To secure a fair distribution of the benefits of cooperation

7.1 The Principle of Equal Basic Rights

The basic rights are to protect the development and exercise of the moral powers. The first principle, accordingly, reads: "Each person is to have an equal right to a fully adequate scheme of equal basic rights and liberties which is compatible with a similar scheme of liberties for all" (*PL*, 5, 291). Since *adequacy* here refers to the development and exercise of the moral powers, the basic rights are all and only those rights necessary for the adequate development and full exercise of the two moral powers. This is Rawls's contractualist criterion of basic rights (*JaF*, 45, 112, 169; *PL*, 74, 187, 293, 297, 308, 325; *CP*, 313).

Rawls employs the criterion to identify three groups of basic rights (*PL*, 310–24, 334–5, 409–19; *JaF*, 45, 112–3). These groups have the same level of priority, but differ according to how they are tied to moral powers. The first group contains rights that are necessary for the adequate development and exercise of the sense of justice. These *political rights* include freedom of political speech and assembly, freedom to form, join, and leave political parties, equal voting rights, and rights to run for public office. The second group contains liberties that are necessary for the adequate development and exercise of the capacity for a conception of the good. These *liberties of conscience* include freedom of religious, philosophical, and moral thought, and freedom to start, join, and leave a religious or philosophical community. The third group contains liberties that are necessary for guaranteeing any of the liberties established as basic in one of the first two groups. Rawls thinks these *supporting rights* include liberty and integrity of the person, the rights and liberties covered by the rule of law, rights of privacy, and rights of personal property. Sometimes Rawls indicates that liberties of movement and occupation are basic as well, but other times he keeps them off the list of basic liberties (*PL*, 181, 228, 308; *CP*, 313, 362, 366).

Apart from security of personal property (and perhaps liberty of occupation), *the various economic rights are not basic*, but are protected merely by the presumption of liberty (*TJ*, 42, 43, 82; *PL*, 228, 232, 298, 335, 338, 363; *JaF*, 114). Rawls does not discuss in detail why the economic rights are not basic, but, given the contractualist criterion of basic rights, the argument must be that they are not necessary for the adequate development or full exercise of either of the moral powers.

The value or worth of rights and liberties depends on one's opportunities for exercising them, including what sorts of wealth and income one receives. Thus, the worth of basic rights depends on how well one does with respect to the other primary goods, and this means that inequalities in wealth and income translate into the unequal worth of basic rights. Rawls does not see a problem with permitting unequal worth of basic rights (*PL*, 324–31). Inequalities of wealth and income are permitted only to maximize the position of the least advantaged as required by the difference principle; so, the unequal worth of basic rights is permitted only where it is necessary to increase the worth of rights to the least well-off. This argument does not, however, work for the political rights, since the aim here is to ensure that all equally gifted and motivated members have a roughly equal chance of influencing policy and attaining public offices (*PL*, 327, 358). Rawls accordingly argues that the political rights must have *fair value* to all citizens, so that political influence is unaffected by economic inequalities. The way to achieve this fair value is to minimize the influence of money on the political process.

What, then, justifies the first principle and its priority? Why do the parties in the original position favor all conceptions of justice that secure this list of basic rights and give them priority against all other social concerns? The short answer is that all, and only, these rights are necessary for the adequate development and exercise of the moral powers. The development and exercise of the moral powers present two separate aims, and it is relative to these aims that their development and exercise determine the content and priority of the first principle of justice. The aim of the development and exercise of the capacity for a conception of the good is to freely and rationally guide one's conduct over a complete life (*PL*, 332, 418). The aim of the development and exercise of the sense of justice is to build and support a system of political institutions that expresses and maintains fair terms of cooperation.

Each of these aims supports a specific argument for basic rights. For the capacity for a conception of the good, we can say that a liberty is basic, if it is necessary for citizens to freely and rationally devise and pursue a determinate conception of the good of their own. For the sense of justice, we can say that a liberty is basic if it is necessary for citizens to build, support, and abide by just institutions (*PL*, lecture VIII; *CP*, 307–22). Conversely, the *adequate* development and *full* exercise of the moral powers that are protected by the basic rights is simply the development and exercise achieved in these aims. The capacity for a conception of the good is adequately developed and fully exercised when citizens freely and rationally devise and pursue their own determinate conceptions of the good. The sense of justice is adequately developed and fully exercised when citizens understand, affirm, and take as directive the requirements of justice when called upon to act as citizens. When all citizens have developed and exercise their sense of justice, and know that other citizens do so as well, society is well ordered: it realizes the requirements of justice, because the citizens affirm, deliberate, and act from these in matters of public interest.

To clarify how the basic rights are necessary for the development and exercise of the moral powers, we can look at the two main groups of rights that Rawls argues are necessary and see what we can glean from his arguments: the liberties of conscience and the political rights.

Rawls identifies three reasons why the liberties of conscience – the liberties of religious, philosophical, and moral thought – are necessary to adequately develop and exercise the moral power to freely and rationally devise, revise, and pursue a conception of the good life (*PL*, 312–4; *TJ*, sect. 33). First, without the liberties of conscience, citizens are not free to make and correct mistakes of their own, to meet and engage with those that disagree with their religious, philosophical, and moral convictions, or to critically reflect on and challenge the convictions that their family or cultural circles affirm. So, the liberties of conscience are necessary for citizens to freely and rationally devise and revise their determinate conception of the good in accordance with their own considered philosophical, religious, and moral convictions. Second, without the liberties of conscience, a majority of citizens might use the coercive powers of the state (or other coercive measures) to determine what sorts of religious, philosophical, and moral views other citizens should pursue or publicly affirm. Third, these liberties are necessary for citizens to confidently affirm for themselves and to others that their determinate conception of the good truly expresses their considered beliefs, values, and ends, and so is worthy of respect and public deference.

The argument for the necessity of the political rights is best presented in terms of the requirements for the exercise of the sense of justice. If citizens are to have an equal say in determining the laws to which they are subject, they must have roughly equal political power – meaning, at least, that they must have equal voting rights and equal access to the public exchange of reasons (*TJ*, 200). So, the full exercise of the sense of justice requires universal suffrage, equal rights to join or start political parties, freedom of assembly, equal rights to run for political offices, freedom of speech, and measures to ensure that inequalities of wealth and social position do not result in inequalities of political influence (*TJ*, sect. 36; *PL*, lecture VIII). (There are hard questions concerning the constitutional design of these liberties: To what extent can majority rule be limited by a bill of rights and judicial review? To what extent should freedom of speech protect revolutionary or seditious agitation? Fortunately, we need not decide these questions here.)

We get another perspective (but the same conclusion) if we view the development and exercise of the moral powers in terms of the reasoning of the parties in the original position (*PL*, 73–7, 310–24). From that perspective, what matters is the relation between the moral powers and the determinate conceptions of the good of those that the parties represent. Ignorant of what these conceptions are, the primary interest of the parties is to ensure the best conditions for devising, revising, and pursuing determinate conceptions of the good in general (*TJ*, sect. 25; *PL*, 304–7). This interest explains why the parties care about the development and exercise of the moral powers.

First, the parties only care for the development and exercise of the sense of justice insofar as the development and exercise of this power serve the pursuit of the determinate conception of the good of those they represent. Even so, there are at least three reasons why the parties care about the development of the sense of justice. Only a society where the members develop and exercise their sense of justice is well ordered, and the parties are interested in securing a well-ordered society since only such is stable for the right reasons, reliably provides the social bases of self-respect for all, and secures conditions of pluralism where the pursuit of the determinate conception of the good of each enhances and enriches the possibilities of others (*PL*, 315–24; *TJ*, sect. 67). Conversely, the parties have no interest in aiming for a fuller development and exercise of the sense of justice (whatever that might be) than what is sufficient for achieving these ends. So, from the perspective of the parties in the original position, the target of their interest in the development of the sense of justice is the point at which the members of society offer and abide by fair terms of social cooperation and create and maintain the institutions that implement these. This target defines the adequate development as well as the full exercise of this moral power.

Matters are a bit more complex for the capacity for developing, revising, and pursuing a conception of the good. Since a determinate conception of the good must be freely devised and endorsed as one's own, the capacity to freely develop and revise one's conception of the good is (from the perspective of the parties in the original position at least) itself an ingredient in the determinate conceptions of the good of members of society (*PL*, 313–4). So, the parties in the original position care about the development and exercise of this moral power both as an instrument for and as an ingredient in determinate conceptions of the good. However, these two interests yield the same target. The instrumental interest in this moral power is satisfied when persons can freely and rationally develop, revise, and pursue a conception of the good of their own. Likewise, for the intrinsic interest: from the perspective of the parties this moral power is an ingredient in determinate conceptions of the good only because and insofar as its development and exercise are necessary to freely develop and endorse one's determinate conception of the good as *one's own* (*PL*, 314).

Here, then, is Rawls's argument against pure utilitarianism. Pure utilitarianism is the single principle (monist) conception of justice that tells us to design the system that can be expected to maximize average utility. If we imagine that the parties choose between justice as fairness and pure utilitarianism, then the parties will choose justice as fairness, for to choose otherwise would be to risk a society where some members are unable to develop and exercise the moral powers of democratic citizenship. The parties will not take such a risk, for, first, it is irrational to gamble with the essential preconditions for living a good life simply for the possibility of receiving more of the nonessential resources; second, the *strains of commitment* commit them to choose only a conception of justice that those they represent can be expected to respect and endorse, even if they are the worst off members of society. The utilitarian conception of justice might leave some members in conditions so bad that they cannot be expected to respect (and even less endorse) the rules of the game that made them miserable.

Justice as fairness, by contrast, secures the preconditions of democratic citizenship for all *and* maximizes the worth of basic rights to the least well-off members of society (because the difference principle secures for them the best material conditions of any accessible system), which means that the least well-off are guaranteed the ingredients of free and equal citizenship and more resources than in any other scheme. Even the least well-off can respect and endorse the rules of a system well ordered by justice as fairness. Thus, the parties will prefer justice as fairness to pure utilitarianism.

In sum: the adequate development and full exercise of the sense of justice is the development and exercise sufficient for citizens to be able to honor and abide by fair terms of social cooperation and support the institutions that express these terms. The adequate development and full exercise of the capacity for a conception of the good is the development and exercise sufficient for freely and rationally devising and pursuing a determinate conception of the good. The parties in the original position will prefer any conception of justice that secures an adequate scheme of these rights over conceptions that do not, since only conceptions that secure an adequate scheme of basic rights for all secure the conditions necessary for the development and exercise of the powers of democratic citizenship that make social cooperation both desirable and possible. The parties know that those that they represent have a higher-order interest in the development and exercise of these powers, so they would not gamble with these for the sake of other goods.

7.2 The Principle of Fair Equality of Opportunity

In the previous chapter we saw that equality of opportunity is the idea that all members of society should enjoy equal opportunities for success. This idea supports the principle that access to careers should be open to talents, but also the stronger principles that require the effects of the social and natural lotteries to be countered as best we can. Rawls states the principle of fair equality of opportunity as follows:

> Those who have the same level of talent and ability and the same willingness to use these gifts should have the same prospects of success regardless of their social class of origin, the class into which they are born and develop until the age of reason. In all parts of society there are to be roughly the same prospects of culture and achievement for those similarly motivated and endowed.
>
> (JaF, *44)*

In addition to nondiscrimination, fair equality of opportunity requires that we seek to minimize the effects of the social lottery, so that "those with similar abilities and skills [...] have similar life chances" (*TJ*, 63). Securing fair equality of opportunity requires that we set the free market system in a framework of political and legal institutions that adjust the long-term trend of economic forces "so as to prevent excessive concentrations of property and wealth [... and] establish, among other things, equal opportunities of education for all regardless of family income" (*JaF*, 44). Notably, fair equality of opportunity does *not* tell us to minimize the effects of the natural lottery.

Why should we go beyond the principle of nondiscrimination and embrace fair equality of opportunity? And if we accept fair equality of opportunity, why not go all the way and require that we also minimize the effects of the natural lottery? Rawls's reply to the first of these questions marks an interesting contrast between right-liberalism and left-liberalism. (His reply to the second question marks an interesting contrast to socialism, but we won't see this contrast until Chapter 5.)

Right-liberalism, recall, affirms procedural distributive justice and says that the distribution that results from the game of catallaxy (the free market regulated only to secure the system of liberty) is just, no matter what else is true about it. Ideas of equality of opportunity and principles of distributive justice are mistaken, because they require us to interfere with the market in ways that destroy the creative powers of the free economy and violate the liberty of the members of society. Rawls *also affirms* procedural distributive justice, as do left-liberals more generally. As Rawls says, the distribution that arises from free and voluntary exchanges within a fair system of rules is just, no matter if it conforms to some pattern:

> The correctness of the distribution is founded on the justice of the scheme of cooperation from which it arises and [...] A distribution cannot be judged in isolation from the system of which it is the outcome [...] If it is asked in the abstract whether one distribution of a given stock of things to definite individuals with known desires and preferences is better than another, then there is simply no answer to this question.
>
> (TJ, *76)*

Rawls's embrace of procedural justice means that he accepts Hayek's claim that there is no way to judge the justice of a distribution except by looking at whether it came about through voluntary transactions against a background of just rules. Yet, Hayek and other right-liberals mistakenly believe that the idea of procedural justice can be used to support the conclusion that the pursuit of equality of opportunity or other principles of distributive justice is misguided. For the question remains: What is the just system of rules of the economic game whereby the distribution of resources takes place? Hayek and right-liberals need a separate argument to show that principles of distributive justice can have no role in the design of the rules of the game (the basic structure), and they do not provide this argument. Hayek's argument directs us to the question of what the fair and just rules of social cooperation are – but it does not give us the answer to this question. Rawls and other left-liberals argue that fair and just rules must satisfy fair equality of opportunity.

Here's why: it is unfair when access to attractive positions and offices and the various economic and cultural opportunities that such access provides is determined by the wealth and power of one's parents or other relations, rather than on one's own talents and efforts. The system of liberty allows prospects in life to be determined by the wealth and privileges of one's parents and their connections to a wider social class. Over time, this will lead to a society where the distribution of opportunities is increasingly skewed in favor of those who are already rich or are born into rich families. A system of rules that allows such inequalities of opportunity to arise and be reproduced across generations is not fair to those who are born with fewer opportunities for success. Fairness implies some sort of equal chance of success for those of equal talents. So, to ensure fairness in the game of cooperation, we should try to minimize the effects of the social lottery through the rules of the game.

Note that Rawls sees *no unfairness* in our different natural and social circumstances as such. The facts that some are born more talented than others and that some are born into more resourceful families (as defined in the previous chapter) are neither just nor unjust – they're just facts that we have to deal with. What is just or unjust is how we deal with these facts – and especially how our institutions allow these facts to influence the distribution of opportunities, wealth, and income:

> The natural distribution is neither just nor unjust; nor is it unjust that persons are born into society at some particular [social] position. These are simply natural facts. What is just and unjust is the way institutions deal with these facts. Aristocratic and caste societies are unjust because they make these contingencies the ascriptive basis for belonging to more or less enclosed and privileged social classes. The basic structure of these societies incorporates the arbitrariness found in nature. But there is no necessity for men to resign themselves to these contingencies. The social system is not an unchangeable order beyond human control but a pattern of human action. In justice as fairness men agree to avail themselves of the accidents of nature and social circumstance only when doing so is for the common benefit.
>
> (TJ, *87–8)*

To limit the effects of the social lottery, society should limit the accumulation of wealth across generations, provide for equal access to education for all, and ensure that all members of society have access to basic healthcare. These measures are not, of course, sufficient to eliminate the effects of the social lottery, but the things we would have to do to completely eliminate them would violate basic rights. Our opportunities are as much determined by the cultural, emotional, and intellectual resources of our families as by their wealth and social influence. Though we can counter the effects of the latter, there is very little we can permissibly do to eliminate the effects of the former. Even with a well-funded and well-functioning system of education for all, some will fare better in this system because of the cultural, emotional, and intellectual resources of their parents. So, we cannot fully secure fair equality of opportunity: "the principle of fair opportunity can be only imperfectly carried out, at least as long as some form of the family exists" (*TJ*, 64). This leaves a question of how we should deal with these sources of unequal opportunity.

Another apparent source of unfairness left unaddressed by a system that secures fair equality of opportunity is that the effects of the natural lottery appear equally unfair. If we should seek to minimize the effects of the social lottery, then why not also seek to minimize the effects of the natural lottery? Rawls's answer is that we cannot minimize the effects of the natural lottery without violating the first principle, but also that it would be stupid to try to do so, since we can use the distribution of natural talents to everyone's advantage. This subject takes us to the second principle of democratic equality, namely, the difference principle.

7.3 The Difference Principle

Recall that Rawls lists the following primary goods: basic rights and liberties, opportunities, wealth and income, and the social bases of self-respect (the latter are discussed in Section 8, below). In the preceding two sections we have seen that the first principle secures equal basic rights and liberties to all, and the first part of the second principle requires fair equality of opportunity for access to offices and positions of employment. The second part of the second principle governs the distribution of wealth and income, and it requires that we design a system where inequalities of wealth and income are to the benefit of the least well-off. This principle, the so-called difference principle, works together with the principle of fair equality of opportunity to secure that the distribution of opportunities, wealth, and income that results from free interactions in the economy is fair.

We should emphasize that the difference principle is *not a principle of allocation*, meaning that it is not a principle we can use to judge any particular distribution of resources. Again, Rawls is committed to procedural distributive justice, in the sense that the distribution of resources is just if it came about by permissible moves made within a just system of rules, roles, and institutions. The only way we can judge the justice of a particular system and the inequalities it contains is by looking at the design of the basic structure of that system and whether the moves that led to the distribution were permissible *in that structure*. If the structure is just *and* the moves were permissible, then the distribution is just, no matter how unequal it is. Of course, Rawls differs from Hayek by insisting that the basic structure is just only if it satisfies the two principles of justice.

The difference principle is a *prioritarian* principle in the sense that it tells us that we should design the system of institutions that maximizes the position of the least well-off. To explain the attractions of this principle, imagine that the parties in the original position are choosing between a set of principles where the only difference is in the second part of the second principle: one conception has the principle of equality, the other has the difference principle (a principle of priority). Now, the parties will agree to any departure from an equal distribution that promises to improve the position of those they represent. Since every member of society is better-off in the system designed to satisfy the difference principle than in the system of equality, the parties prefer the second conception.

Why would departures from equality increase the position of the least well-off? One possibility is that inequalities can increase social productivity by offering incentives for people to train for and pursue careers that exercise their most productive talents, and thereby also facilitate a productive division of labor. When people are paid more to develop their natural talents and use them where they do the most good, then they will tend to do it and everybody will benefit:

> The function of unequal distributive shares is to cover the costs of training and education, to attract individuals to places and associations where they are most needed from a social point of view, and so on. [...] Variations in wages and income and the perquisites of position are simply to influence these choices so that the end result accords with efficiency and justice.
>
> (TJ, *277)*

Recall that fair equality of opportunity allows inequalities that arise from the effects of the development and exercise of natural talents. The fact that persons have different natural talents is not just or unjust, it is simply a fact, and there is nothing we could do to correct it that would not violate basic rights. But that does not mean that the more talented are entitled to whatever they can procure for themselves, as in a system of liberty. Entitlements are defined by the rules of the game, and the question is how we should design these rules so that the distribution of entitlements that results from citizens playing this game is fair:

> [T]he more advantaged have a right to their natural assets, as does everyone else; this right is covered by the first principle under the basic liberty protecting the integrity of the person. And so the more advantaged are entitled to whatever they can acquire in accordance with the rules of a fair system of social cooperation. Our problem is how this scheme, the basic structure of society, is to be designed.
>
> (TJ, *89)*

The difference principle governs these effects of the natural lottery (and also the incorrigible effects of the social lottery) by permitting inequalities of wealth and income that arise from the exercise of natural talents, but only when these inequalities benefit the least well-off. By permitting only these inequalities, they become acceptable to all and are preferable from the point of view of the original position: those who are better-off in the system designed in accord with the difference principle can accept it, because they benefit from it. Those who are least well-off can accept it, because there is no system where they would be better-off.

Next, imagine that the parties choose between the conception that has the difference principle as the second part of the second principle and a conception that instead has the principle of utility (the principle that tells us that we should maximize the average level of wealth and income). Once more, the parties will prefer the conception that has the difference principle, since the one that has the utilitarian principle fails to secure them against extreme poverty. It might maximize utility to have extreme poverty in society – it might increase productivity by putting pressure on unskilled labor to work at low wages – but the parties would not prefer a system with increased average wealth when those they represent might live in extreme poverty, to one that guarantees that no one lives in extreme poverty and where everyone benefits from the inequalities of the system.

The following graph (Figure 3.1) illustrates both what the difference principle requires and the argument in favor of it.

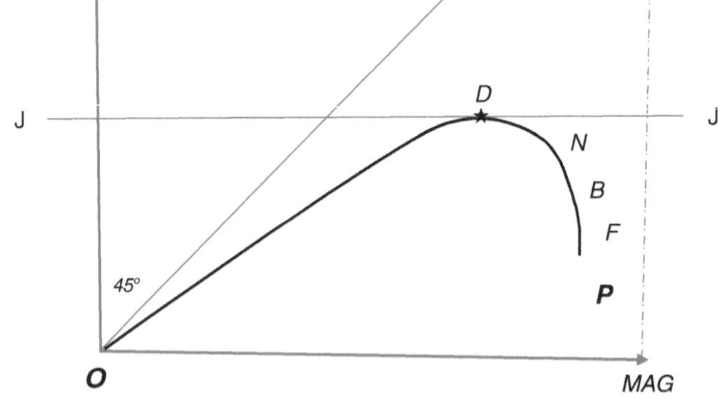

FIGURE 3.1 Illustrating the difference principle. (Adapted from *JaF*, 62.)

The graph shows the distribution of wealth and income between the least advantaged group (the relatively poor) and the most advantaged group (the relatively rich). We can think of the poor as unskilled laborers and the rich as whomever benefits the most from bringing their talents to the marketplace. There will, of course, be numerous groups on the continuum between these, but for the purposes of illustration we can leave those off the chart. Now, the point **O** is the point of equal distribution. The line from **O** that goes northeast at a 45-degree angle depicts a line of equality. By assumption, the only distribution on this line that we can achieve is **O**, since we cannot produce more resources without allowing for inequalities. The curve from **O** to ***P*** is the curve of achievable distributions. The point *D* is the point where the least well-off have as much as they can possibly get. This is the distribution that the difference principle tells us we should aim for. The point *N* is the point that maximizes the production of resources (favored, I believe, by Hayek). The point *B* is the point that maximizes average and aggregate resources (favored by utilitarianism). The point *F* is the feudal point, where the most advantaged group have as much as they could possibly get.

The graph illustrates why Rawls believes that the requirements of fairness and reciprocity are satisfied only by systems that satisfy the difference principle rather than a combination of utility and sufficiency. Rawls states at least three different versions of the reciprocity requirement:

1. *Reciprocity as mutual advantage.* As Rawls says, "social cooperation [...] is always productive," (*JaF*, 61) and by this criterion all cooperators have a claim to receive more from the cooperative relationship then they provide to it: "everyone as a citizen should gain" (*JaF*, 133).
2. *Reciprocity as the contractualist requirement* that the terms of cooperation we offer to others are those we could reasonably expect them to accept as free and equal persons. It is thus not enough that it is to their rational advantage to accept the terms of cooperation; rather they must be terms that we could expect them to accept, apart from their relative bargaining advantage:

> [I]n offering fair terms we must reasonably think that citizens offered them might also reasonably accept them. And they must be able to do this as free and equal and not as dominated or manipulated, or under the pressure of an inferior political or social position. I refer to this as the criterion of reciprocity.
>
> (PL, *xliv, also* PL *16–7)*

Taken together the first two notions of reciprocity set an equal division as the baseline for distributing the benefits and burdens of cooperation, for an equal division is one that all could (1) *rationally agree to* and (2) *reasonably offer to others* as terms of cooperation.

3. *Reciprocity as no one benefitting at the expense of others.* This notion of reciprocity says that all departures from an equal division should be beneficial to all cooperating parties.

Rawls's main argument for the difference principle is that it is implied by the three notions of reciprocity enumerated above. To illustrate why, Rawls refers to the above graph (Figure 3.1) that illustrates the meaning of the difference principle. The idea is that departures from the baseline of equality (the origin point) are permissible, as long as they are to the advantage of both the least and most advantaged groups. Once we reach D, no further moves along the OP curve are permissible, because moves in either direction would sacrifice the interests of the least well-off. The section of the OP curve that lies between D and F is the conflict segment. Here we find the range of gains to the most advantaged group that come at the expense of the least well-off. Any move in the conflict segment requires sacrificing the interests of some for the gains of others (hence the name). Rawls's main argument for the difference principle is that a system that aims for a distribution to the west of the D point forgoes benefits to all, and any system that aims for a point to the east of the D point (say, N or B) sacrifices the interests of the least advantaged group for gains that go to the most advantaged group, which violates the notion of reciprocity as no one benefitting at the expense of others:

> [T]he difference principle expresses the idea that, starting from equal division, the more advantaged are not to be better off at any point to the detriment of the less well off. [...] a deeper idea of reciprocity implicit in it is that social institutions are not to take advantage of contingencies of native endowment or of initial social position, or of good or bad luck over the course of life, except in ways that benefit everyone, including the least favored.
>
> (JaF, *124; also* JaF, *76–7,* PL, *16–7)*

The difference principle, then, tells us to aim for the design of the economic system that is most beneficial to the least well-off members of society. Any improvements to their lot will also improve the lot of the most well-off group, but there are further improvements to the most well-off that the difference principle tells us are impermissible from the standpoint of justice, since these improvements sacrifice the lot of the least well-off for the sake of increasing the lot of others.

8 The Social Bases of Self-Respect

We are now in a position to understand how the principles of justice secure the primary good that Rawls calls the social bases of self-respect, even though this good is not covered by any of the three principles that together define Rawls's conception of justice.

Rawls says that: "self-respect is secured by the public affirmation of the status of equal citizenship for all" (*TJ*, 478). Rawls's claim here is that the principles of justice, publicly affirmed and expressed in the institutions of society, demonstrate to all members of society their equal status as citizens and thereby secure the most important social basis of self-respect:

> our self-respect [...] depends in part on the respect shown by others [...] it is precisely by publicly affirming the two principles of justice on the democratic interpretation that a society [...] makes visible in its institutions the respect that citizens have for one another as moral persons.
>
> *(*CP*, 171; see also* PL*, 81, 318–9)*

So, justice secures the social bases of self-respect, but the principles of justice are not derived from or justified by reference to self-respect, nor is self-respect itself a good that the principles of justice directly govern. Rather, because of how the principles of justice express and secure equal citizenship for all, they also secure the social bases of self-respect.

9 Rawls's Egalitarianism

Is justice as fairness egalitarian? One might think that it is not egalitarian, since Rawls rejects that the principle of equality should govern the distribution of wealth and income. However, justice as fairness is egalitarian in that it begins with an idea of equality – the idea of democratic society as a system of social cooperation among free and equal citizens. It is also egalitarian in that the principles of justice require equal basic rights and fair equality of opportunity. Moreover, even the rejection of the principle of equality is grounded in a sort of egalitarian concern, for the baseline of a fair distribution is an equal distribution, and the focus on the least well-off required by the difference principle does not make sense without this baseline of equality. Here is a passage where Rawls expresses his egalitarianism:

> We can associate the traditional ideas of liberty, equality, and fraternity with the democratic interpretation of the two principles of justice as follows: liberty corresponds to the first principle, equality to the idea of equality in the first principle together with equality of fair opportunity, and fraternity to the difference principle.
>
> *(*TJ*, 91)*

In addition, the idea of reciprocity and the baseline of equality that support the notion of fraternity expressed by the difference principle are also egalitarian. So, though Rawls rejects the principle of equality, justice as fairness is egalitarian.

10 Justice as Fairness versus the System of Liberty

Above, we saw why the parties in the original position prefer justice as fairness to any conceptions that do not secure an adequate scheme of equal basic rights, such as pure utilitarianism. We also saw that the parties prefer justice as fairness to the conceptions that combine the first principle and fair equality of opportunity with either the principle of equality or the principle of utility. The parties know that those they represent will be better-off with the difference principle (a principle of priority) than with the principle of equality, and they are unwilling to risk the outcome that those they represent lack the material resources to live a decent life or to develop and exercise the powers of democratic citizenship, which they might in a system where the principle of utility governs the distribution of wealth and income. Alas, none of these comparisons tell us much about how justice as fairness would do in a comparison with the sort of right-liberalism that Hayek defends.

Rawls never discusses this sort of right-liberalism. The closest he gets is a discussion of a restricted sort of utilitarianism that affirms both the first principle and fair equality of opportunity, but replaces the difference principle with the principle of utility tempered by the principle of sufficiency (*JaF*, 120). It is a bit puzzling that Rawls never engaged directly with right-liberalism. Rawls could not, of course, discuss all the contending conceptions of justice, and his main aim is to show that justice as fairness is superior to single-principle, pure utilitarianism, an aim he can achieve without engaging with right-liberalism. However, right-liberalism was, and still is, one of the main alternatives to justice as fairness, so it would be useful to know how they compare. In this section I run this comparison using the original position, and try to show how Rawls might argue that justice as fairness is superior to right-liberalism. I deal with each part of Rawls's conception of justice in turn: basic rights and liberties, fair equality of opportunity, and the difference principle.

10.1 Basic Rights versus Liberty

The first subjects for comparison are Rawls's and Hayek's views on basic rights and liberties. Rawls identifies a scheme of basic rights and liberties that should be secured equally for all. The basic rights have higher priority than other political concerns, meaning that they cannot be regulated except as needed to secure an adequate scheme of rights for all. Rawls's view differs from Hayek's in several important respects:

- First, Hayek's concern is for *liberty* as such, and state coercion is justified only to protect liberty or to procure funds necessary to pay for government functions. Rawls, by contrast, gives no special priority to liberty as such. For Rawls, liberty is protected merely by *the presumption of liberty*, which requires that that any coercive exercise of political authority must be justified, but allows for many sorts of justifying reasons – political coercion can be justified to secure basic rights, equality of opportunity, and a fair and efficient system for the production and consumption of goods.

- A second and closely related contrast is that Hayek is skeptical of constitutional protection for distinct rights and liberties. Instead, we should secure the rule of law and ensure that state coercion is exercised only to protect liberty and raise funds for government functions. Rawls, by contrast, singles out a list of rights and liberties for constitutional protection.
- Third, insofar as Hayek plays favorites among liberties, his favorites are the economic liberties – freedom of contract, property rights, and limited government regulation of the market – since these are essential to run the game of catallaxy. Rawls, by contrast, does not grant much importance to economic liberties – indeed, his position is that most such economic liberties are nonbasic, which leaves room to design an economy that gives priority to concerns of distributive justice above the interest in free economic agency and its desirable results.
- Finally, Hayek gives no special support to political rights, whereas Rawls singles out these for fair value protection, which also means that Rawls, by contrast with Hayek, requires that the political process be shielded as much as possible from the influence of money.

As described above, Rawls's argument for giving priority to the list of basic rights is that all, and only, these are necessary for the development and exercise of the powers of democratic citizenship. Since the parties in the original position recognize that those they represent have a higher-order interest in developing and exercising these moral powers, they will not risk a system where some members of society cannot develop and exercise them; they therefore prefer systems that secure the equal basic rights and their priority to those that do not. The question is: Does Hayek's system of liberty secure a result similar enough to the first principle and its priority that the parties can trust that those they represent have adequate institutional support for the development and exercise of the powers of democratic citizenship? If so, the parties will be indifferent between Hayek's basic principle and the first principle of justice as fairness.

There is at least one reason to doubt that Hayek's system adequately protects the development and exercise of the moral powers, namely, that it offers no guarantee of the fair value of political rights. So, we might worry that political power in the system of liberty is partially determined by the wealth of citizens, which would fail to secure for all the conditions of democratic equality.

Hayek might reply to this worry that his system secures free and equal citizenship even more directly than Rawls's. In Hayek's system, the limitation of legitimate state power to protections of liberty and the rule of law – which includes formal equality – also limits the threat of capture of political power by the rich (or any other group), for there simply isn't much legislative action to capture. Hayek might add that the Rawlsian system allows exactly the sort of asymmetry of political power that it should prevent, since it allows coalitions to capture the political process and use it to serve their interests. If, say, a coalition of public employees and the relatively poor can provide a majority in favor of increasing the public sector into spheres that should be left to the free market, then Rawls's system permits them to use their majority to create the laws that let them do it. Hayek's system protects against such coalitions by limiting state action to the protection of liberty. Rawls could counter that his system does not permit such a capture of political power by coalitions, since all state activities must be justified by public rather than private reasons – that is, by reference to true political interests such as those of justice or efficiency – and such coalition activities cannot be justified by public reasons.

10.2 Fair Equality of Opportunity versus the Principle of Nondiscrimination

The second subject for comparison is Hayek's and Rawls's views on equality of opportunity. Hayek rejects any principle of equality of opportunity stronger than the principle of nondiscrimination. Hayek's position, recall, is that the best average opportunities are provided in a system of liberty. Rawls, by contrast, affirms fair equality of opportunity, which combines the principle of non-discrimination with the requirement that we seek to minimize the effects of the social lottery (the effects of the natural lottery are dealt with by the difference principle). The main justification for proceeding from the principle of nondiscrimination to the principle of fair equality of opportunity is that the outcome of interactions in the free market are fair to all – and thus also to those who end up being worst off – *only if* the rules of the game give all members of equal talents and motivation an even chance to succeed. To use a common metaphor, for the game of catallaxy to be a fair game the rules must be impartial (which requires nondiscrimination) *and* the playing field must be level (which requires fair equality of opportunity).

The argument for fair equality of opportunity can be divided into two parts. The first part explains why we *should* embrace equal opportunity rather than maximize aggregate opportunities (a utilitarian principle of opportunity) or allow the free market to distribute opportunities simply according to market value (a principle of liberty of opportunity). The second part explains why we *should not* embrace a principle of priority of opportunity that would allow inequalities of opportunity insofar as these give more opportunities to those who have least.

The first part of Rawls's argument is based on the requirements of reciprocity, the strains of commitment, and stability. *Reciprocity*, recall, requires that the distribution of the benefits and burdens of cooperation are advantageous to each against a benchmark of equality, without any group's gains making another group less well-off. *The strains of commitment* require the parties in the original position to agree only to principles that result in a system wherein all can respect and endorse the rules of cooperation in light of how the rules treat them as free and equal persons. *Stability* is a function of how well a system ordered by a conception of justice generates its own support by engendering a sense of justice in the members of society, so that they come to see that their own good is congruent with (best furthered by) the rules of cooperation of a society well ordered by the principles of that conception. The main thought behind these three ideas – reciprocity, strains of commitment, and stability – is that where the rules of a society treat citizens as free and equal, advances their good, and where inequalities are to the advantage of those that have least, that society can (and should) be endorsed by all members, including those who have the least. Such a society will be stable, not merely by virtue of the coercive power of the state, or because the members of society feel helpless to change it, but because they can see that no other society could better serve their interest without sacrificing the interests of some other group.

A society that follows the principles of utility or liberty for the distribution of opportunities fails to satisfy the principle of reciprocity, for in these societies inequalities of opportunity are not to the advantage of those who have less, but serve the end of maximizing average (or aggregate or product) opportunity. Those who have less do so simply because others can have more – not because they themselves benefit from it. Those who have less might not (and perhaps should not) respect and endorse the rules of their society, but may resent these rules as expressing the view that those with more are also more important.

The way this argument shows up in the original position is that the parties have an interest in stability, which means that they prefer societies wherein all members support the rules of society, because they recognize that these rules treat them as free and equal persons and provide them with a fair share of primary goods. Given this interest, and given that the principles of utility and liberty may result in unequal opportunities that make the least well-off worse off than they would be with equal opportunity, the parties will prefer societies that secure fair equality of opportunity to those that distribute opportunities according to the principles of utility or liberty. Accordingly, the parties will prefer conceptions of justice that include the principle of fair equality of opportunity to those that include merely the principle of nondiscrimination, including right-liberal conceptions such as Hayek's.

Why not proceed to a principle of priority of opportunity? The answer, I think, is quite simple: all departures from fair equality of opportunity will make some members of society worse off than they would be with equal opportunity, which means that the principle of priority is not a real alternative. One person's opportunity is another person's lack of opportunity. If the children of the wealthy have better access to education than the children of the poor, then it is hard to see how this could increase opportunities for the poor – even if they have access to education, this education is not of equal quality to that of the children of the rich, and the market value of their education is lower.

One might object that the same goes for wealth and income: the value of money is relative to the supply of money; the fact that some are rich cannot increase the wealth of the poor, since the market value of their wealth is a function of total wealth. This worry leads to the suspicion that the principle of priority makes no more sense for the distribution of income and wealth than it does for the distribution of opportunities, for it assumes that we can make the poorer better-off by allowing others to be richer. The answer to this worry is that the wealth and income regulated by the difference principle is shorthand for access to desirable goods as these are distributed in the market. When the difference principle directs us to maximize the lot of the least well-off, their lot can be measured in terms of wealth and income only in terms of real purchasing power, that is, as substitute for their access to the desirable fruits of social cooperation: goods, services, and so on.

10.3 Priority versus Liberty and Sufficiency

Finally, why should we prefer the difference principle (a principle of priority) to Hayek's combination of the principle of liberty and the principle of sufficiency? Rawls does not give us a direct answer, but what he says suggests an answer that parallels his argument in favor of fair equality of opportunity. The argument is that only the difference principle fully satisfies the requirements of reciprocity, the strains of commitment, and stability (cf. Rawls's abovementioned discussion of restricted utilitarianism in *JaF*, 119–30).

One way to explain Rawls's argument is to look again at the graph that explains the difference principle (Figure 3.1). The difference principle says that inequalities that improve the lot of the least well-off are just, and that inequalities that do not improve their lot are unjust. The difference principle expresses and satisfies the requirement of reciprocity, since relative to the baseline of equality, every permissible change to the design of the basic structure improves the prospects of all members of society without sacrificing the interests of any (illustrated by the northeastern direction of the curve from the point of equality, **O**, to the point that satisfies the difference principle, *D*). This idea of reciprocity is nicely captured in the original position, where the parties can agree to the difference principle, since they know that those they represent will be better-off in the system that satisfies it than in any other system where no one's interests are satisfied for the sake of increasing the interests of others. Now, if we proceed further east on the graph beyond point *D*, the most well-off group in society will be better-off and the product of utilities (if we go to point *N*) or average utility (if we go to the point *B*) increases. However, the increase in utility and the prospects of the most well-off group is achieved at the expense of the prospects of the least well-off. In a sense, the least well-off are now paying for the improvements to utility. This eastward move fails to satisfy the requirement of reciprocity, since at this point the least well-off are simply losing for the sake of the gains of the better-off. The failure to satisfy the requirement of reciprocity translates into higher strains of commitment and lower stability in the same fashion as the failure to satisfy the principle of fair equality of opportunity, since the least well-off members of society have little reason to respect and endorse the rules by which they end up being the least well-off.

Now, Hayek's main argument for the system of liberty (tempered by the principle of sufficiency) is that this system maximizes the average expected welfare of members of society (in the previous chapter, I suggested this should be read in terms of maximizing the product of utilities). This argument relies on the right-liberal belief that liberty is efficient, so that average prospects are maximized in the system of liberty.

We have arrived at a crucial juncture. If Rawls's argument from reciprocity works, then it shows that *even if* we grant the right-liberal belief that liberty is an efficient tool of prosperity, so that the system of liberty maximizes expected welfare, the system of liberty is still *unfair*, for it fails to satisfy the requirement of reciprocity appropriate to a democratic society. For, in the system of liberty, the maximal average prospects might be achieved by making the least well-off worse off than they could be – by sacrificing the interests of the poorest members of society for the sake of improving the prospects of the better-off members of society and thereby increasing the average.

10.4 Summary

One main division between Hayek's system of liberty and Rawls's justice as fairness is their view of the relation between democratic society and liberty. Whereas Hayek, and right-liberals generally, justifies democracy by reference to the value of liberty, Rawls, and left-liberals generally, justifies the value of rights and liberties by reference to the ideal of democracy.

Moreover, because Rawls conceives of democratic society as a system of cooperation between free and equal persons, he argues that the division of the benefits and burdens of society should be fair, and that fairness entails reciprocity; that no group is made worse off simply to make other groups better-off. Fairness and reciprocity permit all inequalities that make the least well-off better-off, but forbid inequalities that increase average or product utility if these make the least well-off worse off than they could be under an alternative system.

In the end, then, if we accept Rawls's conception of democratic society as a system of cooperation between free and equal persons, justice as fairness is superior to Hayek's system of liberty. Hayek might not be terribly troubled by this conclusion, insofar as he does not accept Rawls's vision of society. Hayek does not start with the idea of democratic society, but with the idea of society as a system of coordinated productive activities. If Hayek's idea of society carries no commitment to the idea of cooperation between free and equal citizens, then he need not embrace Rawls's conclusions about what this idea entails.

11 Summary and Discussion: A Democratic Society?

Using again the pyramid figure, Rawls's left-liberalism can be depicted as below (Figure 3.2).

In more detail, Rawls's theory of justice, and left-liberalism generally, can be summarized as affirming the following positions:

- First, the starting point is a particular idea of democratic society. A democratic society, on this approach, is not merely or primarily a forum of self-interested pursuits, but a relation between free and equal persons that come together to *cooperatively* produce desirable goods. While cooperation as free and equal is not an end in itself, it is an ideal of how we should live together.
- Second, because justice begins with this idea of democratic society, the benefits and burdens of society – the benefits and costs of social cooperation – ought to be distributed in a manner that is *fair* to all citizens. What matters is not merely that society produces as much of the desirable goods as possible, but that the goods that are produced, and the burdens that go into their production, are fairly distributed.
- Third, the principles of justice are the basic terms of society understood as a system of social cooperation between free and equal citizens.
- Fourth, fairness requires at least some measure of equality of opportunity and also that material inequalities are acceptable to those who end up with least – material inequalities may be just, but only if they can be agreed to by all citizens viewed as free and equal. Thus, the state has a role to play in securing equality of opportunity and a fair distribution of resources, so that material inequalities are fair to all.
- Fifth, some rights are very important, but the importance of rights and liberties depends on their role in defining and expressing the ideas of democratic society and democratic citizenship – the ideals of democracy. The ideal of social cooperation between free and equal citizens is more basic than, and serves as foundation for, the value of rights and liberties.

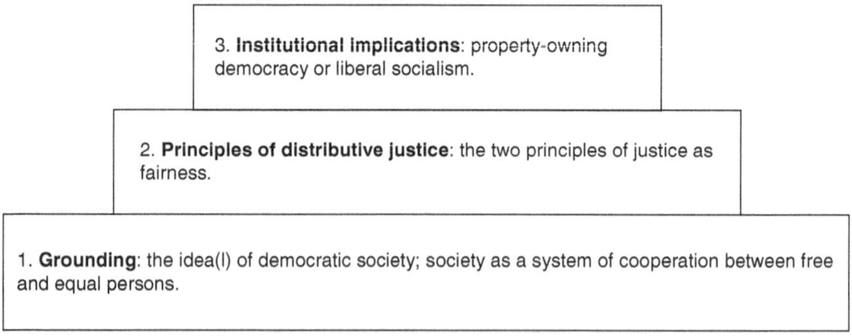

FIGURE 3.2 The main elements of left-liberalism.

The main attraction of this theory is that it starts from a very intuitive and appealing idea – the idea of democratic society. There is widespread agreement that we ought to create and maintain democratic societies. Justice as fairness tells us how to do it. Rawls analyzes the commitment to democratic society into its component parts: the idea of social cooperation and the idea of free and equal citizens cooperating. He then constructs an entire theory of justice from these component parts together with some widely accepted features of the concept of justice. Thus, the main strength of Rawls's theory of justice (justice as fairness) is that it takes a small set of widely accepted ideas – justice, cooperation, free and equal citizens – and constructs a conception of justice from these resources. This conception of justice, justice as fairness, is the answer to the question: What is the best conception of justice for a democratic society?

However, the strength of this theory of justice is also a weakness. Rawls assumes the question – What is the best conception of justice for a democratic society? – and he offers few arguments for why we should understand democratic society as a system of social cooperation between free and equal citizens. Justice as fairness is almost inescapable if you accept Rawls's question and analysis of the terms of the question. But if you think that justice is about something else, or disagree with Rawls's conceptions of justice, cooperation, and citizenship, then justice as fairness is less appealing.

The reach of Rawls's theory of justice is thus limited to those who accept that Rawls's question is indeed the main question of justice, and who also accept Rawls's understanding of the terms of the question. As we shall see in the following chapters, libertarians reject the question, for they think that justice is about something other than democratic society. Socialists, on the other hand, accept the question, but reject Rawls's understanding of the question's components.

Further Reading

The primary sources used in describing Rawls's philosophy are the following (abbreviations for in-text citations in parenthesis):

Rawls, John, 1996. *Political Liberalism, Expanded Paperback Edition*, New York, NY: Columbia University Press. (*PL*).

Rawls, John, 1999a (org. 1971). *A Theory of Justice, Revised Edition*, Cambridge, MA: Harvard University Press. (*TJ*). Notably, this book is Rawls's only monograph, his remaining writings are either based on lectures he gave or articles he published.

Rawls, John, 1999b. *Collected Papers*, S. Freeman (ed.), Cambridge, MA: Harvard University Press. (*CP*). This volume collects most of Rawls's published papers and some of his lectures. It contains Rawls's earlier writings on distributive justice and papers that are helpful for understanding how his ideas developed before and after *A Theory of Justice*.

Rawls, John, 2001. *Justice as Fairness: A Restatement*, E. Kelly (ed.), Cambridge, MA: Harvard University Press. (*JaF*).

Other works by Rawls that are helpful for understanding his theory are:

Rawls, John, 2000. *Lectures on the History of Moral Philosophy*, B. Herman (ed.), Cambridge, MA: Harvard University Press.

Rawls, John, 2001. *The Law of Peoples*, Cambridge, MA: Harvard University Press.

Rawls, John, 2007. *Lectures on the History of Political Philosophy*, S. Freeman (ed.), Cambridge, MA: Harvard University Press.

The literature on Rawls's political philosophy is immense. Below I list some sources that I have found especially useful:

Freeman, Samuel (ed.), 2003. *The Cambridge Companion to Rawls*, Cambridge, UK: Cambridge University Press.

Freeman, Samuel, 2006. *Justice and the Social Contract: Essay on Rawlsian Political Philosophy*, Oxford, UK: Oxford University Press.

Freeman, Samuel, 2007. *Rawls*, London, UK: Routledge.

Mandle, Jon & David Reidy (eds.), 2013. *A Companion to Rawls*, Chichester, UK: John Wiley & Sons.

A thorough explanation of the developments in Rawls's thought that led to the revisions summarized in *Political Liberalism* is:

Weithman, Paul, 2011. *Why Political Liberalism? On John Rawls's Political Turn*, Oxford, UK: Oxford University Press.

Variant defenses and discussions of left-liberalism include:

Anderson, Elizabeth, 1999. "What Is the Point of equality?" *Ethics*, 109: 287–337.

Cohen, Joshua, 2010. *The Arc of the Moral Universe and Other Essays*, Cambridge, MA: Harvard University Press.

Dworkin, Ronald, 2000. *Sovereign Virtue: The Theory and Practice of Equality*, Cambridge, MA: Harvard University Press.

4

LIBERTARIANISM/NOZICK

1 Introduction

As with other theories of distributive justice, libertarianism can be understood both as answers to questions about how we should design the political institutions of society, and as the principles which should guide us when we think about such questions of institutional design. In contemporary public discourse, we usually think of libertarianism in terms of the first of these; we think of libertarianism as the family of views which holds that few areas of life should be governed by state-enforced laws. However, for our purposes it is more interesting to focus on the matter of principles – on the question of *why* libertarians believe in limited government. At this level, the libertarian position is best understood in terms of the simple and powerful principle of liberty, which says that all persons ought to be at liberty to decide what to do for themselves, so long as their actions don't violate the equal liberty of others.

It is easy to see how the libertarian principle can support the libertarian view of institutions, for by the libertarian principle the state should not interfere with people's lives, except to secure that their activities are mutually consistent in terms of liberty. The state has a role in protecting its members from violence, thefts, deceit, and so on, but should not engage in paternalist government (requiring seat-belt use, prohibiting drug use, enforcing a particular view of marriage, etc.), or pursue redistributive policies, since such exercises of state power unjustifiably limit the liberty of some members of society (unjustifiably, insofar as these uses of state power are not required to secure the mutually consistent exercise of liberty of all).

The libertarian principle is both simple and powerful. Its power is perhaps easiest to see by noting the relation between liberty and authority. The libertarian principle can be stated as a principle about the limits of authority; no person has authority to coerce another person, unless, that is, that other person is violating someone's rights. This anti-authoritarian sentiment makes powerful, intuitive sense to many people. What gives me the right to tell you what to do, if your actions don't harm anyone (but yourself)? Just as I cannot take your car without your permission, so I cannot force you to paint it purple, take it for a drive, or to wear a seatbelt when you decide to take it for a drive – I do not have the authority to coerce you to act as I think you should. Of course, if you sell the car to me, or if we make a contract that you give me a ride to the train station, or if you agree to wear your seatbelt in exchange for my promise to wear my bike helmet, then such contracts *create* authority relations between us, possibly even coercive authority. If you don't give me the car, drive me, or wear your seatbelt, then I might have a right to use coercive pressure to make you do it – or there might be some public authority (e.g. a state) that I can call upon to exercise this coercive pressure on my behalf (I take you to court for breach of contract).

This original limitation of authority applies equally to individuals and to the state. The state has no authority but that which originates either from the limitation of authority itself, or from contracts by which the state has been granted additional authority. That is, the state may be used to secure that individual rights are respected by all, and it may also have additional authority insofar as it was given said authority by contracts with the members of society. But absent such contracts, the state has no authority beyond that of securing the consistent exercise of liberty of all.

In this chapter we take a closer look at these ideas and try to explain how they support an appealing and powerful theory of distributive justice. We shall see how the principle of liberty is consistent with the coercive exercise of political authority, the basis and reach of property and contract rights, and why libertarians tend to think that the pursuit of equality of opportunity or a fair distribution of wealth and income are both unjustified and unjust. We will explore the libertarian system of ideas and claims by examining the work of a prominent libertarian philosopher, Robert Nozick (1938–2002).

In his book *Anarchy, State, and Utopia* (1974), Nozick gives a clear and persuasive statement of the libertarian principle, the theory of distributive justice it implies, and why we should reject the more expansive theories of distributive justice presented by thinkers like Rawls (on the left) or even Hayek (on the right). Nozick's conclusion is that only a minimal state is justified and that such a state can serve no (re)distributive purpose – the distribution of resources and other advantages in a society should be a function of individual choices and transactions among the members, rather than the pursuit of some principle of distributive justice. In a slogan: only the minimal state is justified – anything "larger" must violate the rights of members of society and is thus illegitimate (cf. Information Box 4.1 The size of the state). However, Nozick's aim is not merely to show that the minimal state is the most that can be justified, for Nozick takes seriously the anarchist challenge of showing how *any* state could be permissible. To follow Nozick's line of thought, it is helpful to start with this challenge and Nozick's reply to it.

INFORMATION BOX 4.1 THE SIZE OF THE STATE

It is often said that libertarians favor a small state, but what does the concept of size mean in the context of the state? The size of a state can be measured in terms of its expenditure (e.g. as a percentage of GDP), in terms of public employment (e.g. the percentage of the population employed by the state), in terms of how many aspects of life are regulated by laws, in terms of the degree to which these aspects of life are regulated by laws, in terms of the number of laws, and so on. Sometimes, and perhaps normally, these go hand in hand. For example, a state that is large in terms of the domain and depth of political authority is also large in terms of the amount of its expenditure and the number of its laws; but there is no conceptual or necessary connection between these different measures of size. An absolute monarch might have complete authority to regulate all aspects of life, and yet exercise this authority without creating many offices or making many laws (one law could be enough: the current will of the monarch is binding law).

Nozick defines the size of the state in terms of the reach of its authority. As he defines it, *the ultra-minimal state* is a state that exercises monopoly on the use of coercion in a given territory, so that no other agent can use coercion (except in cases of emergency). *The minimal state* is a state that exercises monopoly on the use of coercion in a given territory, ensures that the rights of all persons residing in that territory are protected, *and* does nothing else but ensure that the rights of persons are protected – meaning that it does not provide public goods, poor relief, healthcare, education, and so on – except insofar as such provisions are required to secure the rights of members of society. States are "larger" than the minimal state if they pursue goals in addition to securing the original and acquired rights of its members.

2 The Anarchist Challenge

The anarchist challenge is twofold. The anarchist claims both that the state could not come into existence without anyone's rights being violated, and that someone's rights always will be violated by the actions of a state. The first challenge is about the *genesis* of political authority – that the sort of political authority states exercise cannot be created without rights-violations. The second is about the *exercise* of such authority – that the running of a state must involve rights-violations. The main question of this book is about how we should design the state, and in particular the institutions that influence the distribution of economic advantages in society; but if either of the anarchist claims are true, then this is the wrong question, for then we should not have a state in the first place. As Nozick says, the fundamental question of political philosophy is thus not how we should organize the state, but "whether there should be any state at all. Why not have anarchy?" (*ASU*, 4)

To reply to the anarchist and show that a state could be created and function without anyone's rights being violated, Nozick tells a story of how a state could be generated by only permissible (i.e. not rights-violating) moves from a state of anarchy – a state of nature where no political authority exists (cf. Information Box 4.2 States of nature).

INFORMATION BOX 4.2 STATES OF NATURE

A *state of nature* is an imaginary situation which is in some sense (temporally, theoretically, politically) before human beings enter the *state of society*.

In the history of philosophy, a variety of states of nature have served an equal variety of purposes. In one famous version, Hobbes describes the state of nature as a state without a public authority to define and enforce norms of justice. Given an unfortunate confluence of human dispositions, needs, material circumstances, and an absence of public authority, Hobbes argues, the state of nature inevitably becomes a state of war of all against all, where advances of culture, science, and technology are impossible and the life of most people is "nasty, solitary, poor, brutish, and short." As Hobbes uses it, the state of nature serves as part of an argument that reveals the attractions of civil society where all are subject to the power of a sovereign ruler in exchange for peace, security, and access to the various comforts of life.

In reply to Hobbes, Rousseau argues that the desires and tendencies of human beings in the Hobbesian state of nature – which makes it so terrible – are themselves products of human society, rather than fixed human dispositions. To Rousseau, we are greedy, aggressive, dishonest, jealous, vain, and so on because society makes us so, not because such traits are part of human nature. Rousseau's state of nature is a state of near solitude, and thus a state of primordial innocence and happiness – a vision of an original human existence free from the troubles, worries, and empty desires that make the lives of most socialized human beings so miserable.

Locke also rejects Hobbes's vision of the state of nature, but his focus is more on the validity and power of the norms of justice. Where Hobbes argues that the norms of justice have no purchase except in the context of a state, Locke argues that the norms of justice have full power in the state of nature as well as in the state of society. The state of nature is governed by *laws* of nature that require us to take care of ourselves and respect the rights of other persons – rights of life, liberty, and so on.

Yet another way to view the state of nature (suggested by Grotius, Kant, and others) is purely theoretical – as a state of perfect and equal liberty. Here, the state of nature is simply the situation prior to any acquired rights – prior to the creation of any rights to property or to the services of others. In this situation every person has only her natural rights (say, those dictated directly by the principle of liberty). This sort of state of nature is interesting since it allows us to distinguish between natural (in the sense of original) and acquired rights and also to discuss what sorts of interpersonal relations can be permissibly generated from such pure natural rights – including the question of what sorts of political authority are consistent with the principle of liberty.

Note that the transition from the pure state of perfect and equal liberty to a state of acquired rights need not be a transition from the state of nature to a state of civil society. Grotius and Kant, at least, allow that persons can possess acquired rights (including rights of property and contract) apart from membership in civil society. In that case, the transition is from one state of nature (perfect equal liberty) to another state of nature (where various persons possess various acquired rights).

Nozick accepts as a starting point the purely theoretical account of what the state of nature is (the state of pure original equal liberty prior to the acquisition of rights), but he works with Locke's view of the validity and power of rights in that situation, as well as with Locke's account of how one can acquire property rights.

Imagine a Lockean state of nature where there is no political authority – no laws, no police, no courts. Persons in this state of nature are not particularly bad – they're not unusually foolish, greedy, malignant, vain, jealous, or prone to spite or envy – but they are not particularly good; they're not of superhuman intelligence or knowledge, not of angelic virtue, not immune to the opinions of others. In such a state of nature we can imagine that persons are generally disposed to respect the rights of others, at least for the most part and as they understand them. It is thus not like a Hobbesian state of nature where our tendencies towards quarrel and conflict mean that no one can trust others to respect their rights (insofar as we can have rights in a Hobbesian state of nature, but that's a separate question), but neither is it a golden age or paradise.

There are two sorts of rights in this state of nature: original and acquired. The original rights are those that issue directly from the principle of liberty: the right to dispose of oneself as one wants to (as long as one does not violate the rights of others), which entails freedom from violence and deceit, robberies and thefts, and so on.

Acquired rights are the rights that one can earn through one's actions. There are two basic types of acquired rights: property rights and contract rights. Property rights are rights to dispose of things; contract rights are rights to the actions of other persons. One can acquire property rights either by the original appropriation of an object (say, picking wild berries) or by their transfer from others as gifts or in trades. In the latter case, one might have a contract right to this transfer, say, if I trade my newly picked berries for one of your apples (which you got either by original appropriation or from another person who got it by original appropriation or from another person, and so on until we arrive at an original appropriation). In this story, then, all rights originate either in the principle of liberty, original appropriation of goods, or contracts between persons (by consent). The distinction between original and acquired rights can be used to identify two distinct types of states of nature: the state of pure original rights and the state of acquired rights that is still prior to the formation of a civil society. As we shall see below, this distinction is useful for showing how and why the state can come into existence without anyone's rights being violated in the process.

A state of nature – even a state of nature with acquired rights and where people respect each other's original and acquired rights – is a state of anarchy in the sense that people are subject to no political authority; they not subjected to the rule of positive laws. The question is whether a civil state might arise from such a state of nature without anyone's rights being violated in the process. Nozick argues that it can. The starting point of his argument is that the state of nature presents various inconveniences. Even though persons are generally disposed to respect each other's rights, they face the epistemic obstacle of knowing what rights they have: issues of indeterminacy, where it is unclear what rights people have; an assurance problem, uncertainty that others will respect one's rights; and the risks and costs of enforcing one's rights and pursuing reparations in cases where they were violated. For example, I might claim a stretch of land by building a fence around it, but you also make a claim to it by planting your apple trees on it. It's quite inconvenient that there is no set of mutually agreed-upon rules that defines the necessary and sufficient conditions for effective appropriation, that there is no independent body we can turn to for adjudication in cases of disputes, and no police to enforce justice if, in the heat of the moment, I fell your tree and you trash my fence.

So, for a variety of reasons, we might agree (that is, some number of people might agree) to create an independent body that defines the precise rules of our interactions, adjudicates disputes, and helps us enforce our rights. Those who create such a body would naturally abandon their personal right to enforce their rights against others, except in cases of immediate self-defense. The agreement to create a body for the adjudication of disputes and enforcement of rights would thus take place through the mutual contract to abandon our personal coercive rights and to abide by the decisions of such a body (assuming, of course, that this body makes a good-faith effort to remain impartial, and so forth). Nozick calls such an association a "mutual-protection association" (*ASU*, 12), because it is formed for our mutual protection against one another and also from those outside the association that might pose a threat to us.

For further reasons of convenience and cost-efficiency, and in light of facts about the relative advantages of competing protection associations, it is quite possible that over time one protective association will become dominant in an area. However, such a dominant protection association is not yet a state, for, *first*, it does not have a monopoly on the use of force in the area, since there might be other protective associations working there, or individuals might retain partial rights of enforcement; and, *second*, the dominant protection association does not cover all persons living in the area, but only its members.

Nozick needs to explain how two further developments can take place without anyone's rights being violated: first, how the dominant protection agency can acquire a monopoly on the use of force, and, second, how it can come to cover all persons living in a territory. Nozick's account of these developments is complex and technical, so here is the simplified version (see *ASU*, Chapters 3–6 for the details). Our natural right to liberty entails that others cannot coerce us, except when we have violated their rights (or are just about to do so). This liberty also entails a right that others use reliable and fair procedures for deciding if and when we have violated anyone's rights. If a person is charged with a crime and thus becomes a potential subject of punishment, then she has a right to a fair and reliable trial. A correlate of this right is that persons have a right to resist and defend themselves against exposure to procedures that are *not* reliable and fair (*ASU*, 96–101). This procedural right can, and likely would, be invested in the dominant protection agency to exercise on one's behalf against charges of crimes by other agencies or nonmembers. The dominant protection agency would decide whether the procedures of other agencies are fair and reliable, and force them to use only procedures that it deems fair and reliable against its members, and, because of its dominance, other protection agencies would not wield the same power against it (*ASU*, 108–9). So, once a dominant protection agency has come into existence, it, and it alone, will exercise the right to impose its view of the standards of reliability and fairness of procedures in the territory where it is dominant (*ASU*, 108). This asymmetry between the dominant agency and other protection agencies quite clearly gives it a competitive advantage, and the result will be that it will attract the clients of other protection agencies – obtaining a *de facto* monopoly on the use of force (*ASU*, 108).

There might still be independents – nonclients who are unwilling to join the dominant protection agency. Once the dominant protection agency has a *de facto* monopoly on the use of force and power to decide which procedures for the use of coercion are reliable and fair, these nonclients are severely limited in their ability to enforce their rights against the agency's clients – the dominant protection agency might simply prohibit such independents from enforcing their rights on its clients (*ASU*, 110). Such prohibition, however, is permissible only if the nonmembers are compensated for the disadvantage it creates, and the compensation would naturally be in the form of supplying them with the protective services of the agency free of charge or for a fee less than the standard price (*ASU*, 110–1).

A minimal state has now been generated from the original state of nature without anyone's rights having been violated in the process. The dominant protection agency has monopoly on the use of force in a territory, and it protects all persons living in that territory. It ensures that rights are protected, and when they are violated it adjudicates disputes and metes out punishments according to a system that its members deem reliable and fair. This minimal state exercises no functions other than those mandated by the principle of liberty and the various natural, contractual, and procedural rights that can be generated by persons acting in accordance with that principle. The exercise of state coercion is no different from the permissible, self-protective coercive activities of individual persons – indeed, it is generated by the transfer through contract of these individual rights to the state. Thus, the anarchist challenge has been met.

Next, Nozick argues that no state more extensive than the minimal state can be justified. In particular, any state that limits economic liberties, pursues equality of opportunity, or imposes a principle of distributive justice (other than the principle of liberty) is impermissible and unjust.

3 Justice in Holdings: The Entitlement Theory

Nozick says that the subject of distributive justice – or justice in holdings, as he prefers to call it, since he rejects that there is anything in need of distribution or any agent with authority to distribute – can be summarized by the following claim: "a distribution is just if it arose from another just distribution by legitimate means" (*ASU*, 150). The legitimate means are specified by the principles that govern the original acquisition of resources and the interpersonal exchanges of goods and services. Of course, sometimes a distribution did *not* arise by legitimate means – if I steal a car from you, then the distribution where I have the car is not just – so we also need a principle that governs how we should respond to such wrongdoings. But, according to Nozick, the subject of distributive justice is fully covered by the following three principles:

- The principle of just acquisition, which governs the original appropriation of previously unowned resources.
- The principle of just transfer, which governs interpersonal exchanges of goods and services.
- The principle of rectification, which governs how we should respond to injustices (i.e. violations of either of the first two principles).

3.1 Just Acquisition

Imagine that we are in a state of pure, original, equal liberty. All persons have rights to their own person and to do what they want, as long as what they do is consistent with the liberty of others, but natural resources (land, air, water, apples, and so on) remain unowned, and we do not have any claims on the services of each other. Clearly, remaining in this situation would be folly; it would be better if we could use the various natural resources – indeed, we have to use them to survive – so we need a principle that can tell us what sorts of resources we can lay claim to and how we can lay claim to them. We need a principle of original acquisition.

Nozick adopts a Lockean principle of original acquisition (*ASU*, 174–82). According to this principle we can acquire a previously unowned resource by mixing our labor with it – say, by picking the apple, enclosing and tilling the field, mining the ore, and so forth. But our acquisition is subject to two provisos: first, one cannot acquire more than one can make good use of, and, second, there must be "enough and as good left in common for others" (*ASU*, 175). On Nozick's interpretation, these provisos require at least that the original acquisition does not make others worse off, which at least entails that even when we consider the attractiveness of the division of labor (you till the land, I mine the ore, we trade, and are both better off), others cannot be left in severe need by the original acquisition of a resource. For example, a person cannot acquire the only source of an essential resource (say, water or salt).

3.2 Just Transfer

Just transfers are consistent with the principle of liberty, meaning that they express the voluntary choices of the transferring parties. Modes of transfer include gifts, bequests, and trades. Such transfers are justice-preserving, meaning that if a person got her holdings by a just transfer (say, it was given to her), then she has that holding justly, which also gives her a right to sell it. When she sells it, the trade carries the justice of the holding to the buyer. And so on.

Other modes of just transfer involve contracts for service. If we make a contract that I give you my car in exchange for you painting my house (old car, big house) and you paint my house, then you are entitled to the car.

The Lockean provisos also limit just transfers, for the original acquisition of a resource may violate the proviso of not worsening the condition of others by virtue of *how* it is transferred. To illustrate, a person cannot originally acquire all the salt (for it is an essential nutrient), nor can she acquire it by transfers – say, by buying all the salt in the world from others, and then using her monopoly to exploit others for their goods and services.

3.3 Rectification

Unjust transfers disrupt justice. If I stole the car from you, I can't sell it to a third party – and if a third party buys it from me, then she is not entitled to it, for it is yours. The buyer might, of course, be entitled to compensation from me for the damage or loss that she incurred, when it is revealed that the car belongs to you and the car is returned to you. Similarly, if you painted my house, but I already sold the car (or never had one), then you're entitled to some sort of payment of equivalent value as well as compensation for your loss. All such cases are governed by the principle of rectification, which, in the abstract, simply says that we should do our best to rectify whatever injustices have occurred and thereby establish a just distribution – that is, a distribution as close as possible to what it would have been if it had arisen from a previous just distribution by only just transfers.

The counterfactual work required to satisfy the principle of rectification is daunting – how far should we go back? How can we really compensate for historical injustices? Should the Americas be returned to the descendants of the native populations? Can and should the descendants be compensated? These are hard and complex questions – Nozick does not answer them, but indicates that we need to find answers to pursue justice in the world we live in. As a matter of theory, however, the principle of rectification is simple enough: injustices ought to be rectified.

3.4 A Just Distribution: Liberty, Property, and Contract

Nozick calls his theory of justice in holdings the "entitlement theory," for it spells out distributive justice in terms of the entitlements of individuals to holdings. If they got their holdings either by just initial acquisition or just transfer, then they are entitled to them, period. If they did not get their holding in this fashion, then the principle of rectification steps in and directs us to correct whatever injustice taints current holdings. Once the principle of rectification has been satisfied and there are no injustices needing correction in the past that led to the current holdings, then current holdings are just – all persons are entitled to what they have.

If a distribution arose from another distribution by just transfers, then it is just – *no matter what else is true about it*. Degrees of poverty or inequality; facts about personal merit or the distribution of luck; whether people are happy or miserable; such facts are irrelevant to the justice of a distribution. If you want to know whether a distribution of resources is just, you must simply ask whether those who currently hold the resources are entitled to them. If they are, the distribution is just; if not, the injustices that taint it must be rectified. But the justice of a distribution is a function of its history, and if the history is just, then so is the distribution.

4 Why No More than the Minimal State is Just

Nozick constructs the entitlement theory from simple and attractive materials. First, there is the principle of liberty; that people ought to be free to decide what to do for themselves, as long as their actions are consistent with the equal liberty of others. This principle is then given content by three elements: a principle of property rights that governs how people originally can acquire property and what rights of property amount to; a principle of contract rights that governs how people can make exchanges and acquire claims to services from others; and a principle of rectification, which governs how we should respond to rights-violations. By this theory there are four kinds of rights: rights we have simply as persons (innate rights); property rights that we acquire by original acquisition or transfer from others; rights to the services of others that we acquire through contracts; and rights of rectification. The innate rights we have simply as persons include rights to acquire property rights, to form contract rights, to pursue rectification when we are wronged, and procedural rights. However, the actual property, contract, and rectificatory rights a person has depends on what she and others have actually done in the past in terms of original acquisitions and contracts.

Nozick's case that any further attempts at pursuing distributive justice are unjust is equally simple: a person is entitled to her holdings (her property and claims on others) if she acquired them by legitimate means. If she is entitled to her holdings, then (by the principle of liberty) she is entitled to decide what to do with her holdings, as long as her actions do not violate the rights of others. She may sell her knife, hang it on her wall, throw it in the trash, or use it to cut marks in her table, but she may not lodge it in another person's leg or use it to carve marks in their table. If someone takes her knife against her will, then (unless the taking is part of a compensation for a past injustice) it is theft, and thus unjust. Whether the person taking her property is another individual or a government official does not make a difference. Thus, any pursuit of (re)distributive justice that involves taking property is simply theft – an unjust violation of rights. Any attempt at creating a state with functions beyond securing the rights enumerated in the previous paragraph must violate the rights of some members of society, since such functions require funding which can only be obtained through taxation that (unless it was actually agreed to by each taxed member in a past contract) violates the property rights of the taxed. Indeed, Nozick says that such taxation is "on par with forced labor" (*ASU*, 169), for the members of society need to earn some sort of income and so do not have a real alternative to working and paying taxes – they have to work and so are forced to work and pay taxes.

Liberty, says Nozick, upsets patterns, so you cannot have both liberty and patterns. If, for example, you believe that justice requires some measure of equality of resources, then you cannot allow people the liberty of engaging in voluntary transactions, for voluntary transactions tend to create inequalities. Nozick offers a famous example to illustrate this point. Pick your favorite patterned principle of distributive justice (see Information Box 4.3 Kinds of principles of distributive justice). Imagine then a situation where this principle is fully satisfied – everybody has the same, enough, needs are met, or whatever it is. Now imagine that the famous basketball player Wilt Chamberlain signs a contract with the Lakers that grants him a quarter per ticket sold for their home games. Over time, a million people pay for such tickets, earning him a handsome $250,000. Wilt is now richer than other members of society. If you want to recreate your favored pattern, you'll have to redistribute – take from Wilt and give to those who paid him (or something like it). The effect, of course, is that people don't really have liberty to engage in market transactions – Wilt cannot really enter into the contract with the Lakers, the fans cannot pay to watch Wilt, the Lakers cannot sell tickets for the games. In short, liberty upsets patterns, for the voluntary transactions of individuals in the marketplace will tend to upset any pattern and instead create a messy distribution according to a complex function of desires, talents, merits, efforts, and luck.

INFORMATION BOX 4.3 KINDS OF PRINCIPLES OF DISTRIBUTIVE JUSTICE

Nozick introduces two distinctions that can help us sort principles of distributive justice.

Patterned/nonpatterned

The first is the distinction between patterned and nonpatterned principles. Patterned principles require that the distribution has a certain pattern; nonpatterned principles do not present such a requirement. To illustrate, "distribution according to height" or "distribution according to age," are patterned (and silly). Less silly patterned principles include the egalitarian principle (equal distribution), the aristocratic principle (distribution according to rank), and distribution according to need. Nonpatterned principles include the principles of liberty and utility.

End-state/historical

The distinction between end-state and historical principles marks different approaches to time as a dimension of distributive justice. Historical principles say that whether a distribution is just or not depends on its history. The principle of liberty is an example of an historical principle, for there the justice of a distribution depends solely on whether it came about by just moves from another just distribution. End-state principles, by contrast, are nonhistorical. There are at least two sorts of end-state principles: those that measure the justice of a distribution in terms of its present structure, and those that measure it in terms of its relation to future outcomes. The egalitarian principle, for example, looks neither to the past nor to the future of a distribution to determine whether it is just or not. The utilitarian principle looks to the future and asks whether the current distribution will bring about the optimal outcome.

The entitlement theory of distributive justice that Nozick defends is nonpatterned and historical. For him, the justice of a distribution is a function exclusively of the past and independent of conformity to any pattern.

The conclusion that liberty upsets patterns forces us to choose between liberty and patterns, but it does not determine the choice in favor of liberty. However, *if* we accept the principle of liberty as the basic principle of justice, *and if* we accept that from this principle issue various *economic liberties* to manage our property and engage in contractual relationships with others, then we *must* abandon patterned principles of distributive justice, for implementing such principles must violate the rights of individuals to decide what to do with their property and to enter into contractual relations with others. In short, if we accept the principle of liberty, then we must abandon all patterned principles of distributive justice.

The case against patterned principles appears to take the principles of sufficiency, equality, and priority off the table, but leaves untouched the principle of utility – for utility does not require distribution according to a pattern, but rather that we distribute resources to achieve maximal efficiency; that we seek the optimal distribution (where optimality is defined by what is truly of value, say happiness). The principle of utility is an end-state principle (nonhistorical), but not patterned. Yet, the principle of utility is as much an enemy of liberty as, say, the principle of equality, for liberty need not result in efficiency, and when it doesn't we have to choose between liberty and utility.

Here is a point of contrast between Hayek's right-liberalism and Nozick's libertarianism. Where Hayek's case for liberty relies on the marriage of liberty and efficiency – on the claim that the system of liberty will tend to maximize the good – Nozick's case for liberty does not rely on its connection to efficiency or utility. On the contrary, Nozick seems to think that liberty will not generally tend to utility, and that this fact forces upon us a choice between liberty and utility – a choice he thinks must come out in favor of liberty, since the pursuit of utility will tend to justify rights-violations (*ASU*, Chapter 3). It may be that Wilt's additional $250,000 could do much more good if used for healthcare, but that does not give anyone the right to take it from Wilt and use it on healthcare.

Thus, any pursuit of a patterned principle of distributive justice violates both liberty in general and concrete individual rights, and is impermissible. More or less the same case applies to the pursuit of principles of equal opportunity (*ASU*, 235–9). Nozick would not, of course, allow the state itself to engage in any sort of discrimination, for it is obliged to secure rights equally for all who reside in its territory, but beyond that requirement of no public discrimination, the state has no business fighting private discrimination, or working to ensure a level playing field, or anything of that sort. Again, the argument is simple: the pursuit of equal opportunity requires either worsening the situation of those with more opportunity or improving the situation of those with less opportunity. In either case, resources have to be gathered from the holdings of those with more opportunity, but "holdings to which these people are entitled may not be seized, even to provide equality of opportunity for others" (*ASU*, 235).

It is not clear how much damage Nozick's discussion of the troubles of patterned and end-state principles do to theories of justice such as Rawls's (and Nozick seems to admit as much, cf. *ASU*, 198–213). Rawls's theory of justice is not correctly characterized as end-state, for the justice of the distribution of holdings in a society well ordered by the principles of justice as fairness *is* a function of its history. In such a society, people are entitled to their holdings if they got them by acting in accordance with the rules of that society – but these rules need not (and Rawls argues should not) be those defined by the entitlement theory. Nor is Rawls's theory of justice correctly characterized as affirming patterned principles of distributive justice, for there is *no pattern* that a Rawlsian society must achieve. Instead, the two principles of justice of Rawls's theory are meant to guide the design of the system of rules that secures basic liberties, fair equality of opportunity, and that the distribution of wealth and income over time will tend to advantage those who have least. The prioritarian principle embedded as the second part of the second principle of Rawls's theory of justice is, thus, not a principle that prescribes a pattern that the distribution of wealth and income ought to conform to; instead it prescribes how we should think about the design of the system of economic institutions of society. So, in a society well ordered by justice as fairness, persons are entitled to their holdings, if they got them by voluntary transactions that take place in accordance with the system of rules designed to ensure that the accumulative outcome of such transactions over time is fair, and whatever distribution that results from people engaging in voluntary transactions in the marketplace is fair and just, no matter if it conforms to any pattern of equality or merit, or so on.

Rawls's theory of justice thus *does not* justify the violation of the entitlements of the members of society. Rather, it directs us to design the system of entitlements to ensure fairness over time. If, and when, people are taxed on their income or estates, this tax cannot be described as taking from people what they are entitled to; instead, it is part of the system of rules that defines what people are entitled to – people are entitled to their after-tax income and to the value of their estates minus tax.

So, one place where Nozick and Rawls disagree is in how we should think of entitlements. Nozick, and libertarians more generally, tend to think that the system of entitlements is prior to political society and that political society is created to protect and secure our pre-existing entitlements. We have a right to property that the state should protect and respect; we have a right to make contracts that the state should protect and respect; and so on. Rawls, and left-liberals more generally, do not think that the point of political society is to secure pre-existing entitlements or rights. Instead, the system of entitlements should be designed to ensure that political society is just and fair over time. What property and contract rights people should have depends on how we can best design the systems of property and contract to ensure a fair and efficient economy.

There is, then, a basic disagreement between libertarians and left-liberals in their views on political society. For libertarians, political society is created to ensure pre-political rights and entitlements; for left-liberals, political society exists to enable fair and efficient social cooperation, and the system of rights and entitlements should be designed to facilitate and ensure fair cooperation over time.

5 Left-Libertarianism

There is, however, a branch of libertarianism that is concerned with economic equality, not as a requirement of fairness, but as a correlate of individual liberty. This position, known as left-libertarianism, denies the Nozickean principles of original acquisition and transfer of property. Rather than seeing resources as originally unowned and original acquisition as an event that takes place among persons and previously unowned resources, this position views resources as originally *owned in common.* Original acquisition, accordingly, is not a relation between the acquiring person and the acquired object, but *among the acquiring person and other persons*, who by the original acquisition must now access the acquired object through the will of the acquiring person. The relation of ownership is created through the agreement of the wills of all with regard to the object, not through what the owner did to, or with, the object that becomes property. In other words, it is not that I pick an apple from a tree on an unowned plot of land that makes it mine, but that everyone else can agree to my appropriation of the apple.

The original common ownership of all natural resources invites a contractualist approach to private property, where the original acquisition must be one that all could agree to. This contractualist approach, in turn, invites the idea that any system of private property rights must be one that all those regulated by it could agree to from a situation of original equal liberty; and this, in turn, suggests that no person should be left without sufficient resources for living a minimally decent life (since they would not agree to be so deprived of resources). The left-libertarian thus affirms the principle of sufficiency. Indeed, some left-libertarians maintain that natural resources remain common property, and therefore deny that there are private property rights of the sort usually defended by libertarians. Instead, property rights are permissions to use, subject to the equal claim of all to participate in the co-ownership of resources, which makes the use of resources subject to social approval. In this manner, left-libertarians can argue from the libertarian idea of equal original liberty and end up close to a socialist position (which is one reason socialists are very interested in the libertarian ideas of self-ownership and liberty, as discussed in the chapter on socialism).

6 Summary and Discussion

Libertarianism is based on a single and powerful principle, the principle of liberty. This principle is powerful both in its appeal and in its ability to answer questions of justice. Most people would agree that we have authority to decide things for ourselves, as long as we don't wrong others – and that it is deeply problematic when other people force us to do things against our will, even when they can show that it is for our own good. Paternalism, whether individual or political, rubs people the wrong way; "What gives *you* the authority to tell *me* how to live?" is a powerful question. Moreover, the principle of liberty can support a comprehensive theory of justice. When combined with a theory of property and contract rights, the principle of liberty provides clear answers to the main questions of political philosophy: What justifies the state? What are the limits of political authority? How should advantages be distributed between the members of society? The principle of liberty answers the need to protect our liberty and rights (and our consent to do so through the state); political authority is limited to the protection of liberty and rights; advantages should be distributed by voluntary exchanges that respect liberty and rights.

Returning again to the pyramid introduced in Chapter 1, libertarianism can be depicted as follows (Figure 4.1):

3. **Institutional implications**: the minimal state (or any state actually agreed to by all).

2. **Principles of distributive justice**: the principle of liberty.

1. **Grounding**: we should respect and protect natural and acquired rights as these are derived from the principle of equal original liberty.

FIGURE 4.1 The main elements of libertarianism

Libertarians view society as a series of contracts. The state is special because it has been entrusted to exercise the enforcement of rights on behalf of all, and because one cannot opt out of its authority if one resides in its territory. But the state is not a distinct subject of justice in the sense that it has rights and obligations, other than those that can be created by interpersonal contracts. The state is rather the authority that is contractually entitled and required to enforce justice, which consists in nothing but the rights-respecting behavior of all members of society.

Libertarians thus reject Rawls's claim that the basic structure of society is the first subject of justice, for the first subject of justice is rights and actions – and the rights that matter are not specific to the political relation, but are rather rights that individuals enjoy prior to their relation as members of a state. Of course, in the creation of the state, individuals may give the state authority to enforce rights additional to those they have apart from their membership in the state – but all such additional rights would be created through contract, and so would be based on the rights (including the right to contract) that people have apart from and prior to their membership in the state. The design of the basic structure of society should thus satisfy two considerations: first, the need for institutions that secure individual rights and, second, the means to exercise the actual wills of the members of society, as these were expressed in the contracts by which they created the state. Note that *hypothetical consent* carries no justificatory power here. The fact that I *could have* given you my car, does not mean that it belongs to you; the fact that you *could have* consented to a redistributive state does not mean that the state may take your holdings. If all members *actually* consent to a redistributive state, then redistributive measures would be just, but *hypothetical* agreement is not agreement.

Libertarianism can thus support arguments against expansive government. Government should be limited to the few functions essential to secure the rights of all. Interestingly, though, libertarianism can be flexible when it comes to the functions of government, for contracts can create additional rights that the government should enforce, and the contract(s) by which the state is formed may mandate that it serves additional functions – but only insofar as those subjected to the authority actually agreed to it. In theory, libertarianism can permit just about any sort of state, for any sort of state could be agreed to; but, in practice, the principle of liberty tends to support arguments in favor of a minimal state.

Libertarianism sees economic rights as among the most basic and important rights, for these rights define liberty. Libertarians view property rights and contract rights in terms of especially important liberties – rights to decide what to do with one's property and to contract with others are limited only by the requirement that one's actions do not violate the rights of others. I cannot leave my knife in your leg, but I can sell it to you. I cannot sell it to you if I stole it, or if it was stolen and I bought it (for then it isn't mine to sell), but if it is rightfully mine, I can exchange it for any goods you are willing to trade (e.g. drugs, or guns, or …). As long as our exchange does not violate any rights, it is protected by the principle of liberty and the state has no business meddling with it (unless, of course, we gave it such business through contract).

Libertarians are skeptical of equal opportunity, for they reject that the standards of fairness are really relevant for judging the justice of transactions in the marketplace. What matters is whether people respect each other's rights; if they do, their transactions are permissible and the resulting distribution is just. Whether the transacting parties had equal opportunity for access to advantages is irrelevant to whether their rights are respected in their transaction. Moreover, equal opportunity can only be pursued through the state by the use of rights-violating means. One might pursue it by paying for access to education for the less advantaged, but then one has to tax someone to pay for it, which violates their rights (except, again, if they actually consented to such a tax). Or, one might pursue it by mandating that employers hire equally from different groups in society, but that violates the right to contract of both employers and potential employees. Unless one can show that someone's rights – again, using Nozick's definition of rights – are violated by preferential treatment or unequal advantages, there is no justification for the state to engage in the pursuit of equal treatment or opportunity, and any such pursuit, it seems, violates someone's rights.

In terms of the distribution of wealth and income, libertarians reaffirm the principle of liberty *as a principle of distributive justice.* Assuming that people are entitled to their original holdings, the distribution that results from the voluntary exchanges of the members of society in the marketplace is just – whatever else is true about it. No degree of inequality, poverty, or inefficiency is unjust simply as such – such conditions are unjust only if they were produced by a history of injustices. Conversely, a system without inequality, poverty, or inefficiency is unjust, if it was produced by a history of injustices.

One might worry about the practicality of this insistent focus on the past. It begs questions about the history of how we got to the present that might be hard to answer: How far back should we go to find and rectify injustices? Does every historical injustice, however minute, require rectificatory measures? And it invites conclusions that seem both impractical and harmful, e.g. that the Americas and Australia belong to whatever population(s) can claim to have occupied them first; all others must leave. (Perhaps Manhattan and some of Pennsylvania were contractually acquired from the native inhabitants, but did they truly have a right to sell it? Or did they, perhaps, acquire it by force? Who knows?)

However, impracticality is not, by itself, a serious problem. Libertarianism is a *theory* about justice, not about what we should do. It has implications for what we should do, but its logical truth as a theory stands free of the practicality of its implications. Moreover, libertarianism shares impracticality with other theories of justice. Every theory of justice presents us with requirements that seem hard to satisfy in the real world or that require an uncomfortable reconceptualization of the world we live in. If you live in an unjust world, then justice will seem alien, impractical, and beyond reach – but that reflects the shortcomings of your world, not that justice must be closer to home.

There is, though, one respect in which libertarianism seems especially troubled by the gap between theory and practice, ideal and real. Libertarianism tells us that we must judge a distribution by its history. The libertarian can avail herself of the state-of-nature fiction to make sense of this idea: we start with a situation of pure equal freedom as well as rights to acquire property and to engage in contracts, and then let world history start from there – whenever injustices are done, we rectify them, and so the resulting distribution maintains the justice of the starting point. Assuming a just starting point, the result is just, no matter what it is!

This fiction is useful for showing how states could come into existence without anyone's rights being violated, and it provides a standard of just distribution – the distribution that is untainted by past injustices. However, *no state has such a history and no distribution is untainted* – there never was a situation of original equal liberty; the assumption of a just starting point is *always* false. What we have, instead, is the messy actual history of the world, soaked with injustices at every point. Libertarians, it seems, must either find a way to reset history or accept that no actual state or distribution of holdings can be just. There is a danger here that the need to find and correct all past injustices devours the critical and constructive potentials of the theory, for what we should do to secure justice here and now becomes a question of what injustices happened in the history of mankind and what we can do to rectify them.

Another concern is that the focus on the past seems to allow too much in the present. Recall that (assuming a just starting point) the result of voluntary transactions is just, no matter what else is true about it. This central claim of the libertarian position is troubling, for just about any result we can imagine could issue from such a history of transactions. Factors such as bad personal luck or unfortunate events may lead any number of members of society into extreme poverty – unable to care for their most basic needs or the needs of their children, while other members of society live in extreme affluence. The libertarian sees no injustice in such a distribution, if no rights were violated in its history. A libertarian can, of course, recognize that poverty is bad for the poor and that it would be morally commendable for the rich to assist the poor and do it as a matter of beneficence; or society might create a voluntary insurance scheme that protects against extreme poverty – but neither beneficence nor insurance are required by justice and the entitlement theory sees no injustice in poverty, as such, no matter its extent or degree.

Even worse, perhaps, according to libertarians the rich may legitimately exploit the poor. If the poor are starving, they'll be willing to trade whatever they have for food, but what do they have that they might offer the rich in exchange? Organs and services. The rich could ask for a kidney, eyes, or even a heart, for sexual favors, or a signature to a contract of complete subjection for a definite or indefinite period of time (i.e. voluntary slavery). Nozick explicitly allows contracts for voluntary slavery (*ASU*, 283, 331) – and he *must* do so, since such contracts are covered by the principle of liberty. Recall, by the principle of liberty *any* contract is valid as long as it does not violate anyone's rights. Even a contract that means the death of one party – say, selling a heart in exchange for enough food to prevent one's family from starving in the foreseeable future – can be rational and violate no one's rights. Most would choose slavery, if the alternative was death. Many would choose their own death, if the alternative was the continued starvation of their children. And, of course, where such contracts are made, the state would be *required* to enforce them – the person who resists delivering part of such a contract (his heart, his sexual favors, his enslavement) is violating the rights of the other party to the contract and, as such, should be punished and pay compensation.

Is this grotesque? The state enforcing contracts that entail death, mutilation, or slavery? If it is, then libertarianism is in trouble, for it must accept the permissibility and normative power of such contracts, and therefore the state must enforce them. The libertarian might reply that in the real world, and where Locke's proviso was respected both in terms of original acquisition and transfer, situations that would make such contracts rational would be very rare. Yet, rarity – even extreme rarity – isn't impossibility; the libertarian has to allow that such contracts might be made by members of society and enforced by the state.

The problem, then, is that there might be more to justice than what is covered by the principle of liberty. There seem to be norms of justice that would rule out, say, voluntary slavery and the acceptability of extreme poverty in an affluent society. And if there are such norms, then the principle of liberty is not the whole story about justice, but, at most, part of the whole story, and libertarianism is not an adequate theory of justice.

It should, however, be emphasized that libertarians need not deny that we have ethical duties of assistance or that there are moral prohibitions on domination and exploitation; they merely deny that anyone can be coerced to do, or avoid doing, something unless that action or omission corresponds to someone's rights. So, libertarians can agree that we should help those in need and should not exploit others' misfortune, but insist that it is impermissible to coerce others to be ethical in these ways unless personal rights are at stake. In a sense, libertarianism is optimistic in that it assumes that people will, generally speaking, be ethical, and so will help others in need and abstain from exploiting others' misfortune. If we assume that people are mostly good, then a lot of the worries about libertarianism are unfounded, for people will in fact care for each other and harbor no desire for domination or unethical personal enrichment. Perhaps, surprisingly, this is another point of contact between libertarianism and socialism: like socialism, libertarianism is most attractive when we take an optimistic view of human nature.

Further Reading

My presentation of Nozick relies on the following sources (abbreviation used for in-text citation in parenthesis):

Nozick, Robert, 1969. "Coercion", White Morgenbesser (ed.), *Philosophy, Science, and Method: Essays in Honor of Ernest Nagel*, New York, NY: St. Martin's Press. pp. 440–472.

Nozick, Robert, 1974. *Anarchy, State, and Utopia*, New York, NY: Basic Books. (*ASU*).

Helpful companions to Nozick's *ASU*:

Bader, Ralph M. & John Meadowcroft (eds.), 2012. *The Cambridge Companion to Nozick's Anarchy, State, and Utopia*, Cambridge, UK: Cambridge University Press.

Mack, Eric, 2018. "Robert Nozick's Political Philosophy, *The Stanford Encyclopedia of Philosophy, Summer 2018 Edition*, Edward N. Zalta (ed.), https://plato.stanford.edu/archives/sum2018/entries/nozick-political/.

Wolff, Jonathan, 1991. *Robert Nozick: Property, Justice and the Minimal State*, Cambridge, UK: Polity Press.

Variant statements of libertarianism include:

Brennan, Jason, 2012. *Libertarianism: What Everyone Needs to Know*, Oxford, UK: Oxford University Press.

Lomasky, Loren E., 1987. *Persons, Rights, and the Moral Community*, Oxford, UK: Oxford University Press.

Mack, Eric, 2018. *Libertarianism (Key Concepts in Political theory)*, Cambridge, UK: Polity.

Narveson, Jan, 2001. *The Libertarian Idea*, Peterborough, Ontario, Canada: Broadview Press.

Rothbard, Murray N., 2006. *For a New Liberty: The Libertarian Manifesto, 2nd Edition*, Auburn, AL: Ludwig von Mises Institute.

For statements and discussions of left-libertarianism see:

Mazor, Joseph & Peter Vallentyne, 2018. "Libertarianism, Left and Right" In Serena Olsaretti (ed.), *The Oxford Handbook of Distributive Justice*, Oxford, UK: Oxford University Press. pp. 129–151.

Otsuka, Michael, 2003. *Libertarianism without Inequality*, Oxford, UK: Oxford University Press.

Vallentyne, Peter & Hillel Steiner (eds.), 2000. *Left-Libertarianism and Its Critics: The Contemporary Debate*, Basingstoke, UK: Palgrave Macmillan.

5

SOCIALISM/G.A. COHEN

1 Introduction

As I mentioned in Chapter 1, socialism can be defined in terms of its institutional commitments, but also as a theory of distributive justice. Institutionally, a socialist system is one where the means of production are owned by society as a collective unity rather than by its individual members, and the production and distribution of goods are directed by the state in the pursuit of collectively defined ends. But socialism is also a theory of justice, formed from the principles of justice and view of society that socialists offer to justify the claim that the means of production should be socialized and used for collective benefit. The focus on this chapter is not on socialism as a theory of institutions, but as the theory of distributive justice by which these institutions (or other institutions) are justified.

As in the previous chapters, I use the work of an individual philosopher to articulate the theory; in this case, G.A. Cohen (1941–2009). However, while Cohen does a marvelous job of criticizing other theories of justice and of defending socialism, my focus on his work could be questioned, for some socialists question whether Cohen offers a good presentation and defense of socialism. Of course, my presentation of right-liberalism, left-liberalism, and libertarianism focused on Hayek, Rawls, and Nozick, and each of these foci could also be questioned – indeed, any attempt at presenting these theories of economic justice as unified philosophies must sacrifice some complexity and intratheoretical disagreements to present a clear and coherent theory – but there are at least two reasons why my method of presenting the theories in the light of one of their prominent defenders is especially questionable for socialism. First, socialism is less of a unified theory of justice than the theories presented in the previous chapters. At times it seems as if the only thing that really unites socialists is their institutional commitments – in particular, the wish to find an alternative to capitalism, an alternative where capital is somehow owned and controlled by the whole of society. Different socialists arrive at this commitment in different ways, using different justifications. Second, socialism has yet to receive a philosophical statement and defense with the clarity and power that Hayek, Rawls, and Nozick provide for the other theories discussed so far.

What about Marx? Well, Marxisms are socialisms, but not all socialisms are Marxisms. Marx's teachings were supremely influential on the socialist movements in the 19th and 20th centuries and formed the intellectual basis for the grand (if disastrous) experiments in socialism of the 20th century. But it is a mistake to define socialism in terms of the dogma of Marxism (see Information Box 5.1 Marxism).

INFORMATION BOX 5.1 MARXISM

In this chapter I define and discuss socialism as a theory of justice. As such, I present it as a set of normative principles (principles of freedom and equality) that are justified by a vision of what society is and ought to be about (the achievement of personal and collective virtues), and, in turn, justify a set of institutions (primarily, the socialization of the means of production). Socialism is thus a normative system – a system of prescriptions that issue conclusions about how we ought to live together.

Where socialism is a theory of justice, Marxism is a way to make sense of the world we live in. Marxism has many elements:

- Marxism *explains* why capitalism became the dominant mode of production;
- Marxism *explains and predicts* how capitalism develops over time;
- Marxism *reveals* the hidden structures and social relations of capitalism;
- Marxism *shows* how cultural mores, personal beliefs, and individual desires are conditioned in the capitalist system, and shows us how the role of liberal justice is to justify a state that serves to support the capitalist mode of production;
- Marxism *applauds* the productive powers of capitalism; and yet
- Marxism *diagnoses and criticizes* capitalism as a system of exploitation, alienation, misery, unfreedom, false consciousness, and immoral relations; but
- Marxism *offers a reason to hope* that capitalism contains within itself enough contradictions and tensions that it will collapse onto itself, and at that moment the path will open to a socialist system that employs the productive powers created under capitalism without the attendant ailments; indeed
- Marxism *describes how the transition to socialism might come about,* and thereby also *provides suggestions* for how we might assist in the transition to socialism.

I cannot fill in here the details of the Marxist story or discuss its attractions and problems. Marx's writings are worth every hour you put into them, so I'll just recommend that you spend some time studying them and make up your own mind about the attractions of Marxism.
Marxism is a kind of socialism, but not all socialisms are Marxisms. However, we should not think of the relation here in terms of simple subsets, so that Marxism is simply a form of socialism. Rather, socialism *is* a theory of justice and Marxism *is not* a theory of justice. Marxism contains a theory of justice – indeed, *it contains the socialist theory of justice and is, therefore, a variety of socialism,* but Marxism is much more than a theory of justice. Marxism is, in a sense, a theory of everything human – a theory of history, economics, the state, culture, sociology, psychology, and so on. Marxism concludes in the hope for socialist institutions (the socialization of the means of production) and Marxism to some extent *justifies* these by appeals to a vision of how we ought to live together, but there are many other ways to this hope and many other ways to justify socialist institutions, which is why Marxism is one of many variants of socialism.

What, then, defines socialism? Socialism can be defined both negatively and positively; as a combination of a critique of capitalism and the philosophies that justify capitalism, and as a defense of the socialist alternative to capitalism. As such, socialism is, indeed, first and foremost defined by its institutional commitments, but the terms in which the critique of capitalism is offered and the alternative is defended provide access to a particular view of society as an environment for human flourishing and the socialist principles of distributive justice.

One reason for using Cohen as a representative of socialism is that he does a wonderful job of criticizing not just capitalism as such, but the defenses of capitalism that can be mounted from right-liberals, libertarians, and left-liberals. Using Cohen allows us to continue the discussion of the theories of justice presented in the previous chapters from this critical perspective. I am less confident in using Cohen as representative of the constructive part of socialism (the philosophical defense of socialist institutional commitments). However, I believe that his writings offer a clear statement of socialism as a theory of justice that, while it might not be representative of socialism as such (as indicated, I am unsure that *any* thinker has yet offered a statement of socialism that is representative), is very attractive and merits our attention.

The chapter has two main parts. The first part presents socialism as a critique of other theories of distributive justice. This part runs through Sections 2–4, with a section each for the socialist rejection of the defenses of capitalism that has been mounted by libertarianism, left-liberalism, and right-liberalism. Section 2 is about the socialist critique of libertarianism and revisits the principle of liberty and the subject of proceduralism (the claim that the justice of a situation depends on the justice of the historical transactions that brought it about).

Section 3 is about the socialist critique of left-liberalism and revisits the ideas of fairness and equality of opportunity. Section 4 returns to right-liberalism with criticisms of the principle of utility and the relation between liberty and utility. Additional subjects that arise during these discussions include self-ownership, exploitation, alienation, questions about the "currency of justice" (what justice is about), and the "site of justice" (whether the principles of justice should govern the design of the basic institutions of society or individual choices as they are made within the system of rules defined by those institutions).

The second part (Sections 5–7) presents socialism as an alternative theory of economic life by which socialist alternatives to capitalism can be justified. Section 5 examines Cohen's socialism – how he defines egalitarianism and how this differs from other views; how he links what people should receive from society with what they deserve (merit, or *desertism*); his belief in the conditions of human perfectibility (*perfectionism*); and his belief that concerns about material liberty should be balanced by concerns about our life in the community. Section 6 looks more closely at the link Cohen makes between equality and community, comparing it with the link right-liberals make between liberty and utility. Section 7 proposes a way to see the institutionalist commitments of socialist theories of distributive justice and the other theories discussed in this book within a three-dimensional matrix, and how we might position our design of future policies and institutions within this matrix.

2 Socialism versus Libertarianism: The Question of Liberty

Libertarianism offers a strong defense of capitalism. According to the principle of liberty, all persons have almost unlimited rights to decide how to use what they justly acquired either originally or by transacting with others. Whether bits of the world are or are not employed as means of production matters naught for the entitlements people may have in them. A socialist system *could* arise by voluntary transactions or by some collective, unanimous contract, but even if it did, it would only be just for as long as it expressed the actual agreement by which it was created. (As mentioned in the chapter on libertarianism, *left-libertarians* differ from right-libertarians in that they claim that *original* possession is in common, which means that the rules governing original acquisition differ – original acquisition must be such that it could meet with the actual consent of all, a requirement that also constrains the rules of transfer. However, left-libertarians agree with right-libertarians that there is nothing special about ownership of the means of production, and thus reject the socialist claim that these are subject to special requirements which mandate their continued socialized ownership independently of the system of actual agreements.)

So, while the libertarian theory of justice permits the creation of a socialist system when such can be created through unanimous agreement, the default libertarian system secures personal security, property rights, and freedom of contract – it is a system with a night-watchman state (a state limited to protecting the rights of its members) and virtually no public ownership of the means of production, no restrictions on property rights except those implied by the system of personal rights (we cannot use property to violate the rights of others, but that's the only restriction), and nearly unlimited freedom of contract.

Cohen argues against this libertarian defense of capitalism. First, even if we accept the libertarian theory of justice as liberty, it is not clear that capitalism best serves liberty. Second, we should reject the libertarian theory of justice as liberty. In particular, we should reject libertarian proceduralism; that justice is only about liberty (it is *also* about liberty), and the libertarian theory of liberty as the rights of self-ownership.

If Cohen's critique of libertarianism succeeds, he undermines a powerful defense of capitalism. This should lower our confidence in capitalism as the best and most just system for organizing the production and distribution of goods and services. However, we should remember that lower confidence in capitalism is not yet an argument for socialism.

2.1 Liberty and Liberties

The libertarian argument connects, on the one hand, liberty, capitalism, and economic inequalities and, on the other hand, lack of freedom, socialism, and equality. We must choose between liberty and equality, and the choice should be clear, since only the choice of liberty respects the rights of persons. Moreover, libertarians extend this argument to property rights in both personal and productive property, so that liberty mandates absolute liberties of property and contract (unless these rights have been alienated through actual consent). The libertarian argues that these liberties of property and contract, in turn, are respected only in a minimally regulated capitalist system; the role of the state is to guarantee liberties and the state is prohibited from engaging in the regulation of the economy or taxation, except insofar as is necessary to fulfill such guarantees.

Cohen argues that even if we grant the assumption that liberty is the sole concern of justice, it is doubtful that liberty is best secured by the unrestrained capitalism that libertarians favor.

Cohen first draws attention to the empirical nature of the libertarian claim. Whether socialism or capitalism best secure liberty cannot be decided in the abstract; it depends on how the systems actually distribute and protect the liberty of their members. Indeed, it may be that a system with socialized means of production employed in a manner that secures some sort of equality of opportunity or even of outcome would also be the system that best secures the liberty of its members (*SFE*, Chapters 1–4; *CEJ*, Chapters 7 and 8).

We should, moreover, question whether the principle of liberty really supports absolute liberties of property and contract. Private property rights are, in essence, rights to exclude other persons from access to the things owned. If I own a car, *I* can drive it around, *you* cannot (without my permission). This is ownership: to have rights to use and to exclude others from using. But once we see that property rights limit the liberty of nonowners, it is unclear why private property rights are good for liberty; for one's person's liberty of deciding what to do with her property in something, is also the limitation of other persons' liberty to use that thing. If a few persons owned all the means of automated transportation, then the rest of society would have extremely limited liberty of movement. Similarly, if a few persons owned most of the land in an area, then the rest would have limited freedom to move across or otherwise enjoy said land. It is unclear why interference with the liberties of ownership would not increase liberty overall:

> The government certainly interferes with landowner's freedom if it establishes public rights of way and a right for others to pitch tents on his [the landowner's] land. But it also interferes with the freedom of would-be walkers or tent-pitchers when it prevents them from indulging *their* individual inclinations. [...] incursions against private property which *reduce* owners' freedom by transferring rights over resources to non-owners thereby *increase* the latter's freedom. In advance of further argument, the net effect on freedom of the resource transfer is indeterminate.
>
> (SFE, *56–7)*

In general, then, private property is both liberty (for the owners) and unliberty (for nonowners) and it is unclear whether a system with absolute rights of private property is better at securing liberty than one with limited property rights. Or, better, there is no reason to believe that the degree to which the institution of private property is absolute in a society is also the degree to which that society secures liberty – the relation might well be the inverse.

A libertarian such as Nozick might reply that their concern is not for liberty as such, and it is certainly not to maximize (or equalize, or sufficientize, or prioritize) liberty itself. Their concern, rather, is with the rights of liberty – rights to decide what to do for oneself as long as one does not violate the equal rights of others. The rights of the owner of the land thus construed *are* violated, if and when the state gives others rights to pitch their tent on her land without permission, whereas her state-supported exclusion of others to access her land would not violate her rights. For, by assumption, she acquired rights of exclusion by the just acquisition of the land (either originally or by transfer), whereas the excluded never acquired any such rights, nor can the state confer such rights on them, for the state does not have them to confer in the first place. On this *moralized conception* of liberty, where liberty is spelled out as the rights or *liberties* people have justly acquired, there is no concern for liberty as such, and it is no complaint against a capitalist system that it leaves the poor unfree, for what matters is not freedom, but that just rights are respected.

Cohen counters that the reason libertarians care for rights is that they care for liberty (and the reason that their appeal to rights is persuasive is that we should care for liberty). This care should lead them to doubt the attractions of private property and unrestrained capitalism: "libertarian capitalism sacrifices liberty to capitalism, a truth its advocates are able to deny only because they are prepared to abuse the language of freedom" (*SFE*, 37). Yet, libertarians need not be moved by this accusation, for they have a concept of liberty – liberty as self-ownership – and the rights of liberty that can be generated from this concept do seem to favor the unlimited rights of property and contract, which, in turn, can support the case for unrestrained capitalism.

Once the libertarian specifies that the liberty that matters is self-ownership, it seems that their position regains internal coherence, for the way to protect liberty as self-ownership is to protect the liberties of property rights and freedom of contract – to be a self-owner is to have authority to decide how one uses oneself and one's possessions. However, specification also limits the power of libertarianism, for there are fewer reasons to accept the principle of self-ownership, and more reasons to reject it, than the principle of liberty itself. Below, we look at Cohen's discussion of self-ownership, but first it is useful to treat Cohen's critique of another part of the libertarian theory of justice, namely, its *proceduralism*.

2.2 Against Libertarian Proceduralism

Libertarians maintain that a distribution of goods and obligations resulting from a history of just transactions is just – that the justice of a situation is a function of the justice of the history that brought that situation about: "whatever comes about by just steps is itself just" (Nozick, *Anarchy, State, and Utopia*, 151). The libertarian principles of justice in original acquisition and transfer define what just steps are. Cohen argues that, even if we accept the libertarian principles of justice in acquisition and transfer (and we should reject them), we should still reject libertarian proceduralism; the justice of situations is not reducible to historical justice (*SFE*, Chapters 1 and 2; *CEJ*, 125–31).

Think of the example of Wilt Chamberlain as described by Nozick. Wilt is popular enough that people are willing to pay an extra quarter to watch him play basketball, and in a year a million people do so. The result is that Wilt has earned a cool quarter of a million dollars more than his teammates, and the fans have spent some of their money on watching him play. Since these inequalities arose by just steps (voluntary transfer), they are, Nozick argues, just – and any attempt at returning to a pattern of equality must take from Wilt what he justly acquired, violating his rights. In general, inequalities will arise in a system that respects voluntary transactions; correcting these inequalities by redistribution would violate the rights of those from whom resources are taken.

One objection to this argument is that the resulting distribution might have further results that are unjust. Say that Wilt and others like him use their newfound wealth to buy up means of production and employ others to produce commodities that they can sell at a profit, investing that profit in further means of production. The iterative result of this process is likely the creation of a class society where some have to work for others who own the means of production. It makes good sense to question whether the resulting situation is just, even though we can find no injustice in its history. This objection says that even if they are true, the principles of justice in acquisition, transfer, and rectification cannot be the *only* principles of distributive justice.

A libertarian might stick to her guns and deny that there is injustice in the imagined class society, for those who end up in the lower and higher classes, end up there by virtue of choices and luck – neither of which creates injustice. But that need not be true. First, because Wilt and friends might buy up enough of the means of production to reduce to subjection third parties who had no part in the series of choices that brought the inequality about. Second, because people will be born into the created system, in which case they have no part in its creation. A libertarian might try to counter the latter problem by imagining some sort of reset at death, so that Wilt's wealth is transferred back into society at that time. This is a weak counter. It is not clear that such a policy would be consistent with libertarian property rights (why would this be a just transfer?), and, even if it was, owners could just exercise their property rights and pass on their wealth before they died.

Moreover, we can easily imagine situations where Wilt would live long enough that the problem remains. If, say, longevity treatments come about (as they will sooner or later), but the treatments are very expensive so that only the rich can afford them (as they will be at first), then Wilt might live to be 300 years old, while the poorer members of society have a life expectancy of, say, 80 years, meaning that Wilt and his fellow capitalists get to exploit multiple generations of poorer people in their own lifetimes. Surely, we can maintain that a class society where some are born into a situation where their choice is between starvation and exploitation is unjust; but, if that's the case, then the justice of situations does not reduce to the justice of the transactions by which it was brought about – *even if* we accept the libertarian principles of justice of acquisition and transfer (as Cohen does not).

So, even if we assume away the enormous historical injustices that underlie the current distribution of wealth – such as slavery and colonialism – and start history from a point with no injustice, the reduction of the justice of situations to the history of choices that brought it about is inadequate. For situations do not result from informed transactions alone, but also from uninformed transactions, contingencies, combinatorial processes, and much else, and these other factors may bring about situational injustice, where there was no injustice in the transactional history by which the situation came to be (see *SFE*, Chapters 1 and 2).

2.3 Against Liberty as Self-Ownership

Cohen's discussion of self-ownership is thorough and complicated. He argues that self-ownership fails to support the Nozickean theory of original acquisition, and that a notion of self-ownership is central to much Marxist thought, but should be rejected, since it is inconsistent with the sort of outcome egalitarianism that socialists must favor. He also restates the critique of capitalism as a system of exploitation without using a notion of self-ownership as premise. I bypass these discussions and instead focus on Cohen's argument against the sort of libertarianism that makes liberty as self-ownership the central concern of justice.

Self-ownership is a concept and a normative principle (*SFE*, Chapters 3 and 9). *The concept of self-ownership* is the subsumption of the self under the notion of property rights, so that persons have entitlements over themselves analogous to the entitlements that they would have over a thing if they had full ownership of it. The *normative principle of self-ownership* says that persons *ought to* enjoy all the rights of property over their own person, so that they, on the one hand, are permitted do whatever they want with their own person, as long as they don't violate the rights of others (similarly to how a person may do whatever she wants with her knife – use it to cut bread, sell it, destroy it, make it into art, leave it to rust in a drawer – but may not use it to damage other persons or their property), and, on the other hand, *do not* have obligations to use themselves in ways that they do not want to, even for the benefit of others. That is, they do not have obligations to others except insofar as they incurred these obligations through voluntary contract; and that no person, therefore, can be forced to help other persons absent such contractually acquired obligations. Thus construed, the principle of self-ownership is a version of the principle of liberty, where liberty is cashed out in terms of the full rights of self-ownership.

Cohen does not think that it can be shown that the concept or principle of self-ownership is false. Cohen *believes* that the principle is false, but that its falseness cannot be *demonstrated.* Instead, Cohen offers a set of reasons that undermine the appeal of the principle and, thereby, undermine the appeal of the sort of libertarianism that relies on it (*SFE*, Chapter 10).

First, Cohen offers reasons to doubt that there are no noncontractual obligations of the sort that the principle of self-ownership denies. Think of duties in the family – your elderly mother falls sick or your brother's car breaks down and he needs your help to get to work. In such cases, it seems we have obligations to assist. Or take cases of easy rescue – a toddler drowning in the pond, Kitty Genovese crying out for help – it seems that we have obligations to assist those in need, when we can do so at little expense to ourselves. If we have such obligations, then it is not true that all interpersonal obligations are acquired by the actions of the obligated parties. In that case it seems that the self-ownership principle is false, and it cannot do the work that libertarianism wants it to do. For then there might be obligations to assist the poor that we can (perhaps should) satisfy through some sort of redistributive taxation, or obligations to third parties to our transaction that we can (and should) satisfy by limiting liberty of contract.

Second, Cohen undermines the self-ownership principle by throwing doubt on the reasons we might offer in its defense (*SFE*, Chapter 10). Two Kantian reasons are normally presented in support of the principle of self-ownership: that respecting the principle of self-ownership is a necessary component of respecting autonomy, or that it is required by the injunction to treat people as ends in themselves.

Against the first of these reasons, Cohen argues that autonomy is a matter of degree and that the degree of autonomy achieved by a person is a function of several factors: the rights that persons have to decide for themselves *and* the rights that others have *and* the resources at their disposal. Thus, it might well be the case that the highest degree of autonomy is achieved by limiting some rights and securing adequate resources for all – two measures that would be prohibited by the principle of self-ownership. So, if we want to secure an adequate, or equal, or maximal measure of autonomy for the members of society, it is likely that we must abandon the principle of self-ownership. So, a principle of autonomy offers no support for the principle of self-ownership.

Against the second reason, Cohen argues that the only way that the Kantian injunction to treat people as ends in themselves and not merely as means can support the self-ownership thesis is to employ the notion of consent – as Nozick indeed does when he writes that his defense of libertarian rights reflects "the underlying Kantian principle that *individuals are ends and not merely means*: they may not be sacrificed or used for the achieving of other ends without their consent" (*Anarchy, State, and Utopia*, 31). Cohen argues that the first part, where Nozick introduces the Kantian injunction, neither implies nor is implied by the second part, where he restates the injunction in terms of consent (*SFE*, 238–43). Nozick's claim is that *actual* consent is both necessary and sufficient for treating people as ends in themselves – a claim that indeed would issue an absolute liberty of contract. But Kant would disagree. Consent is not sufficient, since persons may consent to impermissible contracts, e.g. contracts of slavery or prostitution. And it is not necessary, since the sort of consent that Kant thinks is required to treat people as ends in themselves is normative consent – that is, that they could (and should be expected to) consent to be treated in the fashion under consideration. So, there may be interpersonal obligations that are not generated by actual consent. Of course, this argument leaves open what sorts of obligations of assistance we actually have, and how far the state is permitted to force us to satisfy such obligations, but the point is that actual consent is unnecessary for persons to be obligated.

2.4 Summary

In sum, Cohen argues first, that *even if* we accept the libertarian claim that liberty is the sole concern of justice, we should question whether equality is really the enemy of liberty. Also, we can question whether the libertarian understanding of liberty is the right one, and we can question whether the theory of property and contract that libertarians rely on is implied by the concern for liberty. However, *we should also reject* the libertarian claim that liberty is the sole concern of justice. Other things such as equality or suffering are also concerns of justice.

The justice of a situation, accordingly, does not reduce to the history of transactions that brought it about; the justice of transactions and the justice of situations are distinct domains of justice.

Of course, *liberty matters*, but the liberty that matters is not the system of absolute liberties that Nozick favors, nor should we accept the principle of self-ownership that generates these liberties. Instead, justice is concerned with freedom or autonomy – the ability to do things in the world. We should try to create a free society, a society wherein all members enjoy freedom thus understood, but once we understand liberty as autonomy, it becomes clear that which system best protects and promotes liberty is an open question. The libertarian night-watchman state will provide a high degree of autonomy to the rich, but a very low degree of autonomy to the poor (I return to Cohen's defense of this claim in the section on right-liberalism below). If we want to avoid exploitation and interpersonal dominance, we have to secure that all persons have enough resources and that no persons are forced to work for others. If justice is about *equal* liberty, then we may want to secure roughly equal rights in property and *that* is impossible in a capitalist society – equality of property requires the socialization of property. So, whether we want adequate, equal, or maximal liberty, it looks like we should abandon capitalism in favor of socialism.

3 Cohen versus Left-Liberalism: The Question of Equality

Socialists and left-liberals share many commitments. Both believe that justice may require management of the economy that aims to secure a fair distribution of the benefits and burdens of society, and both can justify redistribution from those who have more to those who have less by appeal to intrinsic rather than extrinsic features of the distribution (that is, by looking at the distribution rather than how the distribution came to be, as the libertarians do, or by looking at whether the distribution brings about the optimal outcome, as right-liberals do). Unlike libertarians, they both focus more on society as a whole than on the rights of individuals, and they both reject that economic justice is all about self-ownership and its exercise. Unlike right-liberals, they both believe that elements of the economy and other institutions (for example, education) must be managed to secure equality of opportunity and a fair distribution of wealth and income.

This similarity of principles and institutional implications can make differences between the two systems of thought less obvious. Instead of broad points, such as Cohen's questions about libertarian self-ownership, we will be examining finer points like differences in the use of incentives to produce maximum benefit for the least well-off. Also, for the first time, we will see how a socialist like Cohen views the motives of people in just and unjust societies, and how this conflicts with Rawls's view of democratic citizenship.

Recall that Rawls defends two principles of justice: the principle of equal basic rights and the principle of democratic equality. The principle of equal basic rights secures for all members of society the institutional preconditions for developing and exercising the moral powers of democratic citizenship, enabling a system of cooperation between free and equal citizens. The principle of democratic equality secures a fair distribution of the benefits and burdens of social cooperation. This latter principle consists of two distinct parts: the principle of fair equality of opportunity and the difference principle. The principle of fair equality of opportunity requires that persons with similar natural endowments and the willingness to use them must have equal prospects for success in accessing careers and offices. The difference principle requires that inequalities of wealth and income must be to the advantage of the least well-off.

Together, fair equality of opportunity and the difference principle express an idea of fairness: the distribution of primary goods other than equal basic rights is fair when the members of society compete for said goods on a level playing field and inequalities of income and wealth are acceptable to those who have least. In such a society, there will be inequalities of access to interesting careers and in the monetary rewards that are attached to different careers; the more talented have access to more interesting and more rewarding jobs. But all members can know that these inequalities reflect ability and effort, and that there is no other social system where those who end up in less interesting and rewarding careers would be better-off.

Thus, Rawls's justice as fairness is egalitarian; it secures equal basic rights and fair equality of opportunity, and it takes equality as the baseline – inequalities of wealth and income must be justifiable to those who have least. But it is *in*egalitarian in the sense that it does not require equal access to the resources useful for living a good life, or that people ought to live equally good lives, or that equally deserving people have or have access to equally good lives. Rawls does not think it is unfair if people with different talents face different life prospects in terms of the careers they can pursue and the rewards that are attached to these careers, as long as the rules of the economy ensure that the better endowed benefit in a manner that benefits (even maximally benefits) the less talented.

The difference principle justifies inequalities of income and wealth when these provide incentives to the talented members of society to train and employ their talents in the most productive fashion, to the benefit of all. We want the steadiest hand to perform the surgery, so we give incentives for those with steady hands to train for surgery and compete for the job; and the easiest incentive, in turn, is to allow surgeons to be paid more than, say, street sweepers. Of course, we also want a qualified broom-hand to sweep the streets, but less is at stake and more people are able to perform the job well enough for us to have clean streets without paying street sweepers as much as surgeons. The street sweeper can accept this outcome, since there is no alternative system where he'd be better-off all things considered (and he too might need surgery). The general idea is to embrace the sort of division of labor that right-liberals find attractive without the result being unfair to those who end up with less; to do so we must allow people's choices of what to do with their natural talents to include consideration of the different economic rewards attached to jobs, even while the system as a whole ensures that those with the least attractive jobs are better-off than they'd be in alternative systems. Inequalities of wealth and income are the expected result, but these are, supposedly, fair and agreeable to all in an appropriately described choice situation (the original position). (See Chapter 3 for the detailed story.)

Cohen thinks that Rawls's embrace of these incentive-based economic inequalities is mistaken and that the argument leading Rawls to this embrace is fallacious. Cohen argues that, first, the difference principle would *not* permit inequalities needed to incentivize productive behavior; second, that we should reject the difference principle in any case; third, that the Rawlsian view of equal opportunity is inconsistent with the argument that shows why we should care about equality of opportunity in the first place; and, fourth, that Rawls misunderstands the site and subject of justice.

As Cohen reads him, Rawls offers the following argument in defense of economic inequality (*RJE*, 19):

1. Inequalities are unjust unless they are necessary to make the worst off people better-off, in which case they are just (= the difference principle).
2. Incentive payments that create inequalities *are* necessary to make the worst off people better-off (= the incentives argument).
3. Therefore, incentive payments that create inequalities are just.

Cohen rejects both premises:

Against 1: If equality is the default of justice, then departures from equality are departures from justice, *even if* they benefit the worst off.
Against 2: Incentive payments that create inequalities are not necessary, for the productive could do the same work without the additional payment as incentive (they could do it to help the poor, in line with the aim set by the first premise).

In the following subsection (Section 3.1), I present Cohen's argument against premise 2. This argument assumes the truth of the difference principle, but rejects that it can justify economic inequalities in the manner ascribed to Rawls. Next (Sections 3.2 and 3.3), I present Cohen's argument against premise 1, which amounts to a rejection of the difference principle in favor of a principle of equality (or merit, as I show). I then introduce and discuss Cohen's claim that Rawls is confused about what justice is in the first place (Section 3.4).

3.1 Against Premise 2: The Incentives Argument

Cohen argues that the difference principle *cannot* justify inequalities used to create incentives for productive behavior by the more talented members of a just society. Why? Because the least well-off would be better-off if the talented trained for and performed productive work without added incentives, for then the resources used for incentives could go to the least well-off – in the limit case we would get fully productive behavior without any economic inequality.

Assume that the better endowed produce the same as the lesser endowed without additional training and that they produce 100% more with additional training. Say that there are only two groups and each produces five widgets if the talented do not get additional training, but the talented produce ten with training (cf. *RJE*, 79). The question is how to divide the surplus. One possible division is 6/9, another 7/8, but another is 7.5/7.5. The latter preserves equality and also maximizes the position of the least well-off.

The better endowed might say that they should get more of the surplus. In fact, they might say that they are unwilling to train and employ their talents if they aren't receiving more than half of the surplus they produce. And if they don't actually say as much, it might just be a sociological fact that people won't work harder unless they get something for themselves in addition to their equal share of the product. In that case the difference principle seems to mandate inequalities, because 7.5/7.5 simply isn't a feasible outcome; maybe the best we could do in terms of the less-endowed group is 7/8, in which case this is the outcome that the difference principle mandates.

Against this conclusion, Cohen argues that, *first*, the better endowed cannot say they want rewards for using their talents without destroying their *community* with the less endowed. Cohen's understanding of "community" is broad; it includes ideas such as caring, justification to each, and reciprocity, discussed below, as well as solidarity, meaning that we are all bound together in a bond we all respect, and we make decisions that protect this bond. *Second*, if it is true of a society that inequalities are necessary to incentivize the better endowed to maximally productive behavior, then this truth reveals injustice rather than that justice requires inequality. The site of justice is not only institutions and laws, but the *ethoi* of individual members of society. So, *third*, a society that allows such incentive-based inequalities is distributively unjust, *by the very standard of the difference principle* that was supposed to justify them, for in that society there are inequalities that are not to the benefit of the least well-off.

3.1.1 The Community Argument

Cohen says that one sort of community we should care about is *justificatory community*, that is, where "there prevails a norm [...] of comprehensive justification" (*RJE*, 43). Comprehensive justification prevails where all norms of interaction can be justified by all to all. But sometimes norms that sound good when stated in the third person cannot be justified by some to others, because the former have a role in making the minor premise in the argument defending the norm true; the incentives argument is one such case. To illustrate, look at the following argument (RJE, 34–5):

i. Children should be with their parents.
ii. Unless we pay the kidnapper, little Daisy never sees her parents again.
iii. So, we should pay the kidnapper.

We can imagine a situation where this argument is sound and persuasive. There might be uncounted reasons for not paying the kidnapper (to prevent other kidnappings), but leaving such aside, the argument looks good. Now think of the same argument, but as it is *made by the kidnapper* (*RJE*, 39):

iv. Children should be with their parents.
v. Unless you pay me, little Daisy here never sees her parents again.
vi. So, you should pay me.

The argument is valid; sound, even. But surely, the fact that *the kidnapper* makes the minor premise (v) true makes this a bad argument. For the major premise (iv) implies that the kidnapper should not have kidnapped Daisy in the first place, and that he should, in any case, return her to her parents whether the parents pay the ransom or not. There is a tension between the norm stated in the major premise (iv) and the fact that the utterer of that norm makes the minor premise (v) true – and this tension makes it a bad argument. The case, Cohen argues, is the same for the incentives argument.

To see how, look at another argument, frequently made against proposals to raise taxes on income (a similar version is often made in favor of lowering taxes on income):

vii. We should aim to maximize the position of the least well-off.
viii. If we raise taxes on wealth or income, the more productive/talented persons will not work as hard, to the detriment of the least well-off.
ix. So, we should not raise taxes.

Again, the argument looks good. But as in the case with the kidnapper, think of the argument as offered by the rich to the poor (in keeping with the by-all/to-all norm of comprehensive justification):

x. We should aim to maximize the position of the least well-off.
xi. If we raise taxes on wealth or income, I will work less hard, there will be less to distribute, and you will be worse off.
xii. So, we should not raise taxes.

Again, the argument might be sound, but it is not a good argument when made by the rich in defense of lower taxes on their income. For the utterer (and her class) makes the minor premise (xi) true, but they would not make it true if they were committed to the norm stated in the major premise (x). If the better-endowed person making the argument sincerely believes that we should aim to maximize the position of the least well-off, then even if taxes are raised she should work just as hard as before.

The tension is created by the fact that the person making the argument is committed to the norm that we should maximally benefit the least well-off, while she says in the minor premise that she is not really committed to this norm, for she won't act for the benefit of the least well-off unless she receives a monetary reward. In other words, commitment to the difference principle commits a person to employ her talents productively without added incentives.

But isn't there a disanalogy between the kidnapper's case and the case of the better endowed? In the latter, the issue is what sort of policies we should make, not a state of affairs and individual choices (as in the kidnapper's case); doesn't this make a difference for the tension in question? Rawls does not maintain that persons should be committed to the difference principle in their individual choices, but only in their collective making of institutions, laws, and policies – when they are voting, or advocating policies, or acting as public officials. The better endowed can make this distinction and say: look, our *institutions and policies* should aim to maximize the position of the least well-off, and I will advocate and vote for such policies, but in my personal life and market interactions I aim to serve me and mine. So, I will not work as hard if you raise taxes, and we'd better keep the taxes low if we care for the least well-off.

Cohen's reply to this objection is that the difference principle should govern individuals, not just institutions, laws, and policies. The *site* of distributive justice is not only laws and institutions, but also the wills and choices of individuals; the political is (also) personal.

3.1.2 The Site of Distributive Justice: The Ethos Argument

Cohen finds two readings of the difference principle in Rawls's writings (*RJE*, 69). The distinction between them lies in different modalities of necessity in the part of the difference principle; i.e. the part that says that inequalities that are *necessary* to benefit the least well-off are just. On the *strict reading*, the difference principle justifies inequalities as necessary to benefit the least well-off "only when they are, strictly, necessary, necessary, that is, apart from people's chosen intentions" (*RJE*, 69). On the *lax reading*, by contrast, the difference principle "countenances intention-relative necessities as well" (*RJE*, 69). Cohen argues that the strict reading is the true requirement of justice, even if the lax reading might be good policy in an unjust society.

The strict reading of the difference principle is required by justice if we assume (as we must) that people in a just society "are themselves attached to the idea of justice and are motivated by it in their daily lives" (*RJE*, 69). Rawls is clear, Cohen maintains, that in a just society, individuals are devoted to justice and are thus motivated to make the choices that best serve the achievement of justice. The members in a just society are, in a word, governed in their daily lives also by an *ethos* of justice (*RJE*, 73, 123): a general disposition to pursue their self-interest in a manner that also serves the achievement of justice. (The ethos of a society is "the set of sentiments and attitudes in virtue of which its normal practices and informal pressures are what they are" (*RJE*, 144).)

So, in a just society, the aim to realize the difference principle motivates individual choices (*RJE*, 69–73, 122–3). This fact also means that in a just society, the better endowed *are not* motivated to pursue their self-interest in a manner where their personal benefit comes at the expense of benefits to the least well-off. And this, in turn, entails that in a just society, the better endowed would not make the justificatory-community-destroying argument that they need incentives to develop and employ their talents productively, for they are motivated to do so simply because doing so helps the realization of full justice.

Think again of the case where the better endowed can increase their productive output by 100% (from five to ten) if they engage in sufficient training and employ their skills productively. Why could the surplus not be divided equally? In a just society, the better endowed would not say that they need the additional benefit as incentives for their training and productive work, for they are motivated to do so by their allegiance to the difference principle. So, in a just society the 7.5/7.5 split is feasible. Since this split is to the advantage of the least well-off, this is the split required by the difference principle. Indeed, it will be very hard for the difference principle to justify *any* inequalities (of the sort that should worry us; more on that below).

Of course, if the well-endowed work harder and need the benefit to sustain their harder work, then they *should* receive more benefit, and this sort of inequality will exist in a just society, but that's not a violation of the norm of equality that Cohen is defending. For the norm of equality that Cohen favors is a norm of *equity*, where equally hardworking people receive equal rewards for their efforts (*RJE*, 57–60, 102–3, 154–5). Slackers might receive less than achievers, but this inequality is a function only of differences in effort, not of differences in endowments. (If some are by nature slackers, then they are not slackers in the relevant sense; slackness here is a function of choices, not abilities.)

3.1.3 The Lax Difference Principle as a Principle for Unjust Societies

If the members of our society are motivated by greed rather than justice, then we might use the lax difference principle, which permits inequalities based on incentives to ensure that the less well-off get as much as they can. But we should not pretend that this use of the difference principle achieves justice. *First*, the less well-off would be better-off in a just society, so the distribution of benefits and burdens is unjust by the strict difference principle, even if the lax difference principle is completely realized. *Second*, such a society is unjust because the difference principle is not yet properly accepted by the members of society; there is no *ethos* of justice:

> If we are concerned about the badly off, then we should sometimes concede incentives, just as we should sometimes satisfy the kidnapper's demands. We are not then acting on the difference principle in its strict interpretation, in which it is a principle of justice governing a society of just people who are inspired by it. We are acting on the lax version of the difference principle, which endorses incentives and has application in societies of the familiar unjust kind. [...] Their stance is then unjust by the very standard that the difference principle itself sets. Accordingly, on a strict view of Rawlsian justice, the difference principle in its lax interpretation [...] is not a basic principle of justice but a principle for handling people's injustice.
>
> (RJE, *83–84)*

To clarify, Cohen draws a distinction between a just *society* and a just *distribution* (*RJE*, 128). A just society is one where all citizens affirm and act upon the correct principles of justice. A just distribution is one that satisfies the principle of fair equality of opportunity and the difference principle. A society where inequalities are necessary to incentivize production that maximizes the position of the least well-off is an *unjust society* with an *unjust distribution*, for the better endowed are not acting on the difference principle, and the difference principle could be better satisfied (the least well-off would be better-off) if the better-off were acting on the difference principle.

The preceding argument assumes that the (strict) difference principle is a true principle of justice. But Cohen also argues that we should reject the difference principle in favor of a principle of equality (as defined above: equal rewards for equal effort).

3.2 Against Premise 1: Defending Egalitarianism

Cohen offers two arguments against the difference principle. The first aims to show that Rawls's argument for the difference principle falls short. The second aims to show that Rawls should embrace a principle of equality rather than the difference principle.

3.2.1 How Rawls's Argument Falls Short

On Cohen's reading (*RJE*, 87–91, 156–7), Rawls's main argument for the difference principle has two moves.

In the *first move,* Rawls establishes equality as the baseline by arguing that inequalities with morally arbitrary bases are unjust. Morally arbitrary bases are facts that have no justificatory bearing on the inequality in question, such as the race, religion, gender, or social class of the unequally situated parties. The idea is one familiar from the principle of merit: inequalities should be based on merits and otherwise are unjust; for example, unequal income should reflect different choices and efforts rather than factors such as race, gender, or, Cohen argues, talents.

In the *second move,* Rawls justifies departures from equality that are to the benefit of those who have least in the resulting distribution (or at least the distribution is not to their detriment). If some have more and none have less, it would be irrational to maintain inequality. Cohen calls this move the "Pareto argument," because it justifies all Pareto superior departures from equality.

Cohen argues that these two moves are inconsistent (*RJE*, 97–109, 159–61): if inequalities with morally arbitrary bases are unjust, as the first move assumes, then they remain unjust, even if they lead to a Pareto superior outcome. It may be that the Pareto superior outcome is *better,* all things considered, but we cannot call it *just,* for in that situation there are inequalities that have morally arbitrary bases – and these are, by assumption, unjust.

To make sense of the preceding, we need to recall that Cohen works with a peculiar (but sensible) notion of equality of outcome, where equality is equity. Cohen's idea of equality of outcome, which he assumes is at work in Rawls's argument for equality as the baseline for assessing distributions, is that of equal outcomes for persons who make equally meritorious choices (i.e. work equally hard). On this understanding of equality of outcomes, it is just if people are unequal in terms of holdings and welfare, as long as the inequalities reflect their choices and efforts rather than morally arbitrary factors. In other words, Cohen's egalitarianism is a version of desertism – that people should get what they deserve and that undeserved inequalities are unjust – and it is this sort of egalitarianism he thinks is justifying the baseline of equality in Rawls's argument. (I return to Cohen's position below.)

3.2.2 Why Rawls Should Be an Egalitarian (or Desertist)

The preceding results in the need to choose between the argument that establishes equality as the baseline and the argument that justifies departures from the baseline (inequalities), but it does not settle which of these we should choose. Cohen argues, however, that the more fundamental commitment is to equality (as equity), which means that Rawls should be an egalitarian of the desertist sort. Rawls's theory of justice should replace the prioritarian difference principle with a principle of merit that says inequalities are *unjust* unless they are based on differences in choices and efforts, so that even inequalities that *are* to the benefit of the least well-off remain unjust if they are based on differential luck in the natural lottery.

3.3 Socialist Equality of Opportunity

We can restate Cohen's argument as a defense of socialist equality of opportunity against the weaker notion of equal opportunity that Rawls defends (which we can call left-liberal equality of opportunity). Both socialist and left-liberal equality of opportunity reject as unjust any sort of discrimination based on factors such as race, gender, sexual orientation, or religious affiliation among candidates for positions in both the private and public sector. Both socialist and left-liberal equality of opportunity also maintain that we should minimize the effects of the social lottery, so that one's prospects at birth do not depend on the social class or other social contingencies that one is born into. However, this leaves the issue of differential luck in the natural lottery: the different talents (including abilities for cultivating talents) that people are born with. (It also leaves the remainder of social luck that cannot be eliminated without abandoning the institution of the family or engaging in other policies that violate basic rights.)

Left-liberals such as Rawls argue that we should allow differential natural luck to result in inequalities of income and wealth, as long as these inequalities are to the benefit of the least well-off. Cohen, and other socialists, argue that this last move is a mistake. For the very argument that brought left-liberals to maintain that we should minimize the effects of the social lottery also shows that we cannot allow differential natural luck to result in inequalities of wealth and income – or if we allow them, we accept injustice for the sake of other values. Differential natural luck is as morally arbitrary as differential social luck, and inequalities from either sort of luck are equally unjust. So, we should, socialists maintain, follow our commitments and require (as a matter of justice) that *all* inequalities based on morally arbitrary factors are eliminated (or minimized). Thus, it is unjust if those with a more useful bundle of natural talents are better-off than the less talented, even if the more talented are more productive and even if their increased productivity is to the benefit of the least well-off:

> the only thing about people's labor that would validate the justice of a difference in the income that they get for it is a difference in the burden of that labor [...] If, being more talented and having suffered nothing special to acquire her talent, A produces more widgets than B, then justice forbids paying A a higher rate per hour.
>
> (RJE, *181)*

Thus, Rawlsians should be egalitarians (or desertists) when it comes to the distribution of income and wealth; economic inequalities that do not reflect different choices are unjust, even if they are to the advantage of the least well-off. Rawlsians should replace the combination of fair (left-liberal) equality of opportunity and the difference principle that together constitutes the principle of democratic equality with just one principle: the socialist principle of equality of opportunity, which also implies the meritocratic principle that inequalities of income and wealth are unjust unless they reflect choices.

It is unclear how bothered Rawlsians should be by Cohen's argument against the difference principle. Cohen's argument relies on the assumption that the (or a) basic commitment of the Rawlsian theory of justice is to the position that inequalities based on any sort of morally arbitrary factors are unfair and unjust, but *this is not a basic commitment of the Rawlsian theory of justice.* Recall, that the basic commitment of the Rawlsian theory of justice is to the idea of democratic society as a system of social cooperation between free and equal persons. This idea issues the further idea of fairness: that the division of the benefits and burdens of cooperation should be fair to all cooperating parties. This idea, in turn, is made sense of via the idea of agreement: the division is fair if it takes place according to principles that all the cooperating parties could agree to as free and equal persons (as analyzed in the original position). So, Rawls need not agree that inequalities that issue from different natural luck are unfair or unjust, and he would reject that inequalities must track a metric of merit or desert (however interpreted).

3.4 How to Think about Justice: Facts and Principles

One of the main disagreements between Cohen and Rawls concerns how facts – including facts about human nature and the human condition – should inform our thinking about justice. Surely, Rawlsians would say, we cannot totally eliminate self-interestedness in human nature; we care for ourselves, our families, and our friends more than we care for distant strangers. If so, human beings might be incapable of the sort, or degree, of virtue needed to work as hard as they can without some self-centered incentive. And, in that case, it would seem that Rawlsians can object to Cohen's arguments that the difference principle justifies inequalities based on facts about who we are, for these are, in fact, required to maximize the position of the least well-off. Moreover, the ethos argument goes too far, for it says that a society is unjust if the members of society do not completely internalize the perspective of justice, but "ought" implies "can," and people cannot be as good as Cohen says they should be, so this requirement should be rejected. At the end of the day, Rawlsians will say, justice is about how we should cooperate, given what we know about human nature and the human condition – including that we're imperfect and compete for scarce resources.

Cohen rejects this understanding of justice, and he rejects that the basic requirements of justice can be informed by facts about human nature and the human condition. Indeed, he argues that the basic principles of justice cannot be informed by *any* facts: "[A]ll [normative] principles that reflect facts reflect facts only because they also reflect principles that do not reflect facts, and that the latter principles form the ultimate foundation of all principles, fact-reflecting principles included (*FP*, 23)".

Cohen's argument for this conclusion is as follows (*RJE*, 229, 232):

(1) There is always an explanation for why a ground grounds what it grounds.
(2) So, whenever a fact *F* supports a principle *P*, there is an explanation why *F* supports *P*, that is, an explanation of how *F* provides a reason to endorse *P*.
(3) And, the explanation affirmed for why *F* supports *P* invokes or implies a more ultimate principle, *P1*, which explains why *F* supports *P*.
(4) And, the supporting framework cannot be endless (i.e. no infinite regress).
(5) *So*, every fact-dependent principle reflects a fact-independent principle.

A corollary of the conclusion is that the most basic grounding of any given system of normative principles must be fact-independent principles. So,

(6) The most basic principles of justice are fact-independent.

If this argument is sound, it establishes that the Rawlsian approach to justice is mistaken. Rawlsians try to theorize justice for men as they are, but the most basic requirements of justice are insensitive to facts about human nature and the human condition. Indeed, if sound, Cohen's argument isn't just powerful against Rawlsians, but against *any moral theory* that appeals to *any* facts in its justification of basic moral principles.

Fortunately, for Rawlsians, Cohen's argument has a couple of weaknesses. Two key moves of Cohen's argument are:

(i) That the explanation for why a fact supports a principle implies a principle (= premise 3);
(ii) That the most basic principles of justification are also the most basic principles of justice (= the move from 5 to 6).

Both of these moves can be challenged. Premise 3 is either false or trivial in a sense that renders the conclusion harmless, and the move from (5) to (6) commits a fallacy of ambiguity.

3.4.1 *Against (i)/Premise 3*

Assume a person who is a hedonist utilitarian, maintaining that the only thing of intrinsic value is pleasurable states of consciousness, wherefore the first principle of justice prescribes maximization of pleasure and the absence of pain. In what sense can it be said that the move from the supposed fact that only pleasure is of intrinsic value to the principle "maximize pleasure" implies a further and more basic principle of justice?

To illustrate, think of Mill's utilitarianism. In chapter four of *Utilitarianism*, Mill infamously appears to commit a fallacy of ambiguity. From the fact that all desire happiness (presence of pleasure appropriately conceived and the absence of pain), Mill infers that happiness is desirable and that only happiness is desirable, and from that he infers that the basic moral principle is the greatest happiness principle, which tells us that an act is right to the extent that it promotes happiness. Mill is not, of course, committing a plain fallacy, but relying on the assumption that what we (rationally) desire is of value. The greatest happiness principle thus reflects the supposed fact that only happiness is of intrinsic value, but not a more basic fact-insensitive normative principle.

Cohen might object that a theory of value cannot yield a principle of justice without the additional principle "promote good," which is a fact-independent principle. But if the ultimacy of such a principle is all Cohen has established, then he hasn't established anything but a triviality harmless to left-liberals. For we can all agree that we ought to promote good and do what is right. These principles are not first principles of any *particular* conception of justice, but of *all*. What matters is, of course, what we mean by good, right, ought, and promote. It is in how these concepts are given content that a conception of justice is made. Surely, first principles of justice are more specific than, say, "do right," and insofar as principles can be both more specific than the general precept and can be grounded in facts, first principles can be fact-dependent.

3.4.2 Against (ii)/the Inference from (5) to (6)

Even if we granted Cohen that facts can ground principles of justice only if there are other principles that explain why these facts support the principles, and thus that any conception of justice ultimately must contain fact-independent principles, the argument does not entail that these fact-independent principles are the most basic principles *of justice*. In short, the move from (5) to (6) commits a fallacy of ambiguity.

To explain, there are at least four different ways in which a conception of justice can be informed by facts and four corresponding roles that facts can play in a theory of justice:

(a) There might be factual preconditions for justice to obtain (e.g. circumstances of justice such as moderate scarcity). We can call such facts justice-enabling.
(b) The content of the principles of justice might be determined by reference to facts (content-determining facts), as illustrated by Mill's utilitarianism.
(c) The principles of justice might be justified by reference to facts (justifying facts).
(d) And, finally, the contingencies of a situation are relevant for what principles of justice require for that situation, so that particular prescriptions must be informed by these facts (application-informing facts).

Even if there must be fact-independent principles at the most basic level *of justification*, there is no reason to assume that these principles of justification are first principles *of justice*.

In what respect are principles of justice fundamental? With respect to justification? With respect to determining the content of principles of justice? With respect to regulating society? There is no reason why we should expect the same principle or set of principles to fulfill these various roles. The substance of Rawls's two principles of justice is based on the democratic idea of society as a system of social cooperation between free and equal citizens. But these fundamental ideas are not themselves principles of justice; *they are more basic than the principles of justice, but are not normative principles.* They are, rather, commitments supposedly shared by those dedicated to constitutional democracy and in light of which we can articulate the basic normative principles that we aspire to live by. Nor do the fundamental ideas directly justify *any* principles of justice. To determine the basic principles of a conception of justice based on these ideas we need to go through some constructive process (such as the original position). So, Rawls's principles of justice are not fundamental with respect to justification; they are, rather, the most basic action-guiding political principles and, as such, they are, for Rawlsians, the fundamental principles of justice.

In effect, Cohen confuses a question of moral epistemology (what justifies principles of justice) with one of morality (what are the first principles of justice). It is true that facts ground no principle without an explanation for how they provide said ground. But to infer from this that the most basic principles of justice must be fact-independent is like inferring that the scientific method is the most basic natural law – it confuses the question of what the principles of justice are with that of how we identify them.

3.5 Concluding Thought

There are three basic disagreements between Cohen and Rawls. First, they disagree about what inequalities Rawlsian justice permits. Cohen argues that Rawlsian justice permits no inequalities based on incomplete devotion to justice in the members of society (even if such incomplete devotion is unavoidable, given the less-than-angelic nature of human beings); Rawls permits such inequalities if they are necessary to better the condition of the least well-off. Second, they disagree about what distributive justice requires. Cohen thinks distributive justice requires that equally deserving people are equally well-off; Rawls thinks distributive justice requires that members of society cooperate on fair terms. Third, they disagree about how we should think about justice. Cohen thinks that the basic requirements of justice are fact-insensitive; Rawls that they are sensitive to facts about human nature and the human condition.

Cohen argues that the difference principle requires us to work selflessly for the benefit of the least well-off. If, as a matter of fact, such selflessness is impossible for most human beings, then injustice is unavoidable (and justice unachievable), but that does not change what justice is – we should not think that the requirements of justice are sensitive to who or how we are. Rawls mistakes what justice is about, according to Cohen, and so mistakenly thinks that justice bends to our imperfect natures.

Even if Cohen's critique of Rawls is flawed, there is some truth to Cohen's main objection. Justice cannot be hostage to who we happen to be. To be blunt: it seems that the difference principle can justify increasing degrees of inequality based on the growing greed of the members of society, which cannot be the right conclusion. So, when we think about justice we should take facts about human nature into account, but we cannot bend justice to who and how we happen to be. And we should not take for granted that the people of today or of human history reveal much about human nature, for human nature is malleable and shaped by social circumstances. The fact that persons here and now are selfish tells us little about the possibilities and limits of selflessness.

So, when we think about distributive justice, our inquiry should be guided by facts about human nature and the human condition, but should take these as potentials. And it may be hard, very hard, to determine what sorts of selflessness we can achieve. Justice might require, and be better served in, a much more selfless society than the ones we know. At least, and this is a theme of the next section, we might worry that any embrace of capitalism – even as tempered by Rawlsian principles – makes justice hostage to human vices.

4 Socialism versus Right-Liberalism

As described in Chapter 2, the heart of right-liberalism is the marriage of liberty and utility. Right-liberals claim that when we give people liberty – understood as authority to decide for themselves what to do in economic and noneconomic matters – we also maximize utility. When people use their own knowledge to pursue their own ends in their own local communities, they make choices that are collectively beneficial. That is, the result of the system of liberty is a spontaneous order process that is super-productive of all the good things of human existence (including liberty itself). Liberty and utility are thus wed both at the normative and descriptive levels in the right-liberal theory of justice. Normatively, right-liberalism says that we should create the society that best provides people with what they want, which includes liberty itself, but also, of course, the many means of happiness (utility) such as peace, stability, comfortable housing, healthcare, education, means for satisfying the pleasures of the palate, art, means of easy transportation, and so on. Descriptively, right-liberalism says that the best way to get all these things that we desire is to give people liberty to make up their own minds about the good life and to pursue it as they wish, as long as they do so without infringing on the rights and liberties of others.

While Cohen wrote a book critical of Nozick and another book critical of Rawls, he did not write a book dedicated to criticizing Hayek (or right-liberalism more generally). Even so, we can construct this critique on his behalf from his various writings. His critique would focus on both the normative principles and the empirical assumptions of right-liberalism. That is, Cohen would dispute that right-liberals provide a good understanding of what we should care about, for the liberty we should care about is not the liberty that right-liberals defend, justice is not simply consequentialist in the manner that right-liberals make it, and we should reject that the main value is utility as right-liberals understand it. In more detail, Cohen would argue that:

1. The right-liberal idea of liberty is impoverished and it is unclear that capitalism provides for the sort of liberty that matters.
2. Justice does not require that we maximally satisfy people's preferences, but that people get what they deserve, and in capitalism people do not get what they deserve.
3. Right-liberals understand utility in terms of subjective states of being (e.g. desire satisfaction), but what really (or at least also) matters is who we are, and capitalism tends to make us bad people.

4.1 Liberty, Poverty, and Exploitation

Some of Cohen's critique of the right-liberal view of liberty was covered above in the discussion of his critiques of Nozick. Like Nozick, right-liberals assume a negative concept of liberty; liberty is understood in terms of absence of interpersonal coercion. Cohen argues that this is the wrong concept of liberty. Instead, we should focus on liberty as the ability to do things. When that is our focus, it is unclear that capitalism is a true friend of liberty, for capitalism tends to empower the few (the rich) at the expense of the many (the relatively poor).

There are, however, two additional parts to Cohen's critique of the right-liberal argument from liberty to capitalism, and each of these touches on well-rehearsed socialist critiques of capitalism. It will be worthwhile to see how these play out in Cohen's philosophy. In both of these, Cohen argues that even if we grant the right-liberals their negative concept of liberty, it remains unclear that capitalism is really a friend of liberty, for capitalism is a system of unfreedom in two ways: it concentrates freedom in the hands of the few and it allows the wealthy to exploit the poor.

4.1.1 Poverty and Freedom

The first argument targets the right-liberal position that liberty and poverty are consistent, since poverty might bring about inabilities, but not liability to interference from others. This argument is an important part of the right-liberal argument against redistributive taxation.

Assume, then, that the liberty we should care about is the one defended by Hayek and similar right-liberal defenders of capitalism, namely, the absence of interpersonal coercion, so that liberty is compromised if other persons are liable to interfere with us. A familiar right-liberal argument goes as follows (*CEJ*, 168):

i Liberty is compromised by liability to interference by others, and not by lack of means.
ii To lack money (poverty) is a lack of means, not a liability to interference.
iii So, poverty does not carry with it lack of liberty.

Right-liberals argue further that:

iv. The primary task of government is to protect liberty.
v. So, poverty relief is not a primary task of government.

Cohen says that left-liberals like Rawls tend to grant right-liberals the first part of the argument (i–iii), but challenge the premise that the primary task of government is to protect liberty (premise iv). Cohen agrees with the left-liberal critique of premise iv, but he thinks that they should not allow the first part of the argument, for all of the premises (i, ii, iv) are false.

Premise i is false since it assumes a mistaken concept of liberty. As Cohen argued in his critique of Nozick, on the better concept of liberty, inability (from lack of means or from other sources) is a sort of unfreedom. Premise iv is false, for liberty is not all that matters: equality and good living matter as well (I describe Cohen's argument for this conclusion in Sections 4.2 and 4.3). And even if premises i and iv were true, premise ii is false. To lack money *is* liability to interference by others. So, even if we mistakenly grant right-liberals their understanding of unfreedom as liability to interference by others (premise i) *and* that the primary task of government is to protect liberty (premise iv), we should still reject their argument against poverty relief. Interestingly, if Cohen's argument against ii is sound, then it raises the possibility that right-liberals should favor a redistributive state, since such a state is required by the concern for liberty, *as they understand it.*

Cohen's argument against ii is complicated, but the main idea is simple: the more money one has, the less interference there will be in one's attempts to achieve goals, so to lack money is to be liable to interference.

Take the poor fellow who wants to visit his sister in another country, but cannot afford the airfare. Should he try to board the plane, he'll be arrested and fined. He is liable to interference, and he would not be liable if he had money; his lack of money is why he is liable to interference. Or, take the poor woman in need of a nice set of clothes for a job interview. She is unable to afford the clothes, and should she try to take them at Macy's she will be resisted, arrested, and fined. She is liable to interference from others because of her lack of money. Her poverty is the source of her liability to interference; it is the source of her unfreedom.

More generally, money serves like keys or entry tickets for a host of places, services, goods, and activities that you cannot enter into, access, acquire, or enjoy without money. If you try to enter, access, acquire, or enjoy these without money, you'll be liable to interference. So, if you don't have money, you're liable to interference in the broad, but very concrete, sense that there's little you can do without other people forcibly stopping you and putting you behind bars.

Of course, money is not enough for most of these services. There must be seats on the plane and clothes in the store, and the airline or store must be willing to sell you their service and goods. Indeed, the airline *could* give the man a seat on the plane free of charge. So, to be precise, money is *an INUS condition* for access to most goods and services – that is, money is an **I**nsufficient but **N**ecessary part of an **U**nnecessary but **S**ufficient set of conditions of liberty. Normally, money is necessary for liberties to access goods and services, but so is the willingness of others to trade (hence, insufficient but necessary), but these goods and services could be delivered for free (hence unnecessary), but that's not usually the case in a capitalist society. There, most market players will require money to play with you – indeed, if you have money, you have all that it takes to get their goods or services (hence sufficient).

This argument has three results. First, the right-liberal argument from liberty to restrictions on the redistributive functions of the state fails. Second, any distribution of money is itself a distribution of liberty, so the question of distributive justice arises again for right-liberals – and they seem unable to answer it, for they say liberty prevents further discussions of distributive justice, but, in fact, we have to ask what the just distribution of liberty is. Finally, if we want to maximize liberty, it is uncertain that the right-liberal "system of liberty" (laissez-faire capitalism) does best, for it tends to concentrate wealth and income in the hands of the few. If we want to maximize liberty then, surely, we should try to provide more liberty for most rather than a lot for the few.

Defenders of capitalism would not, I think, be persuaded by Cohen's argument. First, they would contest that poverty is really lack of the sort of freedom that they think justice is about. In a sense, the poor person and the rich person are both free to take the plane or buy the clothes, it is just that the rich person has more means to take advantage of this freedom. Defenders of capitalism could allow that the poor person is *materially* less free than the rich person, while maintaining that poor and rich are *formally* equally free. Moreover, the freedom we should care about is formal freedom, for the system of liberty simply is the system of formal freedoms given full institutional expression and guarantee, and it is the security of this system which enables the productive powers of a free civilization. The marriage between liberty and utility, the capitalist could maintain, is the marriage of formal freedom and utility, so, even if it is true that poverty is material unfreedom, this unfreedom is not a direct concern of justice.

Moreover, the capitalist could continue, since it is dramatically productive, capitalism provides more of the material means for exercising our freedom than any other system. Where do the planes come from? The development of commercial flight? The computer that we use to book the tickets? The nice clothes at the store? Because of capitalism, we have means of transportation available, while competition drives down the price so that more and more people can afford to use them. Initially, air travel was exclusively for the wealthy, but now most people can afford the trip. Surely, the poor are better-off because of the increased means for enjoying their freedoms, even if they are not as materially free as the rich to actually enjoy them. Again, the Hayekian defense of capitalism says that it makes more of the good stuff available for most. If you agree with Cohen that the good stuff is freedom, then capitalism brings more freedom to most. It does not bring equal *material* freedom, but it does bring equal *formal* freedom, maximizes material freedom in the aggregate, and ensures that even most of the poor have more material freedom than they would have in any feasible alternative system. Cohen has not established a capitalist principled commitment to *equal* material freedom, and they would reject it. Without such a commitment, it seems that capitalists are off the supposed hook.

4.1.2 Capitalism and Exploitation

An old and honorable complaint against capitalism is that in capitalist societies the rich exploit the poor. A person exploits another when she uses the fact that the other person has no reasonable alternative to accepting her proposal for unfair employment or exchange to get her to agree to such unfair terms. (Marxists employ another concept of exploitation as simply the extraction of surplus value by capitalists; see Information Box 5.2 Two concepts of exploitation.)

INFORMATION BOX 5.2 TWO CONCEPTS OF EXPLOITATION

Socialists endorse two concepts of exploitation. In both, exploitation happens when employees (workers) are exploited by employers (capitalists) and their exploitation consists in unfair terms of employment; typically, that these terms permit unsanitary or unsafe working conditions, require long and irregular working hours, or that the pay is unfairly low.

The two concepts of exploitation are distinguished by whether or not they count coercive circumstances as a necessary condition for exploitation. On the account presented in the text, *it is not enough* that employees work according to unfair conditions, it must *also* be the case that they have no reasonable alternative to accepting these unfair conditions of employment (they are, in short, forced by their circumstances, which the exploiter may or may not have a hand in creating, to accept these terms at the pain of being unable to satisfy their basic needs or the basic needs of their dependents).

On the alternative account of exploitation, *it is enough* that the terms of employment are unfair. Thus, Marx's most quoted definition of exploitation defines it in terms of the extraction of surplus value by the capitalist, which need not take place by virtue of unreasonable alternatives.

The distinction between these concepts of exploitation is crucial. The former sort of exploitation can be dealt with by offering reasonable alternatives to unfair employment contracts. The latter sort of exploitation seems inevitable in a capitalist society. However, the former offers a much stronger moral critique than the latter. If the millionaire decides to work on unfair terms for McDonalds, then she is exploited according to the latter definition of exploitation, but not the former.

Paradigmatic cases of exploitation involve exploiters who get exploitees to trade or work for them on terms they would not accept if this were not their only alternative to starvation or similar deprivation (e.g. sweatshops, forced sales to a monopsony).

Exploitation involves three sorts of unreasonableness: unreasonableness of the alternatives to employment or exchange, unreasonableness in the terms of employment or exchange, and the unreasonableness of the exploiter who proposes and follows these terms of employment or exchange.

Marx famously berated capitalism's tendency to exploitation. Workers in 18th and 19th century Europe had few alternatives other than to work on the terms proposed by capitalists, and thus ended up working long days for subsistence wages. And it should be obvious that exploitation is still a problem. All over the world, people face a choice between homelessness, food insecurity, and an inability to satisfy other basic needs, or accepting terms of employment that they would reject if not for the unreasonableness of the alternatives.

Socialists argue that capitalism inevitably (or always) creates exploitative relationships between capitalists and workers, for workers have no reasonable alternative to work – without working, they and those that depend on them face homelessness, starvation, and lack of access to education or healthcare – and capitalists exploit that fact to offer them unfair terms of employment, where workers are paid just enough to scrape by, while the capitalists extract the lion's share of their product's value and use it for their own purposes (as capitalists and as individual consumers).

Cohen does *not* endorse this argument, for he thinks that the argument fails (see *SPU*). It is *not true* that workers have no alternative to working for a capitalist, for they might start their own business and make their way into the capitalist class themselves. Since workers are not forced to work for capitalists, it is not true that capitalism inevitably is a site of exploitation in the sense alleged by the standard socialist critique.

However, Cohen argues that capitalism *is* the site of exploitation in another sense. While it is false that individual workers are exploited (for individual workers are free to pursue alternatives to employment by capitalists), it is nevertheless the case that workers *as a class* are exploited; they cannot collectively leave their situation as workers, and so must, as a group, seek employment with capitalists and on the unfair terms dictated by capitalists.

To explain, imagine that a number of people, say 100, are locked in a room (*SPU*, 9–11). There is only one door. Strangely, the door has a sensor that will allow the first three people who try to leave the room to leave it; then the door will lock forever. Now, it is true that each person in that room is *free* to leave. But it is also true that as a collective, these 100 *are not free to leave*, for only very few could leave, and then the rest would be permanently locked in the room. This example mirrors the freedom of workers to leave the proletariat (i.e. to leave their condition as workers forced to work for capitalists); it may be that a few can manage to self-employ their way out of the proletariat, but in a capitalist society there must be workers (and many of them) and only a few of the many workers could manage to leave it at any point. To improve on the example, we can imagine that the door allows three persons to leave per hour and that another person enters the room every time a person leaves, mirroring the continued unfreedom and reproduction of the working class. In that scenario, the door is never locked for good, but it remains impossible for the group to leave their condition of collective unfreedom, even though each, individually, is free to leave.

So, capitalism is the site of exploitation since *workers as a class* (collectively rather than individually) are forced to work for capitalists and on the unfair terms that capitalists dictate.

Again, defenders of capitalism have a strong reply to the charge of exploitation, but it requires some compromise with the central tenets of right-liberal defenses of capitalism. Since exploitation is a function of both the terms of employment and of the available alternatives to employment, worries about exploitation can be removed by manipulating the terms of employment and by providing reasonable alternatives to exploitative contracts. In other words, a society that regulates terms of employment so that they cannot be exploitative is a society where exploitation is *illegal*. So, minimum wage laws and laws regulating work conditions and hours can all be part of creating a society without exploitation. Likewise, if the state serves as employer of last resort, or if there is a strong welfare state with adequate supports for the unemployed, or if there is a guaranteed basic income, or similar measures are in place that guarantee that the basic needs of all citizens are met whether they are employed or not, then there cannot be any *legal* exploitation.

Both sorts of measures require compromises with right-liberal commitments, but not to the degree that they cannot be provided in a capitalist society of a sort that Hayekians could embrace. Measures that regulate terms of employment require compromising with freedom of contract, since capitalists and workers alike will be unfree to engage in exploitative terms of cooperation. The second sort of measure requires some sort of redistributive activities of the state; to fund the provisions for guaranteeing that the basic needs of all are satisfied the state must tax the richer to provide for the poorer, a sort of taxation that is loathed by most right-liberals. Yet, again, it seems that such a taxation scheme would be fully consistent with the basics of a capitalist society of the sort that Hayek and others defend. Recall here that

Hayek endorses the distributive principle of *sufficiency*, and if a society satisfies a robust principle of sufficiency, then it seems that there can be no exploitation in that society, for then all are guaranteed that their basic needs are met independently of their employment.

4.2 Liberty and Merit

Above, I've described Cohen's arguments that *even if* distributive justice is all about liberty, and *even if* we grant right-liberals their favored conception of liberty, a socialist system might be better than a capitalist system in terms of providing liberty to the members of society. Of course, Cohen does *not* accept the right-liberal position that distributive justice is all about liberty (or its supposed partner, utility). Cohen argues that distributive justice is about *desert*. Distributive justice requires that people get what they deserve, so that one's fate in life is a function of effort and choices rather than morally arbitrary factors.

In a capitalist society, advantages are distributed through the interplay of a variety of factors, including natural endowments, social circumstances, luck in health, choices, luck in the marketplace, and value. In this context, value should be understood as market value broadly construed, so that one has more value the more remuneration one is able to collect from one's efforts, which, in turn, will be a function of one's inputs as these are of value to the market. To simplify: if you bring average coding skills to the job market, you'll have higher market value than if you bring excellent child-rearing skills. This difference in value does not reflect a judgment of the worth of the activities, except insofar as these are valued by the market. Surely, it is more valuable to create good people than good software, but the supply-demand function for coding skills versus child-rearing skills makes it so that coders earn more than daycare teachers.

Hayek would agree that the resulting distribution of wealth and income fails to track *merit*; in a capitalist society, the distribution of society's benefits and burdens is not a function of whether people do honest, hard work in worthwhile pursuits as much as of differences in abilities, social circumstances, and simple brute luck. He also argues that this disconnect between distribution and merit is not a problem, for, first, the result is that all (or most) have better access to the means of a good life, and, second, we could not create a meritocratic society without creating a dystopia where the state monitors and regulates all aspects of human existence.

Against this sort of position, Cohen argues that, clearly, distributive justice requires that people get what they deserve and that they get what they deserve if, and only if, the distribution of advantages is a function of the choices people make, rather than various sorts of luck or how their abilities happen to be valued by capitalist producers. In Section 5 below I try to describe in more detail the foundation and results of this position. Here, what matters is that capitalism – even according to its most ardent defenders – distributes benefits and burdens such that those who have less or more do not *deserve* to have less or more. If the principle of merit is a true principle of distributive justice for the case of society, then this is a serious complaint against capitalism. And if socialism would do better at distributing advantages according to merit, then this is also an argument for socialism.

Of course, as a critique, this argument has limited appeal, since it presumes what defenders of capitalism deny; that the principle of merit is a true principle of distributive justice for society. If, indeed, capitalism maximizes utility by giving people liberty, then it is unclear why we should let concerns about merit block the creation of utility through liberty. Indeed, it seems that defenders of capitalism could use a version of the leveling down objection (see Chapter 1, Information Box 1.1 The leveling down objection) against Cohen's position. If it is true that some are better-off and no one worse off in a capitalist society when compared to feasible meritocratic alternatives, then it would seem irrational (since it serves no one) to choose the meritocracy.

Cohen would not, on the other hand, be terribly worried by this objection, for it presumes that the concerns of justice are reducible to concerns about individual well-being, and he denies this assumption: justice requires a distribution according to merit, and if some are worse off in a just than in an unjust society, then that's simply the price of justice. Justice is not our only concern, and we might not be willing to pay this price, but that does not, Cohen would argue, change what justice requires.

In this debate, then, defenders of capitalism and Cohen-style socialists simply disagree about the nature of distributive justice – both what it is about and what it requires. Hayekians are, at bottom, consequentialists, and as such cannot allow that justice would require us to sacrifice well-being to give people what they deserve, as Cohen maintains it does. In this debate, socialists and right-liberals start from different assumptions, and the debate ends in a stalemate. Cohen's critique thus highlights an intuitively appealing view of the nature of distributive justice and show that defenders of capitalism cannot accommodate this view.

But Cohen does more than this, for he would also argue that the Hayekian theory of the good or well-being that serves as input in his consequentialist defense of capitalism is too narrow. What we should care about is not merely that people get what they desire, but that they live good lives in community with others. This critique is the subject of the following section.

4.3 Community, Virtue, and Alienation

In the pure case of market interactions, the agents are governed by a self-serving sort of reciprocity: they give in order to receive, and not because those they interact with need what they provide. Indeed, in the pure case, market agents would prefer to receive without giving anything in return. There is an alternative mode of reciprocity that we all know from friendships, families, or camping trips: communal reciprocity. In communal reciprocity, people provide for each other due to: "the antimarket principle according to which I serve you not because of what I can get in return by doing so but because you need or want my service, and you, for the same reason, serve me" (*WNS*, 39).

The contrast between market and communal reciprocity lies primarily in motives – why persons do what they do when engaged in reciprocal exchange. In market reciprocity, we are willing to produce for and serve others, but only in order to receive products and be served ourselves. In communal reciprocity, by contrast, "I produce in the spirit of commitment to my fellow human beings: I desire to serve them while being served by them, and I get satisfaction from each side of that equation" (*WNS*, 41).

The motives that correspond to market reciprocity are, Cohen argues, fear and greed. We are driven by the desire to get as much as we can for ourselves and by the fear that others might take advantage of us. Accordingly, in market exchanges:

> I give as little service as I can in exchange for as much service as I can get: I want to buy cheap and sell dear. I serve others *either* in order to get something that I desire – that is the greed motivation; *or* in order to ensure that something that I seek to avoid is avoided – that is the fear motivation. A marketer, considered just as such, does not value cooperation with others for its own sake: she does not value the conjunction *serve-and-be-served* as such.
>
> (WNS, *42)*

In a communal exchange, by contrast, the motive includes the desire that others do well through the cooperative activity:

> A nonmarket cooperator relishes cooperation itself: what I want, as a non-marketeer, is that we serve each other [...] The relationship between us under communal reciprocity is not the market-instrumental one in which I give because I get, but the non-instrumental one in which I give because you need, or want, and in which I expect a comparable reciprocity from you.
>
> (WNS, *43)*

As Hayek explains so well, the magic of capitalism is that it harnesses self-interest to the common good, so that people act in a manner that is good for all simply by pursuing their own ends and with no care for the common good. The problem, Cohen says, is that it runs on foul motives to bring about the desirable result. While an economy running on fear and greed might be very productive, it is morally repulsive to relate to other persons through these motives. In the market relation, other persons are seen as things – levers and obstacles – that we should manipulate to maximally satisfy our greed and quell our fears. The market relation thus fundamentally violates the Kantian injunction to treat people also as ends in themselves and never merely as means, for other persons *are* treated as mere means to best satisfy the interacting agents' preferences.

There are, then, two distinct problems with the capitalist mode of relating persons as competitors in the marketplace. First, market reciprocity makes community impossible, for community obtains between persons that care about each other in the manner of friendship rather than as competitors, so that they act to serve each other because each needs the others' service, not simply for their own gain. Second, the psychology of marketeering is morally repugnant. So, both at the collective and individual levels, capitalist society makes the economy the site of moral failures; it undermines true community between the members of society, and it makes the individual members vicious – driven by greed and fear to relate immorally to their fellows.

In a word, capitalism is *alienating*: it breeds immoral psychologies and undermines the achievement of true community. It might be very productive, but this attraction comes at a very high moral cost. In exchange for the material comforts that capitalism provides, we pay the possibility of living together as we ought – in the manner of friendship – and support the making of vicious, morally despicable human beings.

So, when defenders of capitalism count the consequences we should care about in terms of peace, stability, liberty, and material comforts, they leave out two values that matter as much, if not more; the values of community and virtue. In a word, Cohen defends a *perfectionist* theory of well-being against the utilitarian theory assumed by Hayek and like defenders of capitalism. What matters is not so much that we get what we desire, but that we desire the right things; these include how we relate to each other and who we are. The success of a society cannot be measured by how much it produces of the goods and services we want, but by how well it allows for and cultivates real community and morally attractive human beings.

By Cohen's argument, capitalism destroys community and makes us morally despicable, and that, surely, should count against it. Socialism, Cohen argues, would do much better at allowing real community and human virtue to flourish, for a socialist economy does not rely on the competition of self-interested agents to power production and distribution. In a socialist economy, the productive process is geared towards the satisfaction of real needs rather than corporate profit, and the producers are driven by their desire to assist each other rather than to maximize how much they can procure for themselves. In socialism, the economy is not mere coordination or cooperation, but true community.

Is the socialist vision of *the economy as community* utopian? Could we really create a society where all love all in the manner of friendship and where all serve each other without regard for personal gain? Cohen says that we don't know, but also that it does not really matter whether socialism is utopian. For, first, the criticism of capitalism as destroyer of community and corrupter of the soul is true, whether or not socialism offers an alternative (or whether there is *any* alternative that would do better). Second, we should all agree that *if* socialism is possible, then it is better than capitalism, because it adds both community and virtue to the goals of society. Thus, we should all be socialists as a matter of ideal theory, even if, at the end of the day, we realize that socialism is unachievable. The fact that we cannot reach the grapes does not mean that they are not the sweetest. By analogy, Cohen argues, even if socialism is beyond reach, it is still the best system.

5 Cohen's Socialism

Cohen does not provide a clear statement of what socialism is or what particular principles of justice he defends. However, the discussion above reveals that his position is a sort of pluralism – meaning that it consists of multiple principles – and also provides a clear statement of some of these principles.

One way to express these is to identify the particular reasons that Cohen thinks a socialist design of the economy is preferable to capitalism. To repeat, here are his main criticisms of capitalism:

- Capitalism leads to an unfair distribution of the benefits and burdens of cooperation.
- Capitalism fails to provide real freedom to most members of society.
- Capitalism destroys the ties of community.
- Capitalism makes us bad people.

From this we can infer that a socialist design of the economy is preferable because (or insofar as):

- A socialist economy secures a fair distribution of the benefits and burdens of cooperation.
- A socialist economy provides real freedom to its members.
- A socialist economy relies on and supports ties of community.
- A socialist economy allows us to become good people.

The first contrast between capitalism and a socialist economy is about distributive justice in the narrow sense; it is about fairness in the distribution of the benefits and burdens of cooperation. The other three contrasts are about the consequential effects an economic system has on those related within it. Accordingly, we can group these into two sorts of criticisms and two sorts of principles employed in Cohen's argument for socialism: the argument from fairness and the argument from consequences.

5.1 The Argument from Fairness

Cohen maintains that fairness requires linking how people do in life with what they deserve. That is, Cohen affirms a principle of merit as the basic principle of distributive justice. In particular, Cohen's principle says that "differential advantage is unjust save where it reflects differences in genuine choice [...] on the part of the relevant agents" (*CEJ*, 60). Cohen argues that this is an egalitarian idea, since it secures that equally deserving people are equally well-off in terms of access to advantages (*CEJ*, 59, 69). To further explain this principle, it will be helpful to look closer at the three parts: the currency part (advantages), the egalitarian part, and the merit part (desert).

5.1.1 Advantages

Amartya Sen famously asked the question for egalitarians: Equality of what? (See Further Reading in Chapter 1 for reference.) Some egalitarians say that people should be equally well-off and thus define the metric of equality in terms of welfare. Others say that people should have the same amount of goods and thus define the metric of equality in terms of resources. Sen argued that each of these positions has problems. If people should be equally well-off, then people with expensive tastes or those who have cultivated weird desires for expensive goods should receive more than those who have cheaper tastes or who have cultivated less demanding preferences, and that seems unfair to the less expensively inclined. On the other hand, if people receive the same resources, then those who need more resources (say, those who suffer handicaps that need resources and assistance to function at the normal level, however we define normal) will be worse off simply by virtue of that need, which also seems unfair. Sen proposes that we should focus instead on capabilities, so that people should be equally well-off in terms of what they can do.

Cohen does not follow Sen in turning to the metric of capabilities, for he thinks that the concept of capability is murky and subject to ambiguities (*CEJ*, Chapters 1–3). He also thinks that we cannot abandon the metrics of welfare or resources entirely, for clearly their distribution matters – and they matter (or are subject to norms of fairness) independently of how they serve in relation to capabilities. Moreover, Cohen believes that Sen's argument is powerful against outcome egalitarians, but less powerful against those who instead focus on equality of opportunity. If, say, we shift from equal welfare to equal opportunity for welfare, then the egalitarian position does not maintain that those who cultivate expensive preferences should receive more resources, for they chose to cultivate them and are thus responsible for their costliness.

So, Cohen proposes that we think of the metric of equality in terms of equal access to advantages. *Access* is a mode of opportunity, so we should ensure that people at birth have equal access to advantages when measured over a complete lifetime. And *advantages* include resources and welfare, but also the other things people need to live well (cf. *CEJ*, 4, 61–5).

5.1.2 Equality

As mentioned above, the equality that Cohen's principle demands is not an equality of outcome (that people receive the same at the end of the day), but an equality of opportunity (that people have the same access to advantages). The idea is that if all persons have equal access to advantages, the advantages they end up with are determined by the choices they make, so that those who make the same choices receive the same amount of advantages in life. Those who start from a more challenged starting point should be compensated for these challenges: "we should compensate for disadvantage beyond a person's control" (*CEJ*, 20). Those who cultivate expensive tastes should not be compensated for that disadvantage, but those who suffer handicaps should.

5.1.3 Merit

Inequalities of advantage should reflect people's choices rather than luck, so that "the inequality that egalitarians seek to eliminate is that of disadvantage that is due to brute luck" (*CEJ*, 69). The idea, then, is that people's fate – or the fate they enjoy relative to the fate of others – should be a function of the choices they make in life rather than morally arbitrary factors. Thus, egalitarians like Cohen "object to all and only those inequalities that do not appropriately reflect choice. They object to inequalities that are caused by brute luck" (*CEJ*, 116). This position is usually called "luck-egalitarianism," but the name is a bit misleading. What matters is that equally deserving people have the same access to advantages, and luck (good or bad) is a source of inequalities that are undeserved and thus should be corrected. It is, Cohen argues, *unfair* when people's relative access to advantages is a function of luck rather than their choices.

It is worth noting that, because the metric of merit is choice and responsibility for one's advantages, Cohen's egalitarianism justifies inequalities where these are based on choice. So, if there is equality between two groups in society, but one of these got most of their advantages by virtue of choices they made, then the other group – the ones who did not make such choices – *should be worse off*, and justice demands taking from them what they don't deserve.

In capitalism, the distribution of advantages is largely a function of luck – the wealth and social status of the family we are born into, the education we receive, how well our investments do, who we meet, what illnesses we get, and so on. In socialism, by contrast, the state can design an economy that does not reward luck as much, and it can actively seek to correct the effects of luck.

5.2 Cohen's Perfectionist Consequentialism

Securing fairness in the distribution of the benefits and burdens of cooperation (in Cohen's terms: advantages and disadvantages) is not enough to create a good society. Even if we eliminate the effects of brute luck on the distribution of advantages, there will still be inequalities based on the choices people make, including choices to seek out luck by taking risks (so-called option luck). These inequalities might undermine the achievement of true community among members of society (cf. *WNS*, 34–8). In addition, equality of access to advantages as Cohen recommends does not by itself suffice to provide the means for material freedom or a society hospitable to virtue, so these ends – community, freedom, and virtue – add additional requirements or considerations that we should include when we decide how to live together and what economic system we should choose. Cohen, of course, believes that they all recommend a socialist design of the economy.

5.2.1 Community

Cohen discusses three kinds of community. First, there is justificatory community, which obtains when the norms that govern interactions between the members in a community can be justified by all to all. Second, communal reciprocity obtains when the members of society are motivated in their interactions in the manner of friendship, so that their interactions are governed by the desire to serve each other. Third, there is community of care and understanding when all members of society care for and can relate to each other as equal members of the community.

Justificatory community is tied to the principle of equality of advantage, since all inequalities in a society governed by that principle are justifiable to all by all as a function of the choices each has made from a standpoint of equal access to advantages. The other two sorts of community are not directly tied to the principle of equal access to advantages. Community-as-friendship simply recommends that all interpersonal dealings, including economic ones, be governed by the more attractive reasons of community rather than self-interest. Thus, this second form of community has no direct relation to the principle of equal access to advantages. Community-of-care, however, might be in direct conflict with that principle, for even inequalities that are justified (and thus *required*) by the principle of equality of advantages can undermine the community of care and understanding. As Cohen says, there cannot be full community between the very rich and the poor, even if their inequality reflects only choices and thus is justifiable by all to all, because then the poor and the rich will labor under different challenges to such an extent that they won't really be able to relate to each other (cf. *WNS*, 35–7).

Therefore, Cohen argues, our concern for community should restrict the principle of equality of access to advantage. Even inequalities that are mandated by the principle of equal access to advantages are impermissible, if they undermine (to a sufficient degree) the achievement of community.

Capitalism fails to provide for each of the three sorts of community, for, first, the distribution of advantages is not justifiable from all to all, since it reflects morally arbitrary factors (e.g. luck and ruthlessness in the pursuit of economic opportunities); second, our economic dealings are governed by market forces rather than communal reciprocity; and, third, the divisions between the classes of society prevent communal care and understanding among equals.

Socialism can do better on all three counts. It can secure that inequalities are justifiable, it structures the economic sphere to work without the competition that relies on market reciprocity, and it tempers all inequalities enough that communal relations are possible. At least, that's the hope we can hold for a socialist economy.

5.2.2 Material Liberty

Cohen does not dispute the right-liberal argument that we should care about liberty, nor does he dispute that we should care about utility, but he would argue that the right-liberal argument mistakenly sees one (liberty) as the means to the other (utility), where the two are actually ontologically tied together. If by utility we mean the various means of getting what we want, then these *are the means of exercising our formal liberty*, so liberty is not a means of utility; rather, utility is the means for enjoying our liberty. Or, even better, utility understood as the many products of the economy is nothing but the materials by which we have *material* liberty. These means are also the means of happiness as preference satisfaction, but happiness itself does not seem to rank high on Cohen's list of things that truly matter. Instead, what matters is that we have the means to pursue our ends, meaning that we have material liberty for all.

Cohen acknowledges that it is unclear whether a capitalist or a socialist design of the economy would do best at providing the materials of material liberty, but he can argue that the right-liberal defense of capitalism fails to realize that this is the liberty we should care about, and also that *if* capitalism does better at providing these means to all, that would be coincidental and not by design. Moreover, Cohen would argue that what matters is not merely that all have the means of material liberty, but also that these means are fairly distributed. In other words, the means of material liberty is one advantage that should be distributed fairly, in accordance with the principle of equal access to advantages. Only a socialist system is designed to (and can be expected to) combine the interest in providing the means of material liberty for all and the interest in securing that these are fairly distributed – and, therefore, a socialist economy, by contrast with capitalist economies, can be expected to secure a fair system of material liberty for all.

5.2.3 Virtue

Capitalism makes us bad people, Cohen argues. But why think that a socialist economy would do any better? The answer is that socialism does not rely on, and so does not engender, the moral psychologies of a possessive and competitive society – it does not rely on or engender the motives of fear and greed, but instead relies on and engenders the motives of benevolence and trust. In an economy governed by communal reciprocity, all provide what they can because others need their help, and they also all expect to receive what they need because they need it. In other words, a socialist economy, where communal reciprocity governs and the moral psychologies of the members of society have fully internalized the motives appropriate to communal reciprocity, would realize the socialist principle of distribution: from each according to their abilities and to each according to their needs (*CEJ*, 219–20). That is attractive in itself, but it is even more attractive since it allows the development of truly admirable and virtuous human beings and the exercise of their virtues.

5.2.4 Socialism as Perfectionism

Each of the three ends of Cohen's socialist consequentialism are objective goods: true community, real human freedom, admirable human character. These three together provide values that we should care about and that socialism promises to provide, and their opposites – social disunity, unfreedom, and vice – are disvalues that we should expect to dominate in capitalist societies. Or so Cohen argues.

There is, here, a very interesting analogy and contrast between the right-liberal sort of argument that ties liberty to consequentialism of the utilitarian sort and the socialist argument that ties equality to a consequentialism of a perfectionist sort. The distinction between utilitarianism and perfectionism lies in their value theories. Utilitarianism and perfectionism are both consequentialisms, but utilitarian consequentialisms define good and bad consequences in terms of *subjective well-being* (pleasure and pain, preference satisfaction or dissatisfaction, happiness or misery), whereas perfectionist consequentialisms define good and bad consequences in terms of *objective well-being* (communal relations, virtue and vice, freedom).

Socialism combines a perfectionist consequentialism with a principle of equality (in Cohen's version, the principle of equal access to advantages). What matters is not merely that we are happy. The serf and the lord might both be happy while they live undesirable lives without community, freedom, and virtue. What matters, then, is that we live truly good human lives in community, with freedom, and with virtue.

Socialists argue that only a socialist society provides the circumstances wherein these objectively good human existences can be realized. They also argue that only a socialist society can provide for distributive justice in the form of distributions where all get what they deserve. There is, then, a marriage in socialism analogous to the marriage between liberty and utility that we found in right-liberalism, namely, a marriage of equality (or equity) and perfection.

Given the pluralist tendencies of the socialist theory of distributive justice, it is hard to provide a simple depiction of it, but Figure 5.1 is an attempt to fit it into the pyramid illustration introduced in Chapter 1:

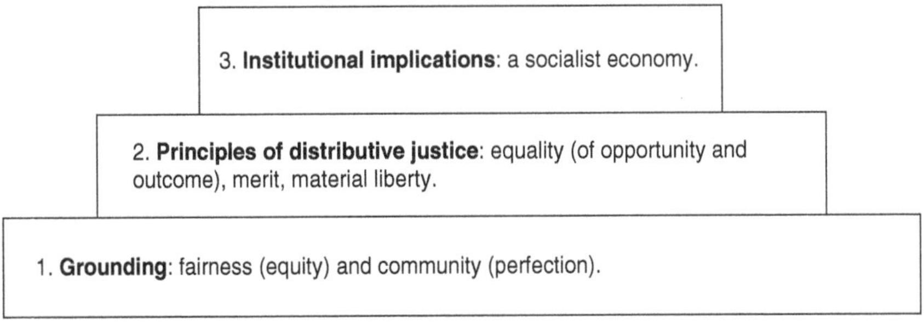

FIGURE 5.1 The main elements of socialism

6 The Marriage of Equality and Perfection

In my discussion of right-liberalism I raised doubts about the marriage of liberty and utility that is the core of that theory of justice. Right-liberalism is based on the belief that giving people liberty also maximizes expected utility. This is a very optimistic belief, but defenders of capitalism have some empirical basis for it. At least, it seems that the story of how the world broke the Malthusian trap and became a very nice place to live for an increasing number of people, has a lot to do with the spread of capitalism understood as a system of economic liberties together with private ownership of the means of production. Of course, any historical phenomenon has many causes and it is impossible to single out any particular cause of economic progress as primary, but capitalist societies tend to be wealthier than noncapitalist societies, whether we draw that comparison in time or space, so the marriage of liberty and utility might not be so tenuous after all.

Socialists argue against the relevance of this supposed marriage of liberty and utility, for they think that justice is about other values (or different conceptions of these values). We should instead care about equality and perfection (as defined above), and they seem to hold that equality and perfection go hand in hand – that there is an analogue marriage of equality and perfection.

However, it seems harder for socialists to point to empirical facts or inter-societal comparisons in this marriage of equality and perfection similar to those that defenders of capitalism rely on to support their faith in liberty joined with utility. Socialists can point to empirical facts to support their critique of capitalism, for experience supports the worries that inequality undermines community, that capitalism concentrates real freedom in the pockets of the rich, and that capitalism makes it easier for members of society to develop various vices connected to competition for scarce resources in an unfair playing field: envy, spite, resentment, greed, malice, and the various patterns of actions associated with these. However, there is limited empirical basis for claiming that socialism would do as well (or better) in these respects. The claim that there is a direct link between socialist egalitarianism (in the form of the principle of merit) and the elements of good living (community, liberty, virtue) is an empirical claim, and must be tested by reality, not theory.

7 Capitalism, Socialism, or Something In-Between?

In this chapter I've described the socialist arguments against capitalism and how these arguments also deliver a positive case for socialism. Throughout I've described this choice as a binary – we must choose between capitalism and socialism – but that description is oversimplified, for there are intermediate options. There is a spectrum between capitalism and socialism, and we can (and, in reality, do) choose to aim for an economy that lies on one of the points between the extremes of this spectrum.

Indeed, the spectrum is a space, for I've defined capitalism in terms of three dimensions and socialism lies at the opposite end of each of these dimensions.

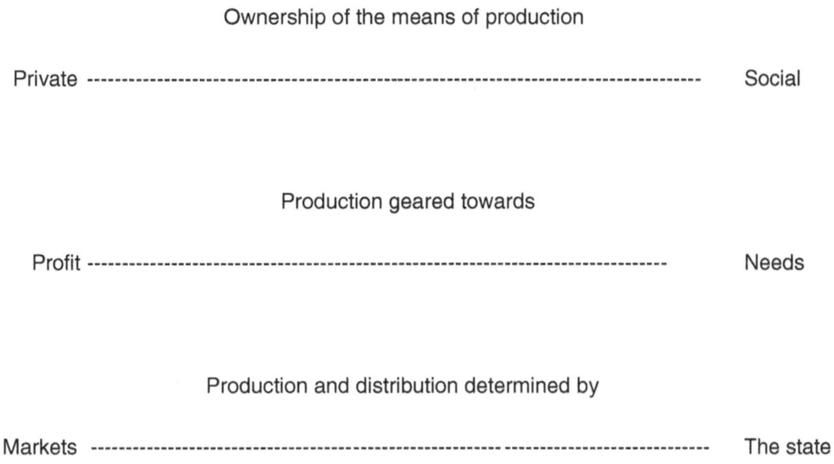

FIGURE 5.2 Capitalism versus socialism: three continua

Capitalism was defined (Chapter 1, Section 2.3) as involving private ownership of the means of production, a system of production and distribution geared towards profits for the owners of the means of production, and a system where market forces determine what is produced, how much of it is produced, at what prices, and where it is sold, and so on. Socialism, by contrast, is a system where there is socialized ownership of the means of production, production is geared towards satisfying collectively defined needs, and some collectivized planning decides what is produced and who gets the products. The choice between these two systems, then, should be understood as a choice of where to land in these three continuums (Figure 5.2).

While there are some linkages between these, the linkages are weak enough in theory that we could aim for economies lying on any combination of points in the above-defined space. So, the debate between socialists and defenders of capitalism is a debate about two things: first, what we should care about when we decide where to land in this space and, second, where we should aim to land. In this chapter, and in the book more generally, I've focused on the first of these debates – the debate about the true principle of distributive justice – for it is the answers to this debate that will tell us how we should conduct the second debate – the debate about institutional design.

Further Reading

The primary sources I have used in describing Cohen's political philosophy are the following (abbreviations for in-text citations in parenthesis):

Cohen, Gerald A., 1983. "The Structure of Proletarian Unfreedom", *Philosophy & Public Affairs*, 12 (1): 3–33. (*SPU*).

Cohen, Gerald A., 1995. *Self-Ownership, Freedom, and Equality*, Cambridge, UK: Cambridge University Press. (*SFE*).
Cohen, Gerald A., 2000a. *If You're an Egalitarian, How Come You're so Rich?* Cambridge, MA: Harvard University Press.
Cohen, Gerald A., 2003. "Facts and Principles", *Philosophy & Public Affairs*, 31 (3): 211–245. (*FP*).
Cohen, Gerald A., 2008. *Rescuing Justice and Equality*, Cambridge, MA: Harvard University Press. (*RJE*).
Cohen, Gerald A., 2009. *Why Not Socialism?* Princeton, NJ: Princeton University Press. (*WNS*).
Cohen, Gerald A., 2011. *On the Currency of Egalitarian Justice and Other Essays in Political Philosophy*, Princeton, NJ: Princeton University Press. (*CEJ*).

Other works by Cohen that are useful for understanding his version of socialism are:

Cohen, Gerald A., 1989. *History, Labour, and Freedom: Themes from Marx*, Oxford, UK: Oxford University Press.
Cohen, Gerald A., 2000b. *Karl Marx's Theory of History*, Princeton, NJ: Princeton University Press.
Cohen, Gerald A., 2012. *Finding Oneself in the Other*, Princeton, NJ: Princeton University Press.
Cohen, Gerald A., 2013. *Lectures on the History of Moral and Political Philosophy*, Princeton, NJ: Princeton University Press.

There are innumerable alternative statements and defenses of socialism. I have found the following useful:

Harrington, Michael, 1989. *Socialism: Past and Future*, New York, NY: Arcade Publishing.
Levine, Andrew, 1988. *Arguing for Socialism, Revised Edition*, London, UK: Verso.
Przeworski, Adam, 1985. *Capitalism and Social Democracy*, Cambridge, UK: Cambridge University Press.

6

CONTRASTS

1 Introduction

In this chapter I sharpen the contrasts between the theories of distributive justice described in the previous chapters by describing their views in each of several dimensions. Recall that theories of distributive justice can be described as having three parts: foundational ideas and values, normative principles, and institutional commitments. These are also levels of theorizing, in the sense that the institutional commitments spell out how the normative principles can be satisfied and these principles, in turn, express the prescriptive dimension of the foundational ideals. Here, I go into more detail for each of these levels to summarize and contrast the main theories of distributive justice. This chapter explores:

Foundational ideas and values

- View of society;
- View of the person;
- Philosophical framework appropriate for thinking about justice;
- Primary virtue of a just society.

Principles

- General normative requirements;
- View on economic rights;
- View on equality of opportunity.

Institutions

- Choice of economic system;
- View on democracy.

Though I introduce some new ideas in this chapter and refine other ideas, the chapter travels some ground already covered in the previous chapters and some repetition is unavoidable. My hope is that the presentation of this chapter helps deepen your understanding of the theories, but also that it helps you get a sense of the big picture – that is, that after reading this chapter you sense the whole map of the landscape of theories of distributive justice rather than merely the individual members, and that you begin to understand both *how* these four theories are related as members of a finite set of theories of distributive justice, and *why* these four are the main theories of distributive justice. In the following and final chapter I elaborate on these insights.

2 Foundational Ideas and Philosophical Frameworks

One of the main takeaways from the study of theories of distributive justice as conducted in this book is that their disagreements about how we should organize society stem from underlying disagreements about which principles of distributive justice should guide this design, *and that this disagreement about principles stems from different views of society and personhood.* In the end, these four theories of distributive justice are founded on four distinct views of society and personhood which, in turn, support different frameworks for thinking about distributive justice.

2.1 Foundations of Right-Liberalism

Right-liberals see society as an emergent solution to coordination problems. Societies are patterns of behavior, social roles, and attendant social norms that evolve over time in response to the challenges of the human condition. It is a fact of human existence that we can live better as members of societies than by ourselves, for in societies we can assist each other in the achievement of our various ends – we can better enjoy both happiness and liberty as members of societies where our security is protected, activities are coordinated, and labor can be divided among us. Societies ought to be structured to best achieve the various ends that explain and justify them. Right-liberals argue that these ends are best achieved via the powers of free enterprise, private ownership of the means of production, free market exchange, and so on; this is the marriage of (economic) liberty and utility that holds together the right-liberal theory of distributive justice. It is a marriage that combines factual and normative claims in a powerful syllogism:

1. We ought to create the society that best secures the happiness of its members;
2. The system of liberty is the society that best secures the happiness of its members;
3. *So*, we should create the society that best approximates the system of liberty.

The factual and the normative premises of this syllogism can be (and have been) challenged. As described throughout this book, left-liberals, libertarians, and socialists all reject the normative premise (premise 1), but the point here is that the normative premise of the syllogism is founded on a view of what society is all about – namely, for its members to get what they want.

The basic framework for thinking about social organization, the state, and the design of the economy is thus a sort of indirect consequentialism. The state is simply another tool that emerged because it is useful for helping us better satisfy our preferences. The role of the state, then, is to secure the background system of rules that allows the system of liberty to function. The state should provide security of property and contract, work to prevent market failures such as monopolies, and assist in the provision of public goods. The central virtue of state institutions is efficiency: their excellence consists in being the most efficient instruments for the achievement of the happiness of the members of society.

The view of personhood that attends the right-liberal vision of society is that of persons as pursuers of maximal satisfaction of their preferences – i.e. as maximizers of expected utility. The person is conceived of as rationally self-interested. Rational self-interest is not egoism; rather, it means that persons try to maximize the satisfaction of their preferences, where preferences might or might not include the interests of others. An egoist has only her own happiness as motive; a rationally self-interested person may have the happiness of others among her motives. An egoist has no concern for moral restrictions on her behavior, except insofar as respecting these restrictions helps her achieve her own happiness; a rationally self-interested person might (but also might not) have among her interests an interest in behaving in a morally defensible fashion. The right-liberal conception of the person is thus not unnecessarily bleak or amoral, since it allows that altruistic and morally motivated behavior can be rational; but the right-liberal conception of the person is agnostic and nonjudgmental in that it does not require altruistic or morally motivated behavior. The person pursues the maximal satisfaction of her preferences. Rationality itself only constrains the formal properties of her preferences; it does not subject her preferences to substantial normative judgment, nor does rationality require that choice options be limited to those that withstand moral scrutiny by some moral standard external to rationality. The moral strictures that count are, rather, the rules that coordinate individually rational behavior for the benefit of all.

This view of the person is well developed and powerfully employed in the field of economics, which has had some success in describing and predicting human behavior. Decision theory and game theory have done much to study the details of this model of human behavior, and also promise to turn it from a descriptive into a normative theory – that is, a theory that can tell us what we should do to maximize the satisfaction of our preferences, given what we know about the world and other agents.

It is notable that the normativity of the right-liberal conception of the person is extremely limited: it is the normativity of rationality understood in terms of formal restrictions on the person's preference order and the consistency of their choices with what they prefer and know about the world. A person's preference order should satisfy minimal strictures of completeness, transitivity, symmetry, and, perhaps, a few others (see Informaton Box 6.1 The formal principles of rationality); and among the available choice options persons should pursue the one that has the highest expected utility, where utility simply means satisfaction of a weighted index of their preferences.

INFORMATION BOX 6.1 THE FORMAL PRINCIPLES OF RATIONALITY

Unlike a substantial description of rationality (which is the domain of ethics), a formal description of rationality (the domain of so-called decision theory) says nothing about what we *should* want, but merely lists a number of requirements on what we want and what choice options we should pursue, given what we want. The formal principles of rationality, accordingly, are of two kinds: those governing our preferences and those governing our choices.

There is some disagreement on what the necessary and sufficient principles for a rational preference order are, but there is consensus that our preferences should satisfy these minimal requirements:

- Completeness: for any two preferences, one is preferred to the other or they are equally preferred.
- Transitivity: for any three preferences, if the first is preferred to the second and the second to the third, then the first is preferred to the third. (Similarly for indifference: if a person is indifferent between two preferences and between one of these and a third, then she is indifferent between all three.)
- Symmetry: for any two preferences, if one is preferred to the other, then it is not the case that the other is preferred to the one.

These principles define minimal rationality of preferences. Once we have a rational preference order, we can combine it with our understanding of the world to rank different choice options according to how well they can be expected to satisfy our preferences. How exactly to define "expected" and "satisfy" are subjects of debate, but most decision theorists endorse some version of the principle of expected utility, which says that:

> Among choice options, it is rational to choose the one that has the highest expected utility; correlatively, it is irrational to choose a choice option if one or more of the alternative options have higher expected utility.

The expected utility of a choice option can be calculated as the summed products of utilities and probabilities of the possible outcomes. If, say, choice option "*a*" has five possible outcomes and these have utilities u_1, u_2, u_3, u_4, and u_5 and probabilities p_1, p_2, p_3, p_4, and p_5 respectively (probabilities must sum to 1), then the expected utility of that choice option is:

$$EU(a) = p_1 u_1 + p_2 u_2 + p_3 u_3 + p_4 u_4 + p_5 u_5$$

Once we have calculated the expected utility for all choice options, they can be ranked from high to low, and the principle of expected utility says that the rational choice is the option with the highest expected utility. If there is a tie for the highest expected utility, then the principle of expected utility does not provide a way to choose between them – in that case this principle would be indifferent, meaning that each option is equally good.

Right-liberals can take pride in the minimalism, broad appeal, and realism of their conception of the person. They take the accepted view of personhood from economics – a view that does not assume that we are motivated by moral considerations and does not tell us to become better persons than we already are – and then construct a vision of society from that, namely, society as the coming together of persons for mutual benefit, given their preference orders. The right-liberal view of society, then, is not an ideal to be pursued, but a hypothesis of how and why human societies exist; and the ideal is simply the society that best answers the why of this hypothesis.

2.2 Foundations of Left-Liberalism

Left-liberals do not see society primarily as a system of coordination between rationally self-interested persons; nor do they work from an understanding of how societies actually evolved to solve problems of coexistence. Instead, left-liberals claim that embedded in modern liberal democracies is an ideal of democratic society, namely, the ideal of society as a system of social cooperation between free and equal persons. Left-liberals claim that this ideal is explicitly or implicitly assumed by various central texts and practices of liberal democracies: constitutions and bills of rights, court procedures and procedural assumptions and habits, canonical speeches and writings, and the political debates surrounding elections and referenda. The central shared assumption of all these texts and practices is the democratic ideal. The left-liberal project can thus be conceived of as seeking internal consistency in the norms and practices of liberal democracies, and then telling us – that is, we who are committed to the ideal of liberal democracy – what this ideal really is and thereby informing our deliberations about how we can realize it.

Since the ideal of democratic society is one of cooperation rather than coordination, left-liberals argue that the pursuit of happiness – whether individual or in the aggregate – is subject to norms of reciprocity and fairness. The role of the state is to ensure that our rationally self-interested behavior takes place according to rules that make sure our choices are consistent with, and eventually express, the ideal of democratic society, which also requires that the benefits and burdens of social cooperation are fairly distributed among the members of society. Society should, of course, pursue efficiency as the right-liberals understand it, but this pursuit of efficiency is cooperative and must take place within, and is restricted by, rules that secure ongoing fairness.

This relation between utility (efficiency) and fairness (reciprocity) is repeated in the left-liberal conception of the person. Persons are conceived of as both rational and reasonable. That is, persons are rational in that they can order their preferences in accordance with the formal strictures of rationality, and choose among choice options in the manner that maximally satisfies their preferences; but persons are also reasonable, which means at least three things. First, reasonable persons do not allow unreasonable preferences to motivate their behavior, that is, they are not (or should not be) motivated by desires to dominate or belittle others, or by sadistic desires, or in other ways to find happiness in the misfortunes of others. Second, reasonable persons do not allow unjust choice options to figure into their ranking of choice options. It might be that a person could maximize her expected utility by engaging in rights-violating behavior, but a reasonable person would not consider that a live option. Third, this behavior-restricting side of reasonability also has a societal and principled direction. Reasonable persons would not propose unfair terms of cooperation to others, but are willing to offer and abide by fair terms of cooperation, as long as others are willing to do the same. In this manner, the notion of reasonability is tied to the idea of reciprocity, for reasonable persons are (only) willing to engage in cooperation with others on terms that these others could be expected to accept as free persons and from a standpoint of equality. This idea of reciprocity, in turn, points us to contractualism as the natural framework for thinking about principles of justice, for contractualism says that the basic normative principles of society are those that all members of society could agree to as free and equal persons.

Where right-liberals work from the descriptive to the normative (from the explanation of why we have societies to how we should organize them), left-liberals work from the normative to the ideal and then back to the normative. Left-liberals start with a disorganized set of norms and practices and work these into ideals of society and personhood, and these ideals of democratic society and democratic citizenship, in turn, can then be used to construct a framework for thinking about our basic normative commitments – the framework is the idea of the social contract (or the original position) and the normative commitments are the principles that issue from the properly constructed framework (that is, the principles of justice as fairness). Once the principles are in hand, they can direct our assessment of how our society falls short of complete justice and what we should do to get closer to our ideal of a democratic society.

2.3 Foundations of Libertarianism

Libertarianism does not start with a normative conception of society or personality. That is, libertarians reject that there is some ideal of society or personhood or some specific end (such as happiness or perfection) that should guide our political choices. What matters for libertarians is that people freely choose what to do for themselves and as collectives, and whether their choices make them happy, or good, or collectively achieve an ideal of democratic society is neither here nor there when it comes to thinking about the requirements of justice.

So, in terms of a vision of society, the libertarians see a society created through the voluntary choices of its members – and any society thus created is ideal, since it expresses and is consistent with the liberty of its members. There is no utopia, but a vision of society as realizing whatever utopias its members have and agree to try to create together (cf. Nozick's *Anarchy, State, and Utopia*, Chapter 8). Just about any sort of society is permissible, be it a Hayekian system of liberty, a Rawlsian democracy, a socialist commune, or even monarchies or aristocracies designed for the benefit of one or some, as long as these are created through the voluntary consent of the members. And only for that long; since no person could be subjected to the authority of others except through their consent, these societies must be continually regenerated through the consent of new generations.

The state, meaning the institutional body entrusted with the authority to use force to secure the rights of its members and to tax its members for that purpose, is special in that it can extend its authority even to those resting within its territory who do not explicitly consent to become subjects to it. The state is simply a comprehensive and dominant protection association – it is not a tool for the pursuit of some common good, except the good of security of rights, and any attempt to use it to promote the happiness of its members, their virtue, or external standard of distributive fairness is impermissible, unless, of course, the members all agreed to use it for that purpose.

The conception of the person embedded in the libertarian theory of justice is that of the person as self-author, meaning that persons have authority to decide for themselves what to do, rather than be subjected to the authority of others, except where they violate the rights of others. All are equally limited by the natural and acquired rights of others, but when all act within these limits, any set of choices and outcomes resulting from those choices realizes the libertarian ideals of society and personhood as exercises of mutually consistent liberty.

The libertarian views of society and personhood are at the same time extremely permissive and extremely restrictive. They are permissive, insofar as a person can be and do whatever they want, as long as they respect the rights of others, and since any social organization that can be generated by voluntary consent could be just. They are restrictive, insofar as they limit political authority to the minimal state and what is generated through actual consent.

2.4 Foundations of Socialism

Like left-liberalism, socialism works from ideals of human society and personhood, but unlike left-liberalism, socialism does not elicit these from the public political culture of liberal democracies, but rather constructs them from philosophical ideals and then uses them to criticize liberal democracies. As I reconstructed socialism in Chapter 5, this theory of justice rests on ideas of how human beings ought to relate to themselves and each other. Socialism is, in a word, a sort of perfectionism; it presents us with a vision of what we ought to be and how we ought to relate to each other and elicits from this vision the principles of justice that fit this vision. The structure of socialism is like that of right-liberalism in that it starts with an end and then presents the principles of justice as means to that end, but, unlike right-liberalism, the end it starts with is not happiness or preference satisfaction, it is not utility or *subjective* human goodness (happiness); instead the end is *objectively* good human living (perfection).

It bears repeating that my reconstruction of socialism as a perfectionist sort of consequentialism could (and likely would) be contested by many socialists. Some socialists might argue that what defines socialism is the principles of justice that socialists affirm – primarily principles of equality of opportunity and outcome – and the commitment to a socialized economic system as an alternative to capitalism. Other socialists might argue that there are other foundational views of society and personhood than those I have articulated on behalf of socialism.

Nevertheless, perfectionism offers a defense of the socialist principles of justice and institutional commitments, and there are additional meta-theoretical reasons to read socialism along these lines (I return to these meta-theoretical reasons in the following chapter).

The main ideas of socialism as I understand them, then, are that persons ought to realize their potential for good human living in productive society with others, which implies that they ought to relate to others in the manner of community and friendship (as ends in themselves), rather than as obstacles and opportunities for the maximization of rational self-interest. The socialist can thus accept the formal constraints on rationality discussed in the presentation of right-liberalism, and the constraints on preferences and choice options discussed in the presentation of left-liberalism, but add substantial positive demands on what people *should prefer*. That is, socialism as I understand it argues that the preference orders of persons ought to incorporate the ends of others as if they were their own ends – just as we (should) do in families and close friendships, but extended to all members of society (in the limit, to all of humanity so that humanity should be a community).

The ideal of society, accordingly, is that of *community*, of people living together and cooperating in the manner of friendship, so that all contribute what they can to the cooperative enterprise, because it helps others (and not merely to help themselves as in the right- and left-liberal ideals). In such a society (and in our attempts to approximate the ideal of such a society), the state serves as an instrument to achieve and maintain this end; the state of affairs where all develop and exercise their economic powers in a cooperative venture that benefits all and *because* it benefits all and not merely for self-interested gain.

3 The Subject, Role, and Principles of Economic Justice

Because of their different visions of society and personhood, the theories support different views of what economic justice is about and issue different principles of economic justice.

3.1 Economic Justice and Right-Liberalism

For right-liberals, justice is the rules that best allow us to achieve the ends of society: the liberty and utility of its members. The main virtue of just institutions is thus one of efficiency, of maximally well supporting the achievement of these aims.

Right-liberals argue that the aims of liberty and utility go hand in hand – this is the marriage of liberty and utility that I've described as the nodal belief of right-liberalism. Because they believe that liberty and utility go hand in hand, right-liberals can reaffirm these values as also the principle requirements of justice. That is, the requirements of justice are mainly two:

- First, the principle of liberty, which says that that all members of society should be free to decide for themselves what to do as long as their choices do not violate the equal liberty of others.
- Second, the principle of utility, which says that the state should play a supporting role in promoting utility.

The principle of utility also can support a sufficientarian principle, so that one of the supporting roles of the state can be to secure that no member of society lives in absolute poverty – not because poverty itself is unjust, but because (and insofar as) it is an enemy of utility.

3.2 Economic Justice and Left-Liberalism

For left-liberals, justice is the rules that secure a fair system of social cooperation between free and equal persons. The main virtue of just institutions is that of fairness, of treating members as free and equal and securing that their dealings in the economy are consistent with the basic norms of reciprocity and fairness appropriate to a democratic society.

These norms are defined by the three principles of justice as fairness. All members of society should enjoy the basic rights sufficient to enable their cooperation as free and equal persons – that is, the full development and exercise of the moral powers of democratic citizenship. Members should carry only a fair share of the burdens of cooperation, and should thus enjoy fair equality of opportunity for access to the various positions and offices through which cooperation is conducted and to which the benefits of cooperation are attached. And those who receive least of the benefits of cooperation should receive more than the least well off would in an alternative economy.

3.3 Economic Justice and Libertarianism

For libertarians, justice is the rules that define the system of original rights, rights acquisition, and the exercise of original and acquired rights. A society is fully just when persons enjoy their rights as these have been generated through the permissible exercise of their original rights from a situation of original equal rights, or when all rights-violations have been rectified. The main virtue of just institutions is thus that they secure basic and acquired rights, settle disputes about rights, and effectively rectify any rights-violations.

There is only one principle of justice in the libertarian theory: the principle of liberty. People should be free to decide what to do with and for themselves, as long as they don't violate the equal liberty of others. The libertarian method is to tie the principle of liberty to the rights that people may have, so that all rights are of three kinds: first, rights of liberty (to not be interfered with unless one violates the rights of others); second, rights that define how this original liberty can be exercised to acquire additional rights by original acquisition or by interpersonal agreements; and, third, these acquired rights. The libertarian can thus say that there are no rights other than those that define and are mandated by the principle of liberty.

3.4 Economic Justice and Socialism

For socialism, justice is the rules that best allow us to achieve the ends of objectively good human living: personal self-realization in community with others. The main virtue of just institutions, accordingly, is one of efficiency, of maximally well assisting us in achieving this end.

Socialists argue that community presupposes equality – equality of status and power, equality of opportunity, and equality (or equity) of outcome in the sense that equally deserving persons are equally well-off. Where the right-liberal sees a marriage of liberty and utility, the socialist sees a marriage of equality and perfection: the way to objectively good human living is material equality. Socialists will also insist that a socialist society is one where the members are happy and free, and freedom is itself an aspect of objectively good living. But, I do not think that socialists are committed to happiness as a requirement or concern of justice; rather, we want to be happy and it is reassuring that socialism promises a society where happiness is possible for all.

4 Economic Rights and Liberties

One way to pursue the distinction between the different theories of distributive justice is to focus on their different theories of economic rights and liberties. *Rights* are normative relations between persons; relations such as privileges, claims, powers, and immunities. A system of legal rights distributes these relations and thereby defines what is legally permitted, prohibited, and required for a given domain of justice. *A liberty* is a right that protects some sphere of activity (or bundle of activities) from interference so that, first, neither the state nor other citizens may interfere with the exercise of that activity except for weighty reasons, and, second, the state has an obligation to protect citizens in the enjoyment of that activity. In short, the state must respect and protect a liberty. How weighty the reasons for interference must be depends on the level of priority of the liberty.

The (written or unwritten) constitution of a legal system normally defines how legal rights can be generated and enumerates basic rights. Such *basic rights* typically combine different incidents: they grant some privilege, claim, or power to all citizens, require that the state secures these rights from infringement, and also grant immunity from having these rights taken away or altered by the state or members of society; basic rights are, in short, inviolable and inalienable. Different theories about the normative origins of basic rights (why some rights are basic) can generate different views on the priority of basic rights (the level of priority basicness confers) and different lists of basic rights (what rights are basic).

The weight of a right is how important it is relative to other social concerns. In terms of liberties, weight determines the limits and obligations of political authority: the weightier the liberty, the less that sphere of agency can be regulated for the sake of other social goods (and the more important is its protection). In theory, there is a continuum of weights, but the three important ones are:

- Absolute liberties (highest weight): where the sphere of agency can be regulated only to secure that *it* is respected and protected for all.
- A basic liberty (medium weight): constitutional guarantees, where the sphere of agency can be regulated only to secure the full scheme or system of basic liberties is provided equally for all.
- The presumption of liberty (minimum weight): where the sphere of agency can be *regulated for the sake of other social pursuits* such as utility or fairness.

Economic rights are concerned with economic agency: work, investing, banking, the production and consumption of goods and services, exchanging or contracting for goods and services in the marketplace, the activities engaging property, and so on. Economic liberties are economic rights that protect various aspects of economic agency from interference by the state or other persons. These include: liberties of working (to employ one's body and mind in productive activities according to terms to which one freely consents); liberties of transacting (to save and invest, to start, run, and close commercial enterprises, to hire workers, display, advertise, and sell one's products or services); and ownership rights (to hold and transfer property, to sell, invest, bequeath, consume, destroy, or otherwise do as one pleases with one's resources).

One divisive question is whether we should grant any economic liberties the status and priority of basic rights: Which, if any, economic liberties are basic rights? To be clearer, it's helpful to distinguish three dimensions of the answer to this question; that is, a theory of economic liberties specifies the three parts of the answer to this question:

1. Range: What economic liberties should the members of society enjoy?
2. Significance: What is the weight of these liberties (what reasons are sufficiently strong to limit or otherwise regulate the exercise of these liberties)?
3. Grounding: Why do these liberties have this level of priority?

The question, then, is which economic liberties should have which weights and why. The four main theories of distributive justice can be distinguished by their answers to these questions.

4.1 Economic Rights and Liberties in Right-Liberalism

Recall that right-liberalism is a sort of indirect utilitarianism. The main goal is social prosperity (the happiness of the members of society), but this goal is pursued via the system of liberty, that is, the system of rules that secures a wide range of economic liberties for all members of society. Individual choices made within this system of liberty need not aim to promote social utility, for (so right-liberals believe) the self-interested pursuit of personal utility that takes place within the system of liberty will tend to promote social utility – at least in the aggregate and in the long run.

Right-liberals thus grant high priority to the full range of economic liberties. Indeed, right-liberals tend to treat economic liberties as on par with the other basic liberties common to liberal democracies, such as security of the person, freedom of religion, and freedom of speech. Of course, this indirect utilitarianism implies that economic liberties can be regulated as needed to secure social utility – but in this they remain on par with other rights and liberties given high priority by right-liberals.

The instrumentalist defense that right-liberals provide for rights and liberties can be a weakness. Right-liberals may be criticized by utilitarians that question the importance of rights for the promotion of utility; if what we really care about is promoting happiness, then we should violate rights when it promotes happiness to do so. Conversely, right-liberals can be criticized by less utilitarianly inclined liberals such as libertarians, who argue that the indirect utilitarian framework fails to capture the normative importance of high priority liberties, which is precisely their ability to trump and override utilitarian (or other consequentialist) justifications of law or policy.

Another problem is that the indirect utilitarian argument cannot establish that economic liberties should be *equally* enjoyed by all members of society, for a system of unequal economic liberties might better promote social utility; an outcome that seems contradictory to the liberal tradition that right-liberals claim to carry. At best, right-liberalism provides a conditional justification for equal economic liberties, a justification that depends on empirical beliefs that might be false.

4.2 Economic Rights and Liberties in Left-Liberalism

Left-liberals tend to assign economic liberties low importance. According to Rawls, only two categories of economic liberties should enjoy the priority of a basic right: the right to possess and have exclusive use of personal property, and free choice of occupation. Apart from these two, the activities of economic agency can, and should, be regulated as needed to realize the fair value of political liberties, equality of opportunity, and a fair and efficient distribution of income and wealth.

Unfortunately, Rawls does not offer much of an argument as to why most economic liberties have low priority. Given his contractualist framework and the role of basic rights in enabling social cooperation between free and equal persons, and how he understands this cooperation as engaging the two moral powers, his argument must be that most economic liberties are *not* necessary for the adequate development or exercise of either of the moral powers. But the details of this argument are unclear. It is clear why Rawls needs to establish that only a limited range of economic liberties are basic rights, for if they all were there would be little the state could do to secure the other principles of justice as fairness – i.e. fair equality of opportunity and the difference principle – and Rawls's justice as fairness would then require a Hayekian constitution of liberty! But the need for an argument is not an argument, and it is unclear how Rawls's argument would go.

4.3 Economic Rights and Liberties in Libertarianism

Libertarians are inclined to grant the full range of economic liberties the highest priority. Natural rights of noninterference combined with rights of acquisition and transfer, and whatever one has acquired by a justice-preserving transaction, entail that persons should enjoy maximal freedom to decide what to do in their economic affairs. The full range of economic liberties can thus only be regulated as needed to secure that all enjoy their original and acquired rights – and cannot be regulated for the sake of efficiency or fairness.

One difficulty for libertarians is that the libertarian view of economic liberties seems to carry some costly commitments. If economic rights are absolute, there is very little the state may do to protect the poor from exploitation or to provide for those who cannot provide for themselves; for any pursuit of a sufficientarian guarantee seems to require (redistributive) taxation that is proscribed by the economic rights protecting property.

Moreover, if freedom of contract is absolute, then libertarianism seems to allow contracts of prostitution, slavery, and perhaps even the sale of bodily organs such as kidneys or hearts. These permissions are concerning, especially so in light of the impermissibility of the state serving a role in limiting absolute poverty. The absolutely poor might face a choice between starvation and a terrible contract – a mother might have to choose between her kids starving and a contract to sell her heart in exchange for food for her children. The libertarian position seems to permit the situation of poverty that creates such choices, to sanction such contracts, and even to require that the state use its power to enforce them, insofar as they are fully informed and voluntary. If this conclusion is absurd, then there is a fault somewhere in the libertarian position.

4.4 Economic Rights and Liberties in Socialism

The views sketched above rely on the distinction between liberty and ability or "freedom." A citizen's liberty is the set of liberty rights that the state ought to respect and protect. Ability or freedom is what a person can do with her liberties, the set of options available to her. Liberals – whether right-, left-, or libertarian – see the abilities and means needed to exercise one's liberties as conceptually and normatively distinct from liberties themselves. A person can be said to fully possess a liberty even if she is unable or lacks the means to exercise it; a person too sick or too poor to travel has no less liberty of movement than the healthy or wealthy, though she is, of course, less free to travel than the wealthy and the healthy. The liberal approaches to liberties all maintain that the main role of the state when it comes to (economic) liberties is to respect and protect these liberties, not to secure for all the abilities and means needed to exercise them (left-liberals maintain that the state should provide for the means for exercising political rights in order to secure equal political power for all citizens and also require that all have a fair share of the means for exercising their rights and liberties).

As described in the chapter on socialism, socialists reject the liberal distinction between liberty and freedom and object to what they see as a liberal conflation of "inability" and "lack of means." Lack of means, especially money, legally restricts the exercise of a liberty. This objection can support two further socialist critiques of liberal theories of economic liberty. The first criticism is aimed at the right-liberal view of economic liberties as the primary instruments of social prosperity: if basic rights are enjoyed only when the necessary means for their enjoyment are available, then the economic liberties can and should be regulated as needed to ensure for all citizens the means for enjoying the full scheme of basic liberties, *whether or not the economic liberties themselves are basic.* For socialists, a thorough regulation of the activities of economic agency is thus consistent with taking the full range of economic liberties as basic. Second, if having a liberty includes having access to the means to exercise it, then having an economic liberty includes having access to the means to engage in that sphere of economic agency. The right to property is not, as liberals tend to understand it, a negative right that protects holders of property against interference from others; rather, the right to hold property is exactly that, a right to actually hold property. So, if the liberties of ownership require that all members of society have more or less equal access to ownership of property (whether personal or productive), then the economic liberties can be protected and respected only in a system that secures access to equal ownership of property for all, that is, in a socialist economic system with socialized ownership of the means of production.

Thus, socialists can agree with liberals that the state has a role in protecting economic liberty, but maintain that liberals mistake this role. When the liberal state "respects" economic liberty by not regulating economic agency and ownership of productive property, the members of society are prevented from taking democratic control of their economy and thereby securing true economic liberty for all. When the liberal state "protects" economic liberties by forcefully preventing interferences with the established entitlements of a capitalist society, it enforces a distribution of entitlements and contractual obligations whereby the majority of citizens have no capital other than their human capital, and so are prevented from enjoying their economic liberties. Socialists thus argue that the liberal theories of economic liberty serve as part of the ideology of capitalism that justifies using the state as a means of oppressing the unpropertied classes.

5 Equality of Opportunity

The notion that the members of a society should enjoy equal opportunity for access to careers and offices is hard to deny. There is a sense that without equality of opportunity a society must be straightforwardly unfair; the members play the game for advantages on an uneven playing field, where the outcome of this game is a result of their unequal opportunities as much as of their choices or luck. Few believe that economic justice requires equality of outcome, and it is often offered as reply to outcome egalitarians that unequal outcomes are just, as long as they result from choices made within a system of equal opportunity – suggesting that equality of opportunity is at least a minimal requirement of distributive fairness, and perhaps also all there is to it. But, where left-liberals and socialists have different views on what equality of opportunity requires, right-liberals and libertarians reject that it is a requirement of justice at all; in part, at least, because they reject that economic justice is about fairness.

5.1 Equality of Opportunity and Right-Liberalism

Right-liberalism rejects that justice is about fairness and argues that the pursuit of equal opportunity undermines the creation of social utility. There should not, of course, be any discrimination in laws, the administration of the state, or the labor market. The state must treat all members equally, so public discrimination is out of the question. Discrimination in the labor market is also impermissible. The most productive system rewards value, which is invariant with the usual bases of discrimination such as race, gender, or religious affiliation. Right-liberals can question whether it is necessary to have anti-discrimination laws on the books, for, in theory, the market should give a competitive edge to employers who do not discriminate as these can draw from a larger talent pool. Yet, there might be instances where this is not true (say, if most of the consumers of a product in the service sector are white and prefer white employees), in which case right-liberals can accept anti-discrimination laws.

The right-liberal rejection of equality of opportunity as a norm of justice has three parts. First, justice is about utility and liberty, not about fairness, so the usual reasons offered in favor of equality of opportunity have little traction in the right-liberal framework. Right-liberals can allow that a system without equal opportunity is not fair, but that's not the same as *un*fair. It is not fair when people get sick or someone wins the lottery, but that's not the same as saying it is unfair – the standard of fairness simply doesn't apply to these cases, and right-liberals argue that the same goes for the distribution of economic benefits and burdens.

Second, right-liberals argue that the pursuit of equality of opportunity requires intrusive and destructive government interference with many spheres of society. To equalize opportunity, we might have to limit what the talented may do with their talents; and full equality of opportunity seems to require intrusive interference with how families decide to invest their resources.

Third, if what we care about is opportunity, then why not seek to *maximize* the opportunities available to members of society rather than equalize them? This variant of the leveling down objection points out that it is very easy to equalize opportunity; we can simply eliminate all but one sort of education and one sort of job, but that would hardly be a desirable society. It is better to create a society where there are opportunities for all members to develop and pursue their own ideas of the good life, and if we want to maximize opportunity we should institute the system of liberty, where the choices of each continually create new opportunities for others.

5.2 Equality of Opportunity and Left-Liberalism

But, left-liberals say, justice *is* about fairness – what matters is not simply that we maximize utility or opportunity, but that we cooperate as free and equal persons in the pursuit of utility and opportunity. Cooperation should be fair, and so must secure equality of opportunity for all. We should not, of course, try to eliminate the differential distribution of natural talents or invest all our resources in developing the talents of the less talented. We should, rather, allow the market to reward value by paying the talented for the profitable employment of their talents, but we should also see to it that the economic inequalities thus generated do not undermine the fair value of political rights, and aim to ensure that these inequalities satisfy the notion of reciprocity appropriate to democratic society – meaning that these inequalities should be to the advantage of the least well-off (as required by the difference principle). Moreover, while the state may not intrude on the right of families to choose how to invest their resources (for such intrusion would violate the rights of the first principle), the state should nevertheless seek to minimize the effects of the social lottery by making sure that access to education and healthcare is equal and adequate for all, no matter their family or economic circumstances.

This, then, is the left-liberal idea of *fair equality of opportunity*: the distribution of the benefits and burdens of social cooperation, should, as far as can be achieved without violating any basic rights of citizens, be a function of talents and choices. The distribution of the economic benefits of cooperation is also subject to the further requirements of the difference principle.

5.3 Equality of Opportunity and Libertarianism

Libertarians find no basis for the left-liberal requirements of equal opportunity. If all start from an initial situation of equal liberty and then exercise their liberty in a manner that is consistent with the equal liberty of others, then all have formal equal opportunity. Various sorts of luck might lead to unequal outcomes, but that violates no rights and so is of no concern to justice.

5.4 Equality of Opportunity and Socialism

Socialists argue that left-liberals fail to recognize that the commitment to equal opportunity is violated insofar as the distribution of burdens and rewards is a function of the differential distribution of natural talents. If the more talented get more interesting, less burdensome, or better paying jobs, then it is untrue that there is equal opportunity between the more and the less talented. So, if we want to secure equality of opportunity, then we must deal with this particular source of inequality. There are many ways to do so, but two stand out: first, we might tax the talented at a higher rate to eliminate the economic inequalities generated by differential luck in the natural lottery; or, second, we might insist that the less attractive jobs are rotated among members of society, so that all members carry their fair share of the burdens. In any case, socialists argue that those who are committed to norms of fairness should embrace the more demanding notion of equality of opportunity as requiring the elimination of effects of both the social lottery and of the natural lottery.

Since fairness is necessary (but not sufficient) for community, socialists should embrace this requirement of equality of opportunity – though they might do so hesitantly, for, at the end of the day, this notion of equality of opportunity as ensuring a fair competition for the sharing of the burdens and benefits of cooperation rests on a mistaken view of what society should be. In a true community, the economy is *not a competition* but a *collaboration* where each supplies what they can for the benefit of all, and in return is supplied with what they need, independently of the "value to others" of what they supply. So, the socialists favor a meritocratic route to the idea of equality of opportunity, a route which says that welfare should be proportionate to merit and that equality of opportunity is a necessary condition for ensuring this proportionality, at least in circumstances where true community is yet to be achieved. In a true communist utopia there would be equal opportunity, but it would serve no role and would not be a requirement as much as a condition.

6 The Choice of Economic System

One of the basic societal choices is the choice of economic system. While there are alternatives, it seems that the main choice is between varieties of capitalism and socialism. As described towards the end of the chapter on socialism, this choice is really a choice of where to aim for on three distinct scales of choice:

1. Whether the ownership of the means of production should be private or social;

2. Whether production should be geared towards profits or needs satisfaction; and
3. Whether production and the flow of inputs and outputs of production should be determined by market forces or by public officials on behalf of society as a whole.

A fully capitalist economy has private ownership of all the means of production, production is geared towards profits for those who own the means of production, and the various parts of the productive process are governed by the choices of economically rational players aiming to serve their own interests by interacting in free markets. Conversely, a fully socialist economy has completely socialized ownership of the means of production, employs the productive processes to satisfy the needs of the members of society, and has the state control production and the distribution of inputs and outputs with that end in mind.

6.1 The Economic System and Right-Liberalism

Right-liberalism implies that we should aim for an economy that is close to the fully capitalist extreme on all three scales. The positive reason is that the system of liberty harnesses private enterprise to social utility. The negative reason is that no alternative to private enterprise can do nearly as well in terms of providing the members of society with what they want. Thus, right-liberals argue, while the productive and distributive processes in a capitalist society are driven by self-interest, no system would actually do better at satisfying the needs of the members of society – not even a system designed and directed for that purpose by the smartest and least corrupt minds of society. A socialist economy cannot achieve the magic combination of rational self-interest, voluntary exchange, the price mechanism, and rewards attached to market value that a capitalist economy achieves so effortlessly. In addition, because of the ignorance of public officials, and because we should expect them to also use their power for their own gain and not purely for the social good, socialist economies tend towards inefficiency and corruption. Thus, right-liberalism says, of the available options, a fully capitalist society maximizes utility.

6.2 The Economic System and Left-Liberalism

Left-liberals are ambivalent when it comes to the choice of economic system. On the one hand, left-liberals are impressed by the productive powers of capitalism; after all, left-liberals view society as a system of social cooperation for the production and distribution of the resources that we need to pursue our various conceptions of the good life, so it is not irrelevant that capitalism seems to do better than other systems in terms of raw productivity. As described above, in theory capitalism provides for a sort of equality of opportunity where people's chances in life are determined at least in part by their talents (by their ability to deliver something that others value), rather than arbitrary factors such as one's race, religion, or the connections of one's parents. There is a deep egalitarianism in capitalism, insofar as the labor market values all persons blindly in terms of what they offer that is of value to potential employers – and, formally, all are equally free to set up their own shop and try their luck at being capitalists.

However, there are some problems that seem inherent to all sorts of capitalism, even the tempered sorts of welfare-state capitalist societies we know from Northern European social democracies, and these problems are so grave that left-liberals might reject capitalism (cf. Rawls, *Justice as Fairness: A Restatement*, 137–8). First, all sorts of capitalist economies allow for vast inequalities of wealth, as wealth (including real capital) tends to accumulate in the hands of some, while others own little more than their labor-power, incidentals, a car, and perhaps their house or apartment. These wealth inequalities tend to aggravate inequality of income from labor, itself already rather dramatic in capitalist economies, since wealth by itself generates income (e.g. rents or capital gains). Moreover, wealth inequality tends to increase faster than the growth rate of the economy, so income from capital grows faster than income from labor (Thomas Piketty explores this tendency in *Capital in the 21st Century*). These economic inequalities are not necessarily objectionable as such from the standpoint of left-liberalism, but they tend to translate almost directly into further, deeply problematic, inequalities of status, political influence, and economic opportunity. The wealthy might use their resources to seek additional political influence – and even if they do not, the mere fact that their wealth gives them access to more political power than less wealthy citizens violates the fair value guarantee for political rights that is required by the first principle of justice. Moreover, the wealthy might use their wealth to purchase better education or other means for increasing the prospects of their children, which violates the sort of fair equality of opportunity required by the second principle.

Moreover, while a capitalist society might provide a sufficientarian guarantee so that no members live in absolute poverty, this guarantee is also part of a system where the least well-off are kept as dependents, without opportunity to enjoy one of the main bases of self-respect; the exercise of economic agency in cooperation with others on a footing of equality. When the social minimum is provided in the form of welfare payments that keep those left without adequate employment opportunities out of material poverty, then these members of society are no longer provided avenues of full and equal citizenship, but are left behind; sacrificed in the service of the higher utility that accrues to the better-off. Capitalism, and the underlying concern for efficiency, permits (might even require) the creation of an underclass of welfare recipients that are effectively barred from participating as equals in the economy and, thereby, from accessing the opportunities and sources of self-respect tied to participation in social cooperation. Such a welfare-state social minimum may suffice to alleviate suffering and avoid unrest and thus serve well when measured by the utilitarian foundations of right-liberalism; but this welfare state also treats the least well-off as a problem to be dealt with, rather than as equal participants in productive processes with equal claims to receive a fair share of the benefits, and to carry their fair share of the burdens of cooperation.

So, left-liberals seem committed to finding an alternative to capitalism, but does that mean they must be socialists? Rawls did not think so. According to Rawls, there are two sorts of economic systems that can satisfy the requirements of justice as fairness: liberal socialism and property-owning democracy. Liberal socialism secures the rights and liberties of the first principle and seeks an efficient economy by employing markets and the profit motive as drivers of production and distribution, even while the ownership of the means of production is fully socialized (the details of how this combination can be made to work is a very interesting question that has been the subject of some innovative work in recent political economy). In property-owning democracies, by contrast, ownership of the means of production may or may not be socialized, but property-owning democracies are committed to finding some way for all citizens to enjoy roughly equal ownership of the means of production – which may be done by distributing the means of production into roughly equal privately owned shares.

Whether, and how, liberal socialism or property-owning democracy offers a truly feasible and efficient alternative to capitalism remains an open question, and it seems to be one of left-liberalism's weaker spots that it leaves us wanting for an account of a feasibly accessible economy that would both satisfy the requirements of justice as fairness and provide an efficient system for the production and distribution of the things we want and for which we cooperate.

6.3 The Economic System and Libertarianism

Libertarianism establishes full capitalism as the default economic system. Freedom of property and contract and the absence of any public authority other than that which is generated by the consent of those subjected to it entails that the state should play no role in owning productive property or interfering with people's pursuit of their self-interest, except as needed to secure the rights of all or as mandated in the contract that created its authority. Such a contract *might* grant the state ownership of some or all the means of production in some jurisdiction and for its duration, so, libertarianism does not disallow socialism. However, this socialism has to be generated by the actual consent of those that are part of the socialist system and from the capitalism that is the default. (Left-libertarians find other ways from the principle of liberty to socialism, cf. Chapter 4, Section 5.)

6.4 The Economic System and Socialism

To no one's surprise, socialism mandates a socialist design of the economy. *Yet*, there is much debate in contemporary socialism about the degree to which one can run a socialist economy – that is, one where the ownership of the means of production is socialized – while at the same time employing the profit motive and free markets to determine who produces what, using what inputs, and selling it at what price. Socialism, as a theory of justice, mandates socialized ownership of the means of production, but might not mandate complete socialism in that it can allow an economy that is closer to the capitalist end of the spectrum in the other two dimensions. This flexibility offers an avenue for socialists that are impressed with the productive powers of capitalism and the way in which these productive powers rely on the profit motive, the price mechanism, and so forth (that is, socialists who are more or less convinced by Hayekian critiques of completely socialist systems with planned economies and so on), and yet want to avoid the structures of inequality, unfreedom, domination, exploitation, and alienation that they see as inevitable consequences of capitalism. The big question is whether it is enough to avoid these capitalist maladies to shed private ownership of the means of production, for these maladies seem equally caused by the other two dimensions of capitalism. Hayekians might smile at the new socialist political economies, for they will say that productivity (utility) and liberty go hand in hand, so the attempt to have one without the other must fail – and also that socialists exaggerate the maladies of capitalism and underestimate what capitalism can become in the future.

7 Views on Democracy

The four theories of distributive justice have different views on democracy. To understand these, it is helpful to distinguish between three different normative concepts of democracy. First, there is democracy as *popular sovereignty*. Sovereignty is authority to make laws and decide in political matters, and this concept of democracy says that political authority must issue from and serve the people (*demos*) understood as a collective entity rather than some subset of the members of the people. This concept of democracy implies the idea of the rule of law, so that political authority must be exercised in accordance with laws that express and serve the will of the people (the general will) rather than some particular person's (particular wills). Alternatives to democracy in this sense are alternative concepts of sovereignty; say, those that place sovereignty in a king or an aristocracy, or those that deny that popular sovereignty is really possible, since there is no such thing as "the people."

The norm of popular sovereignty also has an international dimension to it. By this notion, a nation (or a nation-state) has authority to organize its affairs as it sees fit, free from undue interference from other nations, though subject to constraints such as those of human rights, just war theory, and environmental concerns.

Second, there is the concept of democracy as a way to generate legislation. In this concept, democracy is the collection of procedures that secures citizens equal access to the processes by which laws and political authority are generated. These procedures might include regular and universal voting in free and fair elections, representative legislatures accountable to their constituents, the struggle of free political parties, freedom of speech and the press, the will of the majority or supermajorities carrying the legislative agenda, and so on. There are many candidate combinations of procedures and rights that express this concept of democracy, depending on who gets to vote, whether all votes are equally weighty, what voters get to vote for, how regularly they vote, how large a share of the vote carries the day, and so on. One prominent debate about these questions is among those defending direct democracy (vote is for laws) and representative democracy (vote is for representatives that then legislate). The alternatives to this concept of democracy are alternative views on how legislative authority should be generated, say, by a council of experts, drawing of lots, or despotic government.

The first concept of democracy (as popular sovereignty) does *not* imply the second concept (as procedures for generating legislation), for it may be that alternative procedures, say, a council of experts or a supercomputer, would do better at legislating the will of the people than the people would by voting. The first concept of democracy is about the basic constitutional commitment of society (who rules), the second is about how to carry out this institutional commitment (how rule is generated), and while the two seem naturally inclined to each other, there's not strict implication from one to the other.

The third concept of democracy is democracy as an ideal of free and equal coexistence. Here the norm is that no person should be subjected to or dominated by the will of others, except insofar as they did or could agree to said objection, so that the rule to which they are subjected is nothing but the rule of their own will as mediated by the delegation of authority. Where the norm of popular sovereignty says that the will of the people is the sole source of political authority, this third concept of democracy says that political authority must express the will of individual members of the people. Here, the idea is really one of individual liberty as political autonomy; of individual persons being rulers of themselves, so that political authority must somehow express their own volition. Again, this third concept inclines towards the second concept of democracy as procedures for generating legislation, but there is no strict implication. It might be that, say, a lottocracy (legislators appointed by lot) or a council of experts would do better at issuing legislation that expresses the will of each member of society. It is, in any case, tricky to see how majority rule is consistent with this third concept of democracy, for when the majority carries the day, it does so against the explicit will of the minority. Those who defend this concept of democracy accordingly envision a two-step generation of political authority: first, the members of society agree to be parts of a society where legislation is determined by a voting process and where the majority vote carries the day, and then, secondly, the actual voting by which legislation expressing the will of the majority carries the day. Since all members have (or could have or should have) agreed to this process for generating legislation, they have no complaint even if when they are in the minority. Indeed, it might be said that the legislation expresses their free choice (to be subjected to the will of the majority), and that they are merely forced to be free when they are forced to comply with the will of the majority, for they are forced to comply with their own voluntary choice to be subjected to the authority thus generated.

One could construct a theory of democracy that brings all three concepts together in a unified framework, but the concepts themselves need not be constructed within such a framework.

7.1 Right-Liberalism and Democracy

Right-liberalism reluctantly embraces the second concept of democracy – that is, democracy as political decision procedure – as the least worst of the known alternatives. However, right-liberalism is not committed in principle to either of the first or third concepts of democracy. Right-liberals are wary of the idea of popular sovereignty, as it might imply a notion of collective agency that they reject – there are no agents or will in addition to the members of society and what they want – and also of the third concept, since they see the primary purpose of the political as the generation of rules that best serve the end of social prosperity, whether or not the members of society actually agree that this is the proper end (though they generally would, of course, insofar as social prosperity is nothing but the composite satisfaction of the wants of the members of society). Of course, right-liberals wholeheartedly defend the rule of law and the idea that no person should be subjected to the arbitrary rule of others, but do so without adopting the ideas of popular sovereignty or claims of liberty as political autonomy.

7.2 Left-Liberalism and Democracy

Left-liberals of the Rawlsian variety take the third notion of democracy as their foundational starting point: justice is the rules that allow us to best achieve the ideal of society as a system of social cooperation between free and equal persons. They also tend to believe that democratic procedures (the second concept) are necessary for realizing this ideal, in part for the reasons that Rawls gives when he includes the political rights and liberties in the first principle of justice and argues that political rights enjoy a fair value guarantee. If not for these, citizens could not relate to each other as free and equal in the making of the laws of society – they would not develop and/or exercise the sense of justice appropriate to the ideal of how democratic citizens ought to relate to each other.

7.3 Libertarianism and Democracy

Given its basic commitment to individual liberty, libertarianism can incorporate the third concept of democracy, but give it a stringent interpretation whereby the consent that creates political authority must be actual rather than normative or hypothetical consent. That is, political authority must be generated from the express will of those subjected to it; it does not matter whether they ought to consent to it or what they might consent to under some description of a hypothetical social contract.

Libertarians are, accordingly, not particularly wedded to democracy as a political decision procedure. The members of society *might* decide to use democracy as a decision procedure, but they might not, and it is what they actually agree to in the constitution of political authority that decides what it ought to be. Indeed, libertarians tend to view majority rule with distrust, insofar as it claims to represent the will of all but actually just serves the will of the majority coalitions of the present – and thus normally subjects some members of society to the rule of others, no matter if they agree to be so subjected or not, a clear violation of the principle of liberty and the rights implied by this principle (unless, again, those subjected to the authority actually consented to be so subjected in some real but past contractual event).

7.4 Socialism and Democracy

It is hard to say where socialism stands when it comes to the three concepts of democracy. The question has to be viewed from two directions. First, as I have reconstructed socialism, its allegiance to any of the first two concepts of democracy depends on how well popular sovereignty and democratic procedures serve the ends of personal and interpersonal perfection. But the third concept, that of members of society relating to each other as free and equal persons, *is part of the socialist ideal of community*, and thus serves as one of the foundational values of socialism.

Second, apart from my reconstruction of socialism, most socialists see a socialist economy as mandated by the ideal of democratic equality that is the third concept of democracy, and thus would refuse to yield any ground to the left-liberals in terms of standing on this particular ideal. Instead, they would argue that left-liberals are confused about how we should understand this ideal and what it would take to realize it. Indeed, some socialists argue that the ideal of democracy as a relation of freedom and equality requires that we extend democratic control to economic choices – not merely to the choice of basic rules of the economy, but also to the choices about what is produced and in what ways, an argument that supports socialized control of the means of production and the creation of procedures that secure democratic control of how they are employed.

8 Overview

The schema below (Table 6.1) summarizes the various contrasts I have drawn in this chapter among the main theories of distributive justice. In a sense, the schema is a map of the landscape of theories of distributive justice. As any map does, it leaves out much detail and as such simplifies the landscape, and I am not claiming that the map is complete – for there are theories of distributive justice other than those I have treated in this and the preceding chapters (I return to some of these in the following and final chapter).

TABLE 6.1 Map of the main theories of distributive justice

	Right-liberalism (Hayek)	*Left-liberalism (Rawls)*	*Libertarianism (Nozick)*	*Socialism (Cohen)*
View of society	Association and *coordination* for mutual benefit	Social *cooperation* between free and equal citizens	Voluntary association	(Ought to be) *community*; sharing of ends
View of the person	Rational; satisfies the formal conditions of rationality	(Ought to be) rational and reasonable	Self-author and locus of rights	(Ought to) realize productive potential and be virtuous
Framework	(Indirect) utilitarianism: the marriage of utility and liberty	Contractualism, the idea of democratic society	Liberty and natural rights	(Indirect) perfectionism: the marriage of equity and perfection
Virtue of just institutions	Efficiency (supports spontaneous order, catallaxy)	Fairness	Protect and respect rights and liberties	Enable individuality and community
Principle(s) of justice	(i) Liberty (ii) Efficiency (iii) Sufficiency	(i) Equal basic rights (ii) Democratic equality a) Fair equality of opportunity b) Difference principle	Principle of liberty, respect and protect rights	(i) Equality of opportunity (ii) Equity of outcome
Economic rights	Economic liberties are basic	Most economic rights are not basic	All economic liberties are absolute	Positive economic liberty and rights
Equality of opportunity	Minimal: nondiscrimination (careers open to talents)	Left-liberal (minimize effects of social lottery)	Ultra-minimal: no public discrimination	Socialist (minimize effects of social *and* natural lotteries)
Institutions	Free market capitalism and supporting functions	Property-owning democracy or liberal socialism	Night-watchman state	Socialism
Economic system	Yay capitalism and free markets! (system of liberty)	Free markets regulated to ensure fairness	Absolute property rights and freedom of contract	Yay socialism! (collective ownership of means of production)
View on democracy	Democracy is least worst	Democracy is the point	Unclear, but not a friend of democracy	Democracy is key

Looking at the map, it is, I think, remarkable how the theories occupy distinct positions at more or less every level and in most of the elements that theories of distributive justice generally contain. The takeaway is, I think, that the main distinction between the theories is their different visions of society and personhood. It is because of this basic disagreement that the theories offer distinct principles of justice, different theories of economic rights and views on equality of opportunity, and different institutional commitments, including their stances on the choice of economic system. Because the theories can be distinguished in each of the categories, it is an easy mistake to take their distinctiveness in one particular category as definitive of their difference. Theories of distributive justice are complex beings and must be understood and distinguished from each other as such. Even so, one has not, I believe, understood any of these theories or how the theories differ from each other until one understands how they differ at the most basic level of views of society and personhood and the frameworks for thinking about justice that these views recommend. In the final chapter I elaborate on this claim, suggest some additional meta-theoretical and practical takeaways, and comment on the limitations of this study.

Further Reading

The literature on democracy and democratic theory is vast.
A good starting point is:

Christiano, Tom, 2018. "Democracy," *The Stanford Encyclopedia of Philosophy, Fall 2018 Edition*, Edward N. Zalta (ed.), https://plato.stanford.edu/archives/fall2018/entries/democracy/.

A great source of data on the state and development of economic inequality over time is:

Piketty, Thomas, 2017. *Capital in the 21st Century*, Cambridge, MA: Harvard University Press.

Further reading on equality and equality of opportunity could begin with:

Arneson, Richard, 1989. "Equality and Equal Opportunity for Welfare," *Philosophical Studies*, 56: 77–93.

Arneson, Richard, 2015. "Equality of Opportunity," *The Stanford Encyclopedia of Philosophy, Summer 2015 Edition*, Edward N. Zalta (ed.), https://plato.stanford.edu/archives/sum2015/entries/equal-opportunity/.

Parfit, Derek, 2000. "Equality or Priority?", Matthew Clayton & Andrew Williams (eds.), *The Ideal of Equality*, Basingstoke, UK: Macmillan Press. pp. 81–125.

Scanlon, Thomas, 2018. *Why Does Inequality Matter?* Oxford, UK: Oxford University Press.

Sen, Amartya, 1992. *Inequality Reexamined*, Cambridge, MA: Harvard University Press.

Temkin, Larry S., 1993. *Inequality*, Oxford, UK: Oxford University Press.

An overview of the debate about economic rights can be found in:

Platz, Jeppe von & Tomasi, J., 2015. "Liberalism and Economic Liberty", Steven Wall (ed.), *The Cambridge Companion to Liberalism*, Cambridge, UK: Cambridge University Press. pp. 261–281.

Presentations of varieties of socialism as an economic system can be found in:

Carens, Joseph H., 1981. *Equality, Incentives, and the Market: An Essay in Utopian Politico-Economic Theory*, Chicago, IL: University of Chicago Press.
Roemer, John E., 1994. *A Future for Socialism*, Cambridge, MA: Harvard University Press.
Schweickart, David, 2011. *After Capitalism, 2nd Edition*, Lantham, MD: Rowman & Littlefield.

For discussions of the meaning and attractions of property-owning democracy, see:

O'Neill, Martin & Thad Williamson (eds.), 2012. *Property-Owning Democracy: Rawls and Beyond*, London, UK: Wiley-Blackwell.
Thomas, Alan, 2018. *Republic of Equals: Predistribution and Property-Owning Democracy*. Oxford, UK: Oxford University Press.

7

CONCLUDING REFLECTIONS

1 Justice, Human Nature, and the Human Good

One of the main takeaways from the comparison of theories of distributive justice conducted in the previous chapter is that disagreements about how we should organize the economic system often result from underlying disagreements about human nature and the human good. On the surface we find disagreements about taxation (should we tax income, wealth, or consumption; what should the rate of taxation be; should we tax progressively; and so on), about the supply of education and healthcare (public or private; publicly funded or paid by the users; and so on), about what goods and services we should be permitted to buy and sell in free market transactions (with disagreements about such things as alcohol, drugs, guns, kidneys, children, votes, and sexual favors), and about many other aspects of the design of the economic system. We often see that these disagreements rest on deeper disagreements of principle, e.g. how we should care about liberty and equality, how we should think of fairness, or how we should think about the role of the state. But even these disagreements are just below the surface of a much deeper sea of disagreements, and at the bottom of this sea we find disagreements about how we should think of society, and about human nature, human goodness, and the relation between human goodness and justice.

Theories of distributive justice express views of human society and the human good. Right-liberals and socialists, for example, don't just disagree about the tax rate or the balance between liberty and equality, but about what sort of human goodness justice is about in the first place. Right-liberals have a view of human beings as rational pursuers of happiness, a vision of society as beneficially coordinated activities, and a theory of justice that tells us to maximize subjective human goodness, that is, the happiness of the members of society. Given a set of empirical premises, this normative starting point supports the system of liberty as the proper organization of the economy: a limited set of low taxes; almost unlimited freedom of contract; private ownership of capital; and most services produced and distributed by market forces kept in motion by the profit motive. Socialists, by contrast, work from a theory of what human beings should be. Their focus is not on happiness understood as the satisfaction of the preferences that the members of society actually have or how persons actually tend to engage with others in the market. Instead, socialists work from ideas of what the members of society *should* prefer and how we *should* relate to each other. In terms of economic justice, what matters for socialists is that we create a society of objectively good human living, and, given a set of empirical premises, that this end mandates an economy geared to satisfy true needs, but also, of course, one that is without domination, exploitation, or alienation, and in which the distribution of benefits tracks real merit. Socialists then argue that these requirements are best served through socialized ownership of the means of production and democratic control of the flow of inputs and outputs of the economy.

In this chapter I look more closely at the basic disagreements and what they tell us about:

- The landscape of theories of distributive justice;
- The different sorts of disagreements about distributive justice that we may have;
- Alternatives to the four main theories discussed in this book;
- How the world of theory relates to the political reality of Western liberal democracies; and
- What the future might hold for these worlds of theory and practice.

2 The Right and the Good

To begin, let us recall a distinction drawn in Chapter 1 between teleological and deontological theories of justice. *Teleological theories* define the right in terms of the good, so that justice is the set of principles and rules that, when we conform to it, tends to lead to the most desirable outcome. Different teleological theories disagree about what this desirable outcome is, as in the disagreement between right-liberals and socialists about whether the good is subjective or objective human goodness, but they agree about the priority relation between the right and the good: the good is prior to the right both *conceptually* – we cannot understand the right apart from an independently given theory of the good – and *normatively* – the justification of principles of justice is that conformity with them tends to best promote the good. Teleological theories are often called consequentialist, because they focus on the outcomes or consequences of rules or behaviors.

Deontological theories, by contrast, reject that the right can be understood in terms of the good. Instead, they define the right as the constraints that we must respect when we pursue what is good. According to deontological theories, the right and the good are conceptually independent; neither can be defined in terms of the other. Different deontological theories disagree about what these norms of rightness are – as in the disagreement between left-liberals and libertarians about whether the right consists of norms of democratic equality (fairness) or rights of liberty – but agree that the right is normatively prior to the good in that the pursuit of desirable outcomes is constrained by the norms of rightness.

So, we can already identify two meta-theoretical disagreements about distributive justice:

I. The disagreement between teleological and non-teleological theories. Here the field divides according to whether the right is defined in terms of the good or externally constrains its pursuit.
II. Disagreements about what sort of teleology or deontology is the right one. Here the field divides into disagreements about what is good or what the proper external constraints on its pursuit are.

Following these two divisions, we can define four philosophical frameworks for thinking about distributive justice (Table 7.1).

These divisions take place at the level of pure philosophy, which also means that they are about questions that science cannot help us answer.

3 Why the Landscape of Theories of Distributive Justice Is What it Is

In this book I have discussed four theories of distributive justice: right-liberalism, left-liberalism, libertarianism, and socialism. If my analysis of how these theories are grounded in competing ideas of society and personhood and constructed from the different philosophical frameworks that these ideas suggest is correct, then I have explained why these are the four main theories of distributive justice – both

TABLE 7.1 Philosophical frameworks

Teleological theories		*Deontological theories*	
Justice is the rules that ensure *objective goodness*: good human living	Justice is the rules that ensure *subjective goodness*: happiness (or preference satisfaction)	Justice is the rules that ensure fair social cooperation among free and equal persons	Justice is the rules that ensure that natural and acquired *rights* are respected and protected
Perfectionisms	Utilitarianisms	Contractualisms	Rights theories
⇒ socialism	⇒ right-liberalism	⇒ left-liberalism	⇒ libertarianism

in the sense that these four are the founts from which public reasons are drawn in actual political debates, and in the sense that they dominate the philosophical debate about what principles we should rely on when we conduct this public discussion. If I am right, then, *these four are the main theories of distributive justice, because each corresponds to one of the main candidate conceptions of what justice is all about in the first place.*

When we search for reasons in deliberations and debates about distributive justice, there are only so many resources to choose from. What do we all care about? What is justice about? The main candidate answers are happiness, fairness, liberty, and being good (virtue). The different theories of distributive justice discussed in this book each take one of these as their main focus and then constructs the theory in those terms. Apart from the political philosophies developed by any particular thinker, be they Hayek, Rawls, Nozick, Cohen, or someone else, these four theories of distributive justice are available in theoretical space as coherent explorations of different visions of society, personhood, and basic frameworks. Hayek, Rawls, Nozick, and Cohen are interesting because each of them provides a systematic and thorough exploration of one of these four frameworks, and they bring to our awareness or exemplify what these theories look like in the flesh (or in the word, as it were). Having arrived at this point, we could discard their writings and start anew at articulating each of these four theories in light of our understanding of what they are about and how they are structured from that basic set of ideas.

There are alternatives, of course, and in the following section I look at some of these alternatives. First, however, I want to look briefly at a question that comes in naturally at this point: Can't we be pluralists? Surely, happiness, fairness, liberty, and being good *all matter*, so isn't the truth about distributive justice that none of these theories alone can offer the answer to what we should care about when we design our economies? Can't we combine them in some fashion?

Tempting as this idea is, I doubt that it is a good one, for two reasons. First, these considerations often point to opposing conclusions; conclusions of the sort where accepting one implies the falsity of the others. Think of the choice between capitalist and socialist designs of the economy. For the sake of example, let us grant the empirical assumptions that hold together the right-liberal marriage of liberty and utility *and* the socialist marriage of equality and perfection, and let us also grant that these point to capitalism and socialism, respectively, as required designs of the economy; in that case either one of the theories deems the requirements of the other theory impermissible. As explained in the previous chapters, disagreement arises at every level of theory (grounding, principles, institutions), so if one of these theories is true, the others are false.

In the realm of theory, pluralism requires reconciling contradictions. There may be avenues of reconciliation, but the three most promising seem to go nowhere. The first is to identify a higher-level principle that could allow us to negotiate conflicts among the principles affirmed by these theories, but no such principle is forthcoming, and even if it were, this would just produce a new (fifth) sort of monism. The principle of utility is often defended as the best candidate for a higher-level principle, but accepting it as such betrays the sought-for pluralism. The second strategy of reconciliation is to have priority rules or weights for the different concerns and principles, so that conflicts can be mediated by careful deliberation. But it is hard to see where we could find the needed priority rules or weights. This leaves us with a third option, *intuitionism*, which says that many things matter (it is truly pluralist) and that there is no way to negotiate conflicts other than by intuitive judgment. If, and when, conflicts arise, calm reflection, search for balance, and perhaps aesthetic feelings must decide how to navigate them. Alas, intuitionism is unattractive; it may be the best we can do, but it is also a theoretical and practical surrender that would leave us with no way to negotiate disagreements about justice, for the intuitions of different persons don't agree (and tend to support judgments favorable to the position of the intuiter).

In the realm of practice, without some framework for negotiating the different concerns presented by the theories, pluralism is paralyzed by such conflicts. Without some higher principle or priority rules or weights we can rely on to negotiate conflicts arising from these different concerns, pluralism leaves us with no guidance for what we should do or think about economic justice.

4 Alternatives to the Four Main Theories

There are, of course, alternatives to the four main theories discussed in this book. Some alternatives are radical in that they challenge some basic and shared assumptions of the four theories. Other alternatives are moderate in that they accept the assumptions, but proceed from these in ways not covered by any of the four theories.

4.1 Radical Alternatives

The four theories discussed in this book share these two assumptions:

Justice is real. Justice issues true requirements for how we should organize societies: it is not a mirage or mere ideology.

The scope of justice is human beings. Only human beings have nonderivative moral standing; other beings (animals, plants, species, rivers, ecosystems, etc.) might matter for what justice requires, but if so they matter because of their connection to human beings (say, for their needs, or as their property, or some other reason that ties these nonhuman objects to the nonderivative justice-concern for human beings).

The first assumption is denied by varieties of egoism, some postmodern and neo-Marxist views of the political domain, and some sorts of conservatism. Egoism is, as Rawls says, not really an alternative theory of justice, but a challenge to the enterprise of theorizing justice, for it says that justice is person-relative, so that justice is what serves the interest of the *I* thinking about what justice is. Neo-Marxists tend to see theories of justice as another tool in the struggle for power, typically a tool used by the more powerful to justify their oppression of the less powerful. A theory of justice might be used to justify a system of entitlements, whereby the more entitled and the less entitled alike can share the illusion that their relative lots are fair. Marxists tend to focus on liberation or emancipation as the value we should care for, though it is unclear what caring for such values means apart from the negative injunction to remove systems of oppression and constraint.

Some types of conservatism reject the first assumption (justice is real), in that they see justice as a political dimension of an ethics of authenticity. What matters, on this line of thought, is that society stays true to its history and the ideas that have shaped its history. This history might reveal commitments along the line of any of the theories covered in this book – but it might not, in which case neither of these would be the ideal of justice appropriate for the society in question. The obvious problem for conservatism is that the histories of most societies include ample measures of idiocy and injustice, which makes authenticity a troublesome standard; surely, no country's past can serve as a model for what it should be now or into the future.

Some cynics about justice might say that I get the justificatory structure exactly backward. A theory of justice, they'd say, is always an attempt at justifying institutional structures beneficial to those thinking about them. People start by wanting an institutional design that benefits them, then they go looking for principles that could justify this institutional design, and then, if they are sophisticated, they go looking for a foundational vision that they can draw on to support these principles. However, while this understanding might be true for some political philosophers (and some politicians), I doubt that it is true for all. And, even if it was, it would not really change much, for what we are looking for when we ask, "What does justice require of us?" is the truth about justice. The cynical claim is that we are never really asking that question; instead, we are asking "What is best for me and mine?" But I see no reason to believe that we cannot ask the first question, and I, for one, am very interested in the answer to the first question – and have written this book to explore the main answers to it.

The second assumption (the scope of justice is human beings) is denied by various sorts of environmentalist ethics. According to these, the interests of nonhuman beings are direct concerns of justice, so when we theorize justice and when we think about how to design our economies, we must relate appropriately to the interests of these nonhuman beings in our thoughts and practices. A limited extension of the scope of justice would include sentient beings, as when utilitarians count the suffering of sentient animals as part of the utilitarian calculus of costs and benefits. Even such a limited extension would have dramatic consequences for both theory and practice. If we count the suffering of animals as part of the calculus of utility, then the right-liberal marriage of liberty and utility fails immediately: for, even if the free choices of individual human beings promote human utility, we cannot expect the spontaneous order of a free market society to show any concern for the suffering of animals. Indeed, the market tends to view animals as products and treats them in a manner that leads to massive amounts of animal suffering as a by-product of profit-seeking. In terms of theories of justice, left-liberals, libertarians, and socialists show equal nonconcern for the interests of animals.

Matters get even worse if we expand the scope of moral consideration to plants, nonbiological entities such as mountains or rivers, or any of the collective entities of nature – species, ecosystems, the biosphere. If any of these have a sort of nonderivative moral standing that makes them a direct concern of justice, then all of the theories covered in this book are, at best, incomplete; or, worse, plain false. It may be that the history of theorizing justice in Western philosophy has rested on falsehoods, so that this history must be viewed as wrongheaded and we must start anew at theorizing justice in light of our recognition that beings other than human beings have nonderivative moral standing. However, tempting as this thought may be, it is much easier said than done to construct an environmentally conscious theory of justice. For starters, saying that the scope of moral considerability includes nonhuman beings says nothing about what beings it includes, what moral standing they have, or what requirements of justice are fitting to said moral standing. And there is no consensus at all in environmental ethics about the scope of moral considerability, or what sorts of moral considerability we should grant different sorts of nonhuman beings; the only consensus environmental ethics has thus far achieved is that anthropocentrism cannot be assumed, but needs a better defense than it has hitherto been given. The theories of justice covered in this book rely on the assumption that the anthropocentric perspective is justifiable, but none of them justify it.

4.2 Moderate Alternatives

Moderate alternatives accept the two assumptions about the reality and scope of justice, but occupy different territory in the landscape of distributive justice than either of the four theories. Here, I will introduce two such options: pure-breeds and mongrels.

Like the four theories, the pure-breeds have a single vision of society and personhood and proceed from it, but this vision is an alternative to the visions of the four theories. An example is republicanism. Like libertarianism, republicanism says that justice is all about liberty, but republicanism denies that liberty should be understood along libertarian lines. Instead republicans understand liberty in terms of nondomination; that is, as not being subject to the arbitrary will of others. Republicanism thus requires that all have sufficient resources that no one needs to be subjected to the arbitrary will of another, and different specifications of that requirement result in different republican theories of distributive justice.

Mongrels result from combinations of more than one of the four theories (or other pure-breed alternatives), but break with the systemic entailments from grounding to principles to institutions described in the previous chapters of this book. An example of this approach is the recent development of a market democratic approach to justice (the approach does not yet have a fixed name, we could also call it neo-right-liberalism or neoclassical liberalism). This approach agrees entirely with the left-liberal view of society and personhood, adopts the left-liberal contractualist framework for thinking about justice, and accepts the ideas of fairness and reciprocity appropriate to this framework, *but* argues that the principles of justice that follow from this framework must give high priority to the protection of the economic rights and liberties that right-liberals argue are the drivers of a productive economy. Proponents of this view argue that only something like Hayek's system of liberty can satisfy the demands of justice. Market democrats thus argue that the left-liberal, anti-utilitarian way to think about justice supports almost exactly the conclusions about the design of the economy that right-liberals seek to justify on utilitarian grounds. The market democratic approach does not deny the marriage of economic liberty and utility, but does not rely on it either; rather, theirs is a marriage of economic liberty and fairness, the claim that only in a free market society can the members fully develop and exercise the powers of free and equal citizenship.

Once we break apart the theories along such lines, it becomes clear that the set of theories of distributive justice could have many more members than the four I have focused on in this book. Conceptually, at least, nothing stands in the way of mixing and matching parts of the four theories to construct a theory of distributive justice to one's liking from the various elements (or introduce elements from other pure-breed theories).

Yet, conceptual possibility is not what matters. What matters is also the way a theory of justice proceeds from foundational visions of society and personhood to principles, and from these to institutions; *what matters is the justificatory story* that a theory of distributive justice tells us. And here there are strictures other than the conceptual. It would be hard, I think, to proceed from the socialist vision of society and personhood to a right-liberal view of principles and institutional design. Hard is not impossible; however, the ease of the justificatory story matters, for the strength of justification is a function also of the ease of inferences. There is a reason that the four main theories are what they are: each provides the easiest progression from competing sets of foundations to competing sets of principles to competing sets of institutional designs. Mongrel theories, I believe, have a harder time telling their respective justificatory stories.

5 Disagreements about Distributive Justice

It is not news that we disagree about distributive justice, for few areas of political debate divide people as quickly and as deeply as economic questions. One result of the study conducted in this book is that we can now identify different types of disagreements at the level of political philosophy which can help us better understand what we really disagree about in our discussions of how we should organize economic society. In light of the preceding, we can distinguish between four sorts of disagreement:

- Meta-theoretical disagreements: disagreements about how we should think about justice in the first place.
- Inter-framework disagreements: disagreements between adherents of different theories of distributive justice about how we should organize economic society, based on their disagreement about what the true principles of distributive justice are.
- Intra-framework disagreements: disagreements between adherents of the same theory of distributive justice about what that theory really requires.
- Factual disagreements: disagreements about the empirical dimension of questions of distributive justice.

5.1 Meta-Theoretical Disagreements

Meta-theoretical disagreements occur when we think about *how* we should think about distributive justice. This sort of disagreement is about the choice among the visions of society and personhood that ground the four theories of distributive justice, or among adherents of one of the four theories of distributive justice and those that reject these in favor of either radical or moderate alternatives (as described in the previous section).

These sorts of disagreement are deeply divisive, for they are virtually insoluble. A right-liberal says that justice is the rules that allow us to live together in prosperity, a left-liberal says that justice is about fairness, a libertarian says that justice is about respecting and protecting rights of liberty, and a socialist says that justice is about creating community and the conditions of good human living; there is nothing any of them could say that would persuade the others that they are mistaken. The best any of them could do is to lay out the attractions of their point of view and the detractions of the opposing views, but there are no arguments available that could show that the alternative views are false, for each view is a starting point from which arguments about justice can be drawn.

5.2 Inter-Framework Disagreements

Inter-framework disagreements are based on the principles that each of the theories of distributive justice present as the basic normative requirements of justice. Thus, a right-liberal might argue that we should have a private market for higher education, *because* liberty in the choices of supply and consumption of education channels human and nonhuman resources in an optimally socially productive fashion. Left-liberals might defend a single public supplier of higher education, *because* such a system is necessary to secure fair equality of opportunity for members of society. In a debate between the two, each draws her reasons from the principles of justice that her framework supplies, together with empirical premises. Here, then, are two arguments:

Right-liberal:

1. We should secure the conditions maximally conducive to social prosperity;
2. A private market for higher education is more conducive to social prosperity than a public supply;
3. Therefore, we should secure a private market for higher education.

Left-liberal:

1. We should secure the conditions necessary for equality of opportunity;
2. A single public supplier of higher education is necessary for equality of opportunity;
3. Therefore, we should secure a single public supplier of higher education.

In an actual debate, each will be quick to point to the shortcomings of the other. The right-liberal says "Your view leads to waste and less welfare for members of society!" The left-liberal says "Your view creates an uneven playing field where the kids of the rich have access to better opportunities than the kids of the poor!" In such a debate, both would then reply "No it doesn't!" And then the debate would go back and forth about the merits of these claims about consequences. This back and forth is by no means irrelevant to the question, but it directs (or misdirects) the debate to the empirical question of what would happen and then measures these consequences by the major premise of the challenger's position (i.e. premise 1 in the arguments above).

One problem here is that the debate continues *as if* the positions agree about what we should care about when it comes to institutional design (in the example, the design of the supply of higher education), *but they don't.* Another problem is that it tempts the opposing sides to make false or undersubstantiated empirical judgments, e.g. that the pursuit of equality of opportunity has no cost in terms of foregone prosperity. The more honest reply would run along the lines of "Well, it might, but even if it does, that's not really what matters!" The right-liberal should be ready to allow inequality of opportunity as a price of prosperity, and the left-liberal should be willing to forgo some prosperity to secure equality of opportunity.

It speaks to the attractions of the different theories of distributive justice that political debates tend to get (mis)directed to the empirical questions, for it is evidence of the appeal of each of the concerns that the different theories highlight. It looks like a good objection when the right-liberal identifies prosperity forgone by left-liberal proposals; and it looks like a good objection when the left-liberal calls unfairness on the right-liberal proposal. This often results in the immediate strategy of denying that the opponent's claim is true, for it denies that the position one is defending has any costs in terms of forgoing anything that the opponent seems rightly concerned with (whether it is happiness, fairness, or one of the other main concerns). But pursuing this strategy may cause one to make unfounded and false empirical claims; also, it misdirects our attention from the real and underlying disagreement, which is about normative principle and not matters of fact. The strategy pretends that we are in consensus about what matters and only disagree about how to get it, which is false, for many (most, I think) of our disagreements about economic justice are disagreements about what matters – or about how to balance our competing concerns for what matters.

Either of these disagreements – about what matters or about how to balance different values and concerns – are as inevitable and intractable as the disagreements on what justice is about (cf. Section 5.1 of this chapter). For the choice of principles of distributive justice is based on the founding ideas and frameworks, and it is unlikely that the disagreeing persons agree on what reasons we should rely on in debating which combination of principles we should embrace.

The result of the discussion of meta-theoretical and inter-framework disagreements is troubling. For if it is true that many of our disagreements about economic justice are both inevitable and intractable, then what are we to do? How can we go about creating economic society, if we inevitably disagree about what economic society should be? Here, I think, is one area where democracy as a decision procedure is attractive. If we agree to disagree, and to have our disagreements settled by a political process that represents our different viewpoints roughly in proportion to how they are distributed in the population, then we might agree to settle our disagreements by this process, and democracy offers such a procedure. In a democracy, we might be subject to an economic system we find unjust, but we might be subject to it because it was created by procedures we find legitimate and whereby we had an equal say in the process by which it was created – and we will have opportunities to work to change it in future debates and votes.

5.3 Intra-Framework Disagreements

We also find plenty of disagreements among the adherents to any given framework. Not all left-liberals would agree with the Rawlsian rendition of the principles of justice – and, as I have emphasized above, there is broad disagreement among socialists about what socialism really requires at the level of principle. Socialists variously defend principles of equality, merit, liberty, or some combination of these. The sorts of economic design they propose are functions of these principles, so socialists tend to also disagree about how the economy should be designed. And even if there are agreements within a framework about a basic principle, as when libertarians agree that the principle is the principle of liberty, there can be disagreements about how this principle should be interpreted or what is required to satisfy it. In the chapter on libertarianism I described the disagreement between left- and right-libertarians, which is based on a disagreement about original ownership and the principle of original acquisition of property – a disagreement that exemplifies how even those who agree on the principle can disagree vehemently about what this principle permits and requires.

For these various sorts of intra-framework disagreements to be intra-framework (rather than inter-framework), there has to be consensus on the basics of the framework, that is, on the foundational ideas and the proper framework for thinking about the requirements of justice. Left-libertarians and right-libertarians agree that the foundational idea for all aspects of society is liberty; but affirm different theories about the origins of property rights and, therefore, also tend to disagree about institutional design.

5.4 Factual Disagreements

The preceding sorts of disagreements are normative rather than factual. They are about *what should be* the case, rather than about *what is* the case; they concern norms rather than facts, the prescriptive rather than the descriptive; they deal in the "ought" as opposed to the "is." But, as touched on above, we also tend to disagree about the facts that determine what normative principles require.

Factual disagreements can be found at any of the levels of theorizing justice, and are disagreements about empirical rather than normative questions. As mentioned, factual disagreements tend to dominate actual political debates. And there is a reason for that. It is impossible to prescribe or proscribe any particular constitution, institution, law, or policy without empirical premises, and disagreement about these empirical premises are inevitable. The right-liberal says that lowering taxes leads to more employment; that allowing the market to supply a good or service leads to a more efficient supply; that a mandatory minimum wage leads to less hiring; and so on. Critics of polices friendly to free markets tend to dispute these factual claims rather than the right-liberal principles of justice. Other theories rely on other empirical claims to move from normative principle to prescription of how we should organize society and what we should do, politically, to deal with various social problems as these arise.

Empirical premises, such as the examples from right-liberal arguments mentioned in the previous paragraph, might be true or they might be false. Moreover, whether they are true or false likely depends on the particular societal circumstances (it seems unlikely that these are like laws that are true in all societies at all times) and much depends on the more detailed specification of what's meant by the terms. The truth or falsity of these premises must be decided by the relevant sciences – they are not matters of political philosophy, and political philosophers have no special expertise for answering them. This is an inevitable shortcoming of philosophy as pure philosophy; that it cannot bridge the gap between norms and prescriptions, for the bridge is constructed from empirical premises that philosophers lack the competence and authority to confidently assert.

Of course, the truth of some empirical premises seems invariant across contexts, namely premises about human nature and the human condition. "Humans are by nature incapable of altruistic motives" is an empirical claim, as is its negation. Yet, while such premises seem harder to outsource to relevant sciences – for what science can tell us the potentials of human nature? – it remains true that philosophers asserting them in arguments at best can do so as articles of faith or as warranted by normative premises, rather than as truths that others should believe independently of normative principles.

So, disagreements about factual matters are no less inevitable or intractable than disagreements about normative principles. They are, however, disagreements that political philosophers do (or should) leave to the relevant sciences to settle. What political philosophers can, and should, do is to draw attention to the distinction between factual and normative disagreements, identify the different normative principles that underlie normative disagreements, bring clarity to the presuppositions, attractions, and problems of these normative principles, and ascertain what the best arguments for and against these normative principles are.

6 Distributive Justice in Today's Liberal Democracies

The map of theories of distributive justice provided in the preceding chapters is also, I believe, a map of distributive justice in today's liberal democracies. This means we should be able to explain some things that happen in the political dimensions of liberal democracies by the understanding of the different theories of distributive justice provided in this book.

I have argued that the different theories should be understood as based on competing ideas of society and personhood. These ideas imply what values we should care about, what principles we should rely on in our political-economic choices, and, thus, how we should design the economy. A theory of distributive justice is thus a systematic exploration of an idea of society and personhood; an exploration that has both a conceptual side (what is this value we care about), a descriptive side (how can we best realize that value that we care about), and a normative side (which tells us to do that which brings about the value we care about).

I have also suggested that each of the theories occupies a prominent territory, meaning that the ideas of society and values that the theories are based on are unavoidable; there is no denying the appeal of prosperity, fairness, liberty, or community.

I also believe, though this goes beyond what the book has hitherto argued or suggested, that there is a very limited range of candidate ideas of society and personhood, and of candidate values that justice could be about, and that the four combinations of ideas and values that each of the main theories of distributive justice exemplify are, if not the only ones available, the main candidates – there is, in my opinion, not that much territory in the universe of distributive justice left unoccupied by these four theories. That is, there are not that many stable and attractive combinations of ideas and values other than these four.

If we take these three claims together – that the theories are based on competing ideas and values, that these ideas and value combinations are unavoidably attractive, and that there is little attractive territory left outside of these theories – then this provides a way to explain why the practical politics of liberal democracies when it comes to economic questions tend to be occupied by adherents of these four perspectives on justice.

It may be that the political domain in the US is dominated by just two parties, but look closer and you'll find that on economic questions the parties are internally divided along the lines of the four theories. The Republican Party is split between right-liberals that are all about the conditions of prosperity (utility) and libertarians that are all about liberty. The Democratic Party is divided into three: right-liberal democrats, who agree with the end of prosperity but have doubts about the empirical assumptions that prescribe economic liberty as the only and secure tool of prosperity; left-liberal democrats that take fairness as the main value and tend to emphasize the need for equality of opportunity; and socialist democrats, who believe that we need to create the conditions of real community and emphasize the need for some measure of outcome equality as essential to that end. Other countries exemplify the division between the theories in other ways: in the European countries you'll see parties defending right-liberal views (usually called conservatives or Christian democrats), left-liberal views (e.g. social democrats), and socialist parties. The libertarians are rarely represented by their own party, though the position seems to be asserting its appeal with younger generations.

If this analysis is correct, then it is also true, as the saying goes, that politics is struggle. But it need not be a *mere* struggle for power or a struggle driven by the self-interested desires of various factions and classes in society. It is also *a struggle of ideas* – a struggle between competing, mutually exclusive, internally coherent, and undeniably attractive systems of normative thought that can be constructed from competing ideas of society and personhood and the basic societal values that these suggest. The political struggle about how we should design the economy is also a struggle between the four theories of distributive justice discussed in this book.

7 Directions

What might the future bring for the philosophy of distributive justice? The relation between theory and practice is bidirectional, so it also depends on what happens in the world, which means that it is hard to say much with confidence in reply to this question. Practice outpaces theory – the theories of distributive justice covered in this book arose as responses to practical questions made inescapable by economic developments – but theory tells us how and where we should try to steer practice. The question, then, is what practical tendencies beget theoretical innovations. Interesting predictions are usually wrong. However, some tendencies provide some basis for speculating.

First, then, it seems that questions of economic inequality remain contentious and that philosophy can help clarify these disagreements. Rising inequalities of income, wealth, opportunity, and well-being seem a feature of our world. While these inequalities rise simultaneously with decreases in absolute poverty and increases in average access to the materials of well-being, it seems to many (philosophers and nonphilosophers) that there is something troubling about them.

One question is, which of these inequalities are problematic in themselves and which of them are problematic because they threaten something else we care about? It is remarkable that *none of the theories studied in this book* say that unequal wealth or income is bad as such. Socialists are closest to this position, but they do not quite get there. Some socialists – and Cohen is one of them – embrace a principle of *equity*, so that equally deserving persons should be equally well-off in terms of economic advantages (and, possibly, well-being), but equity requires inequality, for unequally deserving persons should then have unequal access to economic advantages. Other socialists – and, again, Cohen is one of them – worry that material inequalities (of income and wealth, say) must undermine community, and since we ought to live together in the manner of community, we should not accept these inequalities. But that argument does not value economic equality as such, but values it as an instrument of community. Socialists, of course, require a strong sort of equality of opportunity, but equality of opportunity is consistent with just about any degree of inequality of outcome. Other socialists again worry that economic inequality must lead to unequal political power and so defend economic equality as a requirement of democratic equality (i.e. equal political power), but this defense is also of the instrumentalist sort. So, though socialism offers many ways to criticize economic inequalities – and thus many resources for thinking critically about the current trends of increasing economic inequality – even socialism does not find fault with economic inequality as such.

The other theories are even less concerned with economic inequalities, though left-liberals share many of the socialist worries. It may be that economic inequalities are not unjust as such, but it is hard to shake the sense that the degree of inequality we are currently experiencing is wrong.

Of course, *all the theories* agree that if economic inequalities are *generated* by unjust moves or moves made in an unjust system of rules, then they are unjust and should be corrected – though the theories disagree about what constitutes unjust moves or rules. So, every theory covered in this book – even libertarianism and right-liberalism which reject most of the socialist sort of worries about inequality – offers resources for criticizing existing inequalities insofar as they result from unjust moves or rules as judged by the theories.

Second, it seems that we need to think better about alternative economic designs. There are many variants between socialism and capitalism (and possibly alternatives to the two) that we should explore to get a better sense of the options-space for how we might go about realizing the demands of justice.

What section of the options-space we should pursue is a matter of dispute (based on the dispute among the theories of distributive justice), but merely getting a better sense of the options-space would help orient our disagreements. Socialists have done much to present alternative versions of socialism that might compete with capitalism in terms of productivity, while satisfying the socialist concerns for equity, community, and democratic equality. This work is, I expect, driven by the success of capitalism in becoming the dominant way to organize economies, and the sense that the trend is towards increasing capitalism (in all of the three dimensions: ownership of the means of production, use of markets, and the profit motive driving production and distribution) across the globe.

Right-liberal philosophers and economists have not, I think, been equally eager to think about grand questions of economic design. Left-liberals have still to provide a sufficiently detailed description of a system that would satisfy their principles of justice. Rawls and Rawlsians say property-owning democracy and liberal socialism are the best candidates, but leave undescribed what these actually are. If we are to assess the merits of theories of distributive justice, we have to understand what economic systems would satisfy them, both because we can then assess their feasibility and because we can then assess their costs, as measured by the things the different theories care about.

Third, and relatedly, I expect we will see much more work on the international and cosmopolitan dimensions of distributive justice. Great work is already being done in this field, but it seems to me that practice once more is outpacing theory. We now live in a globalized economic system. This system should be subject to political control, which it is not; nor is it clear what such control should look like. Here, the need for theory is clear. The theories of distributive justice described in this book were developed for the domestic domain, so it shall be interesting to see how far they can help us think about the international and cosmopolitan domains, and whether new alternatives will develop to deal with these new questions.

GLOSSARY

Anthropocentrism The view that only human beings have nonderivative moral standing, so that all nonhuman beings (animals, plants, rivers, species, ecosystems, etc.) derive any moral standing they might have from the moral standing of human beings. For example, a cow might matter as property of a human being or as a source of human well-being, but it has no moral standing apart from such relations.

Basic rights Basic rights is a category of rights that has high priority, meaning that basic rights can be compromised only for the sake of better securing of basic rights and not for other reasons that might justify public policy such as the pursuit of efficiency or fairness.

Capitalism A way to organize the economy where there is private ownership of the means of production, the flow of inputs and outputs of production is determined by free markets, and where production is structured to maximize profits.

Catallaxy Hayek's name for the spontaneous order process that is created by a free market economic system.

Citizen A full member of a state. Citizens usually enjoy the full set of political, civil, and economic rights that define citizenship, though there may be exceptions for expatriots or felons.

Coercion The use of force or threats of force by some persons against other persons with intent to control their behavior.

Community A community is a society of persons tied together by shared ends.

Consent To consent is to expressly or tacitly agree to something. Consent has the power to create authority and obligation and is, therefore, of special interest to political philosophy. Political philosophers distinguish between actual consent (where a person did consent), hypothetical consent (where a person would consent), and normative consent (where a person should consent).

Consequentialist A consequentialist moral theory says that the rightness and wrongness of the object it governs (e.g. acts, laws, institutions, constitutions) is determined by its (actual or expected) consequences.

Contractualist A contractualist moral theory says that the rightness and wrongness of the object it governs (e.g. acts, laws, institutions, constitutions) depends on whether those within the scope of that object could, would, or should agree to it.

Corrective justice The subject of justice that deals with how we should think about and correct injustices. The subject includes reparative or rectificatory justice as well as punitive justice.

Democracy, democratic The term democracy has many meanings. Three of these are especially important. First, democracy as the norm of popular sovereignty, which says that sovereignty (the authority to rule) belongs to the people (and thus not to, say, the members of an aristocracy or a monarch). Second, democracy as the idea of political equality, which says that all citizens should have equal political power. Third, democracy as a set of procedures for the generation of laws and executive power (including various rights, voting in periodical free and fair elections, legal structures that define representation, offices and terms, and so on). The term democratic can likewise be used in different senses, some of which correspond to the three senses of democracy, so that a democratic society can be said to be one with popular sovereignty, political equality, or one that secures an adequate measure of the democratic procedures for the generation of political authority.

Deontological A deontological theory is not teleological (consequentialist), meaning that it denies that the right can be defined in terms of the good and it sees the right as constraining what is good or how we may pursue the good. The word derives from the Greek word for duty (*deon*) and deontological theories are sometimes called duty-based, but there are non-teleological theories that are not duty-based.

Desert A measure of what a person would get or how well-off she would be, if her position in life fits her place on a scale of desert. There are many competing accounts of desert, but all of them take desert to be a function of effort and moral uprightness (virtue).

Desertism The moral theory that people should get what they deserve and that we should try to organize society to realize this fit. While a notion of desert can be a notion of merit, there are notions of merit that are not notions of desert, so desertism implies a principle of merit, but there are principles of merit that are not desertist.

Difference principle A prioritarian principle that serves as the second part of the principles of democratic equality in Rawls's theory of justice (justice as fairness). The difference principle that says that inequalities of wealth and income are permissible only if they are to the advantage of the least well-off.

Distribuendum That which is distributed, be it money, power, status, welfare, capabilities, or something else.

Distributive justice A domain of moral theory part of which provides the subject of this book. Distributive justice is the principles that should guide the distribution of a resource or a burden between competing claims to it. Such claims arise in a number of human contexts. One of these contexts is the context of politically organized society with laws that define the rules, roles, and so on of an economic system. A primary subject of distributive justice is this context and how we should design this system of rules and roles.

Economy An economy is a system for the production and distribution of resources. The economy is this system at the level of political society, the rules and roles of which are defined by the various laws, policies, and other regulatives that define the game by which we pursue resources and positions.

Efficiency Effiency is a goal of optimal use of resources (the opposite is waste). Efficiency can be measured in various ways. Popular measures are: Pareto efficiency, where no one could be better-off without anyone being worse off; average utility, where no alternative use of the resource has higher average utility (similarly for product utility or aggregate utility); and Kaldor–Hicks efficiency where it is impossible to find an alternative use of the resource such that those who benefit could compensate those who lose by moving to the alternative.

Egalitarianism/egalitarian The family of positions that affirms the principle of equality. According to egalitarians, persons ought to have the same or be equally well-off in some regard. The specific nature of the position depends on the distribuendum.

Entitlement A legally valid claim, normally acquired by a permissible move in a legal structure (e.g. a purchase).

Equality A relation of sameness in some regard e.g. equal wealth, equal income, equal welfare, equal opportunity, equal merit.

Equality of opportunity The situation where those of equal talent, effort, and luck have equal access to some good or advantage.

Equity A relation of equality within a measure where the related persons might be unequal. For example, equity might require that the equally meritorious persons receive the same income, and thus also require that those of higher merit receive higher income than those of lower merit.

Fairness A requirement of justice emphasized by left-liberals, which says that the terms of cooperation and the distribution of the benefits and burdens of cooperation, should be fair. The left-liberal theory of justice then seeks to answer the question "What is fair?"

Freedom Freedom consists in the ability to do something. It is thus a modal relation of real possibility between a person and an activity. Freedom entails liberty (the absence of interpersonal or legal constraints preventing a person from engaging in the activity in question), but liberty does not entail freedom.

Institutions Systems of roles and rules that structure personal choice and social interaction.

Intuitionism A position in moral theory that claims that there are multiple and irreconcilable sources of normativity and that the best we can do when deciding how to weigh conflicting moral demands is to use intuitive judgment.

Justice, concept of A subdomain of the right that governs political relations and acts. The concept of justice is that all should receive their due.

Justice as fairness The name that Rawls gave his theory of justice, the core of which are his two principles of justice.

Justify, justification Justification is a relation between propositions whereby the truth of one implies the truth of the other.

Left-liberalism The family of theories of distributive justice that takes democratic equality and fairness as the main concerns of justice.

Liberal socialism A system that respects the usual list of rights known from liberal democracies, but organizes the economy on the basis of socialized ownership of the means of production.

Liberalism The family of theories of justice that emphasizes individual liberty as an important concern of justice. Liberal theories of justice share a concern for the rights and liberties known from various lists of individual rights (freedom of thought, speech, the person, and so on), assign the protection and respect for these liberties high political priority, and show some concern for providing to all citizens the means necessary to exercise these rights and liberties.

Libertarianism A species of liberalism; the family of theories of justice that says that the sole concern of justice is liberty and the rights that define liberty.

Liberty A relation between a person and some activity, whereby there is no interpersonal or legal coercion that prevents a person from engaging in said activity. Liberty implies freedom, but not *vice versa.*

Marxism A species of socialism developed by Karl Marx and his followers. Marxists are especially interested in understanding and revealing the true nature of capitalism as a system of exploitation and alienation.

Merit That whereby a person is fit to receive some reward of benefit.

Meritocracy A society where the burdens and benefits are distributed in accordance with an interpretation of the principle of merit.

Moral worth The moral value or virtue of a person. Moral worth is also the domain of morality that governs what human beings should be.

Norm A rule of behavior.

Opportunity Access to some resource or means of advantage such as education, jobs, or offices.

Pareto efficiency See efficiency.

Perfectionism A position in moral theory whereby the right is that which best serves the achievement of objective human goodness (i.e. human perfection).

Pluralism A position in moral theory that says that there is a plurality of true moral demands which cannot be reduced to one common normativity.

Poverty The absence of resources measured either relatively (compared with what others have) or absolutely (as deprivation of something needed).

Premise Part of an argument that serves as support for the conclusion.

Primary goods A concept in Rawls's theory of justice that covers the resources persons are likely to care for simply as citizens and so no matter their particular conception of the good. Rawls lists the primary goods as rights and liberties, opportunities, wealth and income, and the social bases of self-respect.

Principle of equality The principle of equality requires that all have the same of the distribuendum in question.

Principle of liberty The principle of liberty says that all should be free to decide what to do for themselves, as long as their choices are consistent with the equal liberty of others. By this principle, a distribution of some resource is just if it arose from another just distribution by permissible moves, or if all impermissible moves have been rectified.

Principle of merit The principle of merit says that the distribution of the distribuendum should track the merit of the relevant parties. Different distribuenda and different metrics of merit produce different principles of merit. A prominent principle of merit is the principle of desert, which says that the distribution in question should track the deservingness of the relevant parties, but there are non-desertist principles of merit.

Principle of priority The principle of priority says that we should assign differential weights to the interests of persons based on how well-off they are, so that the interests of the less well-off have higher weight than the interests of the better-off. While the relative position of persons thus matters for what the principle of priority requires, its concern is to increase the absolute position of individuals (especially the position of the least well-off), not to equalize their position, which makes the principle of priority immune to the leveling down objection.

Principle of sufficiency The principle of sufficiency requires that all members of society have enough. Different measures of "enough" produce different principles of sufficiency. The standard versions define "enough" in terms of basic needs or minimally decent living, so that all should have enough to live reasonably well.

Principle of utility The principle of utility says that the right choice among available options (for acts, laws, institutions, the design of the economy, etc.) is that which does, or can be expected to, lead to the best overall outcome, where the metric of best (i.e. utility) is defined in terms of subjective well-being. Different accounts of utility produce different principles of utility. In a common version of the principle, utility is defined as preference satisfaction. Different ways of accounting individual utility as part of overall utility also produce different principles of utility. Three accountings are aggregation, averaging, and product.

Principles of distributive justice The basic normative requirements that should guide the distribution of some benefit or burden between those that have a claim to it.

Prioritarianism/prioritarian The family of positions that affirms the principle of priority.

Property-owning democracy One of two economic systems that Rawls argues are favored by justice as fairness, the other one being liberal socialism. In a property-owning democracy ownership of the means of production is widely distributed between the members of society.

Reciprocity As a disposition, reciprocity is a mode of reasonability, i.e. a willingness to engage with others on a footing of equality and to offer terms of cooperation that they could accept as equals – and so is an unwillingness to exploit others. As a requirement of distributive justice, reciprocity says that the terms of cooperation (and the sharing of the benefits and burdens of cooperation) must be such that all cooperators could agree to them as free and equal persons.

Right-liberalism The family of theories of justice that affirms the marriage of liberty and utility and thus argues that the economy should be a system of liberty, i.e. towards the fully capitalist end of the three spectra of economic design: ownership of the means of production should be private, the flow of inputs and outputs of production should be determined through free markets, and the processes of production and distribution should be driven by the profit motive rather than a direct concern for socially defined ends.

Rights Relations between persons that persons in fact have (positive rights) or ought to have. These relations might be claims to property, privileges, immunities, or other. Rights should be both protected and respected by the state, meaning that the state should ensure that rights are not infringed on by other members of society and that the state's activities are limited by rights.

Self-ownership thesis The position that persons have the same rights of ownership over their body and person as they have over property.

Socialism The term socialism is ambiguous between a design of the economy, a set of principles of justice, and a theory of justice. As a design of the economy, socialism is the opposite of capitalism, meaning that socialist systems have a socialized ownership of the means of production, limited use of markets for the distribution of inputs and outputs of production, and production is geared towards needs satisfaction rather than profit. As a set of principles, socialism is not well defined, but the emphasis is on principles of equality of outcome and opportunity. As a theory of justice, socialism is the theoretical structure that issues the relevant principles and justifies a socialist design of the economy.

State of nature States of nature are conditions where some feature definitive of civil society is absent. States of nature are usually thought experiments employed to reveal the attractions of the civil condition, or to think clearly about how we might create a civil condition, or what principles should guide the exercise of political authority in the civil condition, or what the nature and sources of political obligation are.

Strains of commitment The degree to which those party to an agreement (or a social contract) will be tempted to break it.

Subject of justice That which principles of justice apply to. Could be individual acts, laws, institutional design, or the basic structure.

Sufficientarianism/sufficientarian The position that embraces the principle of sufficiency, which says that no person should have less than enough. Different measures of "enough" provide different sufficientarianisms.

Teleological A teleological moral theory defines the right in terms of the good (e.g. utility or perfection). The word derives from the Greek word for end (*telos*), since it says that we should do that which best serves a true conception of the ends we should have.

The basic structure The system of institutions that together define the main roles and rules of citizens. Includes the roles and rules of the economy, the family, and the legal framework that defines the rights and limits of civic associations.

The good The good is the domain morality that covers what is of value.

The original position A device Rawls constructs to make it easier to guide our choice of principles of justice given our commitments to democracy (as an ideal of free and equal cooperation). The original position is a thought experiment, where we imagine that representatives of members of society come together and choose a conception of justice that those they represent will live by. The parties are given a list of candidate conceptions that they then rank by running a pairwise comparison of the candidates until they arrive at a definite order. The ranking is based on the interests and knowledge of the parties. The highest-ranking conception of justice is the best conception of justice for a democratic society.

The right The right is the domain of morality which covers prescriptions for individual or political behavior such as duties or principles of justice.

Utilitarianism/utilitarian A moral theory is utilitarian if it is consequentialist (or teleological) and defines the good and the bad in subjective terms (e.g. happiness verus misery or degree of preference satisfaction).

Utility The measure of the good in a utilitarian moral theory.

Veil of ignorance A part of the original position device from Rawls's theory of justice. The veil of ignorance hides knowledge from the parties that could lead them to propose unfair terms of social cooperation. The veil of ignorance shields the parties from knowledge about who they represent: about their gender, race, skills, wealth, as well as particular facts about their society, such as what sorts of natural resources the society has access to, or the distribution of wealth and opportunities among different classes of citizens. The veil of ignorance lets the parties know general facts relevant for thinking about justice: facts about human needs and psychology; that they are in circumstances of justice; the general theories of sociology and economics; and that their society contains a diversity of philosophical, religious, political, and social doctrines.

INDEX